NGOs IN INDIA

NGOs in India

Role, Guidelines & Performance Appraisal

Edited by

PURAN CHANDRA

AKANSHA PUBLISHING HOUSE
NEW DELHI - 110 002 (INDIA)

AKANSHA PUBLISHING HOUSE
4649-B/21, Ansari Road
Darya Ganj, New Delhi - 110 002
Ph.: 23263193 / 9811582579 / 09435116718
Fax: 011-23263193
Email: ektabooks@yahoo.com
www.akanshapublishinghouse.com

NGOs in India

First Published, 2005
First Reprint, 2008
Second Reprint, 2010
ISBN 81-87606-81-9

[The responsibility for the facts stated, conclusions reached etc., is entirely that of the author. The publisher is not responsible for them, whatsoever.]

PRINTED IN INDIA

Published by Akansha Publishing House, New Delhi and Printed at Harmain Offset Press, Delhi.

Contents

Preface

Non-Government Organisations, popularly known as NGOs or NGDOs, are basically development-oriented voluntary organisations. The term 'voluntary' means serving or acting in a specified function of one's own accord and without compulsion or promise of remuneration; arising from natural impulse; acting or done without any legal obligation. The voluntaryism is the principle of supporting churches, schools and various other philanthropic institutions/causes. From this it is apparent that NGOs are primarily concerned to help the needy. They have some specific mission—having the poor or needy in the centre.

A half century back, the epistemic shift in the voluntary sector was from service to empowerment, development to political action. The drawing edge came from ideological commitment. NGOs, whatever their organisational affiliation may be—Gandhian, religious or Marxist/Socialist—seemed keen to focus on the poor. As NGOs started offering a viable career option, the social base of their cadres slowly started changing. Given the new activity mix, more so of the intermediary support organisations, the emphasis shifted to skill and efficacy. Though we cannot say that the new generation of NGO activists is less concerned about issues related to the poor and deprived. It is that they are more concerned about themselves and thus relate differently to issues of accountability to their respective organisations as also to the people they work for and with.

It is after Seventies of the last millennium, India experienced the amazingly large presence and growth of NGOs. Occupationalism or professionalism entered therein. Resource mobilisation gave them boost. Now these are *professionally* managed organisations—small, operating in a particular region/area, or big as well as MNCs. Likely, collectively emerged the NGO sector. It cannot be said that the NGOs have worked honestly so far. These are blamed to have served personal interests more than the mass interest for which these came into existence.

The new political role, accompanied by radical rhetoric, has generated new pressures from diverse sources on the NGO sector. As a result of the new expectations that NGOs have generated, there is an overloading of demands from the ground. Networking and coordination, combined with servicing grassroots groups and struggles, is a complex task. The inability to satisfy these expectations has led to the trading of vilificatory charges—that NGOs have become corrupt, lazy, used to an easy, cosy and expensive lifestyle, distanced from base communities and groups—some of it unfortunately true.

Towards the end of the millennium, the India faced a daunting situation. More than seven years of attempts at economic liberalisation, designed more to globally integrate the economy and roll back the State even from its constitutionally mandated role rather than 'free' domestic production and distribution, has created a new stratum of the relatively deprived.

The discussion about NGOs and community initiatives and formations thus needs to be located in this context. Issues of accountability and modes to ensure that the NGOs remain transparent have to be tackled with urgency if we are to enthuse are revigorate the sector with a new spirit. Otherwise, notwithstanding greater funding support and glamour, the inflow of devoted and creative people, especially the young, is likely to dry up.

Here in this book, twelve topics are chosen to highlight the NGOs in India, their performance, role, etc. To portray the authoritative account, we have drawn the views, experiences and expressions from leading men of letters and activists. Sometimes we have drawn case study appraisals undertook by various scholars. As the information gathered by one is told and retold again and again this process goes on. As such entire credit goes to those all original contributors.

We are grateful to all those scholars of great merit whose concepts and views are borrowed here. As mainly secondary sources like—books, monographs, reports and journals and magazines are consulted, we owe a deep sense of gratitude to them all—writers, editors and the copyright holders. Finally, we are thankful to our publishers to publish this book elegantly.

—Editor

CHAPTER 1

NGOs in India: Emergence and Role

NGOs or Voluntary organisations in India are shaped by a variety of factors; they have been nurtured and threatened in turn as the dominant political outlook has oscillated between liberalism and statism. Diverse in their functions and purposes, they serve primarily a vast and assorted population of informal workers. A sizable sum from public and foreign sources is expended by this sector. And yet the sector has 'received surprisingly scanty attention from academic researchers and social analysts'. Available literature is limited in its scope and range. What is written falls mainly into two categories: (i) volumes containing accounts of scores of organisations and (ii) detailed portraits of a handful of organisations.

Writings in the first group tend to be impressionistic; the second are usually evaluative, often undertaken at the behest of a funding agency. There have been very few articles studying the phenomenon of voluntary organisations as a whole. A second feature of existing literature on voluntary associations is that there is a dearth of factual information. For example, we do not have even a rough estimate of the total number of voluntary organisations functioning in India; estimates range between 50,000 and 100,000! On the other hand, there are no less than 18 directories of voluntary organisations, compiled for different purposes by various government departments and independent agencies! This massive information is, however, both inadequate and fragmented.

An important reason for this is the absence of an agreed

definition of the basic term. 'Voluntary organisations' vary so much in their size, goals, nature, scale of activities, style of functioning and sources of support that an all-enveloping definition may not even be useful —it may end up becoming a Procrustean bed. Thus, there are no unambiguous answers to relatively simple factual questions, such as how many voluntary organisations are currently active. On the other hand, diverse as they are, voluntary organisations are distinct from both public (government) and private organisations and, accordingly, should be brought under a common conceptual umbrella. Since voluntary organisations do not exhibit characteristics of either public or private sector organisations, the concept of yet another sector—variously called the third sector, independent sector, voluntary sector, or non-profit sector—is necessary to encompass all voluntary associations.

Extreme heterogeneity is one argument against bracketing voluntary organisations under a common label. But then, the same argument can be advanced against lumping widely varying economic and political institutions under their respective sectors. A tea-stall at a street corner belongs to the private sector as much as does the Hindustan Lever Ltd., although they differ in all their characteristics such as the nature and scale of resources employed; the type of product sold; and the level and sophistication of technology used in production, marketing and accounting. Nor do we hesitate to describe as political institutions the UN General Assembly, the Indian Parliament, and a *gram* panchayat, dissimilar as they are. Similarly, voluntary organisations could be placed under a common umbrella, making it possible to view them as members of the same species rather than as merely distinctive entities. Such treatment can bring out their common as well as unique features. Indeed, 'voluntary sector' is emerging as a field of multi-disciplinary research in the West.

Voluntary organisations tend to be emotional and ideological rather than reflective and rational. Accounts of voluntary organisations tend to either praise or denounce diem—what is missing is an effort at understanding and interpreting them. Voluntary associations have been seen alternatively as the 'harbingers of silent revolution'. 'handmaidens of global imperialism', and 'footnotes in India's development'. This chapter considers some of the ways in which they can be understood and interpreted.

Contextual Factors

The cultural conception of society itself can either encourage or discourage the rise of voluntary association. For instance, Indian traditions tend to see society as autonomous and nor subordinate to the State, unlike Confucian and contemporary Chinese concepts of society. This cultural concept partly explains the 'baffling' phenomenon of the continuation of the liberal democratic regime in India in the midst of escalating violence, severe deprivations, and persistent disparities. The same liberal democratic regime, committed to normative pluralism, encourages voluntary organisations. The role of the State in supporting or undermining voluntary associations cannot be overestimated. Just as a liberal democratic regime promotes them, an authoritarian one restricts their growth, and a totalitarian one may obliterate them altogether.

Religion plays an important role in shaping voluntary action, negatively as well as positively. It may promote values which can prove an important source of inspiration for voluntary endeavour. On the other hand, if it is an all-encompassing religion, prescribing every thought and action of the believer, it will leave little space for voluntary effort. Hinduism is not an all-consuming religion and hence allows voluntary effort to flourish. Like religion, secular ideologies also stimulate or deter voluntary endeavour.

Specific environmental factors that have promoted the growth of voluntary associations in India can be summed up under four headings: Hindu traditions, Gandhi's influence, ideology of the Left, and perception of system failure. A number of other facilitating factors have been operational as well.

Hindu Traditions

Voluntary actions are performed of one's free will, impulse, or choice; they are not constrained, prompted, or suggested by another. These actions spring from a variety of sources; some lie within the individual, others in shared experiences.

In the Western societies, voluntary action finds its expression typically in an organisation, a formal and relatively easy to measure manifestation of collective action. Voluntary action in India, however, does not always take the form of an organisation. Many of our charitable customs are individual in their essence; for instance, the tradition of *madhukari* which frees Brahmin students from the trouble of obtaining two square meals a day. The custom of *ramroti* to feed the *sadhus* is another non-organised type of voluntary activity. While highlighting the non-organised nature of the activity, these customs also point to the caste-based character of philanthropy in India.

Like other religious traditions, Hindu traditions also nurture charitable action, although mainly as a religious ritual and within a narrowly defined religious space. The Hindu belief system cherishes service to others, esteems sacrifice and places the highest value on renunciation. The Gita's prescription is to act with no expectation of reward. These values and beliefs promote voluntarism. However, some other Hindu norms, beliefs and practices tend to restrict it. Among them are an emphasis on 'the life hereafter' instead of 'the life herein'; the view that this world is an illusion *(maya)*; and the conviction that one's lot in this life is the result of one's deeds in a previous life *(karma)*. These beliefs tend to downplay the virtues of charity and compassion.

Equally relevant is the kind of importance attached to benevolence by a Hindu priest. He may coax the faithful to give money to restore a shrine, but he is unlikely to urge them to donate money to help the indigent. His role is more of an expert guiding the common man in his search for his own salvation through the labyrinth of rituals, while showing the spiritual path only to the more sophisticated. Finally, there is little incentive to be philanthropic to 'strangers' in the name of religion because Hinduism is non-proselytising in nature.

And yet, charity flourishes in India. It is limited, however, by the Hindu world-view in three ways. First, it would seem that charitable acts are usually performed with the intention of discharging one's obligation towards a departed kinsman or to fulfil promises made to a deity. For example, a man may donate money to an orphanage so that his deceased father's soul may rest in peace or because he has taken a vow to do so.

Second, charity is confined to the religious space; it does not readily expand into the wider, secular space. For instance, going on pilgrimage is important for a traditional Hindu. Therefore, temples and shrines have to be kept in good repair and basic amenities provided to the devotees. It is customary for pious, wealthy families to build dormitories for the pilgrims and provide for their upkeep. Households with more modest means also offer their mite towards the same. Anecdotal evidence indicates that this type of activity dominates philanthropy in India.

Third, when not occurring as a religious ritual or in the religious space, charity takes place in the confines of kinship groups, since Indian cultural norms impose an obligation to tend to the needs of fellow-members of primordial groups such as the extended family and the caste.

Thus, on the one hand, the Hindu belief-system stresses the precedence of society over the State and encourages voluntary action. On the other hand, it restricts its expression to certain channels. It is hardly surprising, therefore, that Hindu traditions are not indicated as providing ideological roots for voluntary action, although Gandhi, Marx, Jesus, and Mohammad are.

Given the limited role of religion in inducing organised voluntary action, the source of inspiration for proliferating voluntary associations must be sought elsewhere. Gandhi's influence, the ideology of the Left, and the perception of system failure suggest themselves as alternative sources.

Gandhi's Influence

The concept embodying the precedence of society over State was strongly reinforced by Gandhiji's distrust of formal power, and was an integral component of both his vision of future India and the path mended for realising that vision. He never held an official party or government position; his renunciation of power bolstered the anti-power orientation that characterised Indian political culture in the early years after Independence.

Second, Gandhiji believed that with Independence, the Congress Party had outlived its utility 'as a propaganda vehicle and a parliamentary machine'. He urged Congress members to leave politics for 'constructive work' which he considered more important. Constructive work does not separate issues of material well-being from those of spiritual well-being; it stresses social and cultural regeneration of the individuals as well as of society as a whole. Gandhiji exhorted Congress members to abjure power and dedicate themselves to pure selfless service to others. He suggested that constructive workers should not aim at entering Parliament, but should work to keep Parliament under check by educating and guiding voters. He called on the Congress Party to turn itself into a Lok Sevak Sangh.

His call to the Congress Party to disband as a political party went largely unheeded, but scores of his followers pledged themselves to a life of constructive work and austerity. Although very few combined the missionary zeal with a complete indifference to their own wellbeing as did Vinoba Bhave, several hunted men and women founded groups and organisations to serve the poor while adopting Spartan life-styles themselves.

Since nationalist mobilisation and the inculcation of Gandhian values had their deepest impact in Gujarat, the state ended up having a high concentration of Gandhian social workers and village-based reform projects. These projects are run by voluntary organisations with those Gandhians and erstwhile Congress Party workers who could not or refused to find a place either in the party or in the government.

Ideology of the Left

The second important source of voluntarism lies in the ideology of the Left. Even before Independence, the growing hegemony of the centrist faction in the Congress Party had brought into open the ideological splits within the party. Consequently, some leftist factions in the Congress Party established themselves as independent political parries and began mobilising and organising people. Later on, party workers, especially of the Communist Party , became disenchanted with the party since it had resolved to function within the framework of parliamentary democracy and competitive electoral politics, attenuating its goals, strategies and tactics. Frustrated as the party workers were by these constraints, they were utterly disillusioned when they found that the party had failed to perform even this circumscribed role effectively. Consequently, many party workers severed their party connections and began to work independently in voluntary organisations.

System Failure

In the 1960s and 1970s, a mood of disenchantment set in.

Both the official planning system and the market economy had failed to make a significant dent in India's problems of poverty and inequality. This gave rise to scepticism about the ability of the institutional structures of democracy—legislatures, parties unions, panchayats—to address the problems and needs of the poor. Formulated policies were not suitable enough to reduce poverty and inequality, and when they were, they were not implemented effectively. The government-sponsored model of development was seen as having failed to deliver benefits to the poor, and the formal political establishment had lost its legitimacy.

More specifically, the Congress Party, a dominant, long-standing institution epitomising democratic processes and norms, was crumbling. The deterioration of the Congress Party disturbed the precarious balance that the 'Congress Party System' had maintained by accommodating diverse claims on the limited resources of the State. This decline in intermediate structures created avoid in the process of political mediation between State and society. To fill the vacuum, 'a new class of social mediators' arose which led local protests and civil rights movements. Thousands of urban, well-educated young men and women, averse to electoral politics, swelled the ranks of activists founding or joining voluntary organisations.

Other Facilitating Factors

If voluntarism was inspired by religion and political ideology, commitment to normative pluralism facilitated its growth. National elites, already steeped in the indigenous cultural conception of society as autonomous of the State, readily embraced normative pluralism. Their commitment has been manifested in several ways. Formally, the Constitution guarantees the right to form organisations to Indian citizens. In addition to this legal provision, certain practices and norms were developed which promoted voluntary organisations.

First, from the very outset Indian policy-makers had

developed a tradition of consulting societal elites and groups. Representative committees were created to secure opinions from various groups in society, and their views were solicited in formulating major domestic policies, even as a centrally planned model of development was adopted.

Second, voluntary organisations were involved not only in formulating policies, but their help was also sought in implementing programmes. The Planning Commission itself had realised at the outset that the task of development was so large and so complex that the State alone would not be able to accomplish it. Accordingly, the very First Five-Year Plan document had carried a plea to voluntary organisations to become involved in the task of development, mainly by implementing government programmes. Appropriate financial provisions were also made for them. Beginning with an allocation of Rs. 4 crore in the First Plan, the voluntary sector has been receiving increasing amounts of public funds. In the place of social and services, was equivalent to Rs. 180 crores; in the Seventh and Eighth Plans it rose to Rs. 200 and Rs. 750 crore respectively.

Finally, the stance of international aid agencies, an extraneous factor has also played a conducive role. In the 1970s, the philosophy and strategy of the international development community began to change. Foreign aid donors started to focus their attention on voluntary organisations as supplementary delivery vehicles for development. They began to channel large amounts of developmental aid to those organisations which worked directly for the poor instead of for the governments. This access to financial resources led to mushrooming of voluntary organisations. Thus, a constellation of events and trends gave an impetus to men and women to establish voluntary associations.

Theories of Origin

Whereas the contextual factors explain the genesis of voluntary organisations in particular societies at specific time-periods, theories of the origins of voluntary associations help explain this phenomenon on a different plane.

Western scholars have put forward several theories regarding the origins of the voluntary sector. The disciplines from which they emanate range from economics and political economy to sociology, political science and anthropology. The theories are partial in that they are not incompatible with one another.

The contract failure theory, an economic theory, explains why particular kinds of goods are produced by voluntary rather than by the private sector. It argues that when consumers feel unable to evaluate accurately the adequacy or quality of the goods, they choose voluntary organisations as suppliers rather than profit-making firms. Consumers distrust for-profit firms for such goods because the manager of a for-profit firm may supply inferior quality goods and pocket the additional earnings thus made. The opportunity to do so does not exist for managers of non-profit concerns as they are forbidden by law from garnering the extra profit. An enlightened consumer thus protects his interests by sponsoring voluntary associations.

The theory as it is formulated does not appear applicable to the Indian situation since in India most voluntary organisations are set up to meet the needs of the vulnerable and those who cannot protect their interests, and to deliver merit goods. A modern welfare state is expected to provide them, but India has failed to do so. The reasons for failure are many: First, the State lacks resources. Therefore, voluntary associations frequently supplement the supply of such goods, e.g., health care. Second, often, negligent public servants fail to perform their duty, even when they have no material gains to derive from this. Of course, there are corrupt officials who can and do subvert enacted policies and reap unauthorised profits from them. In either case, those who are too weak to assert their rights are left out. Third, the weak and the vulnerable often do not know how to access merit goods; sometimes they even have to be convinced of their benefits. These are the tasks that typically a voluntary organisation is capable of, and predisposed to, performing. A vast majority of Indian voluntary associations are set up by the organisers to address this shortcoming of the public system.

The second economic theory, the subsidy theory, argues that nonprofit organisations benefit from a variety of implicit and explicit subsidies, such as exemption from taxes. Thus, once set up, a part of the financial burden shifts to the government, a prospect which acts as an incentive for setting up a voluntary association.

The theory seems particularly applicable to the Indian situation since voluntary organisations here often obtain even their initial funds either from the government or foreign funding agencies. This theory explains the phenomenal growth in the number of voluntary organisations as a result of the abundant availability of funds, both foreign and domestic (mainly overnmental), which began to characterise the voluntary scene from the late 1960s onwards.

The exchange theory offers yet another way of understanding voluntary associations. It views a voluntary association as a benefit exchange: the group organiser offers a set of benefits to the members and receives benefits in return. To join and continue as a member, one may have to pay a subscription, attend meetings, etc. These are the costs a member has to bear to receive the benefits. The organiser, on his part, has to devote time and energy to recruit members and to obtain and deliver benefits to retain them. The organiser's benefits may take the form of fulfilment of much-cherished goals or monetary compensation. The benefits that either party receives could be material, solidary, or purposive. This theory conceives of the organiser as a political entrepreneur. In exchange, the leaders receive returns (i.e., profits). Only a mutually satisfactory exchange—an adequate flow of benefits both to members and organisers—can sustain the organisation. The organiser must earn sufficient returns in the form of membership support to enable him to continue his work of providing the benefits. When benefits or profits diminish or disappear the organisation weakens or closes down. This theory offers a framework for understanding why some organisations thrive and others wither away. The benefit exchange perspective also affords a more balanced view of organisation and particularly of the organiser (entrepreneur): he needs to be seen neither as a pure altruist nor as a crass opportunist, but rather as a rational person.

Activities of Voluntary Organisations

The origins of voluntary organisations, but also their activities can be seen in a new way. Many typologies of voluntary associations have been developed, and the proposed typology makes no radical departure from them. It differs from them only in emphasising the political activities of voluntary associations. The activities can be considered under three heads: *developmental, political* and *catalytic*.

Developmental activities aim at the poor directly. They comprise the delivery of a wide range of services and take various forms. Voluntary organisations may: (i) actually deliver the benefits; (ii) they may act as a bridge, providing information about relevant government schemes to the poor; or *(c)* they may help target groups meet procedural requirements so that the poor may 'reach up and pull down to them the benefits of development.' For example, a voluntary organisation may seek to have all eligible children living in an urban slum inoculated with the triple antigen. In pursuit of this goal, the organisation may set up a clinic in the slum; it may inform the parents in the area about the municipal clinic that immunises children and facilitate their visit to the clinic; or it may help parents fill out a form and obtain the child's birth certificate.

A catalytic activity aims to influence the public in a way which the voluntary organisation expects will initiate action.

As a catalytic activity, a voluntary organisation may launch a public campaign to disseminate information. For instance, it can publish statistics on deaths of children who were not inoculated with the triple antigen with a view to move the public to action. The concerned public may decide to raise resources to start an immunisation programme or persuade the government to do the same.

Political activities, on the other hand, are directed at a governmental authority. The aim is to persuade the authority to take action to create such conditions as would improve the lot of the poor. When a voluntary organisation convinces the municipal health department, a public authority, to launch a scheme to inoculate children in city slums, it is engaging in political action. Political activities are important because they attempt to bring about changes at the policy level. If implemented effectively, the policy-level action can have far-reaching consequences since it encompasses all who fall in the defined category. For instance, if an organisation succeeds in persuading government to fix a minimum wage for the readymade garment workers, all workers in the occupational category will avail of the benefit, whether they are members of the said organisation or not. On the other hand, if the organisation successfully negotiates with the employers to pay higher wages to its members, its members will benefit, but not all readymade garment workers. Organisational members would normally form only a part of a much larger occupational category of readymade garment makers. Thus, if a voluntary organisation engages in a policy-influencing exercise, it can have an impact well beyond its members, transcending its usual, local sphere of influence.

Developmental, catalytic and political activities are not mutually exclusive, and most voluntary organisations pursue some combination of all three, often in conjunction with each other or as a series of successive steps. However, both voluntary associations themselves and the researchers have shied away from focussing exclusively on political activities.

Summing Up

This chapter discusses the contextual factors influencing the emergence of voluntary organisations in India. It then reviewed some major theories of the origins of voluntary organisations and their applicability to the Indian situation. Finally, it presented a framework for classifying activities of voluntary organisations with a view to underscoring the importance of their political activities. It has, in this way, indicated the issues which can, and ought, to be explored. Marx was in despair because everyone was trying so hard to interpret the world, when the point, according to him, was to change it. One could stand his comment on its head: voluntary organisations are so busy transforming the world that it is time academicians made efforts to understand and interpret them!

REFERENCES

Bonner, Arthur (1990). *Averting the Apocalypse: Social Movement in India Today*. Durham: Duke University Press.

Clark, Peter B. and James Q. Wilson (1961). 'Incentive systems: A theory of organisations', *Administrative Science Quarterly* 6, pp. 129-66.

Canaan Ram A., Felice D. Perlmutter and Chul-Hei Kang (1991). 'Voluntary associations: Societal variations in response to human needs', paper presented at the Third International Conference of Research on Voluntary and Nonprofit Organisations, Indianapolis, 11-13 March, p. 1.

Eldridge, Philip (1984/5). 'The political role of community action groups in India and Indonesia: In search of a general *theory'*. *Alternatives* 10, pp. 401-34.

Hansman, H. (1979/80). 'The role of non-profit enterprise', *Yale Law Journal* 89, pp. 835-901.

Hardgrave, Robert L., Jr and Stanley A. Kochanek (1986). *India: Government and Politics in a Developing Nation*. San Diego: Harcourt Brace.

Indian Journal of Public Administration (1987). Special number on 'Voluntary organisations and development: Their role', July-September.

Jain, Devaki (1956).'Struggle against power: Notes on Indian political behavior', *World Politics* 7, pp. 393-96.

Jhunjhunwala, Bharat (1986). 'Voluntary work as countervailing power,' *Economic and Political Weekly* 21.

Karat, Prakash (1984). 'Action groups/voluntary organisations: A factor in imperialist strategy', *The Marxist*, April-June, pp. 19-54.

Kochanek, Stanley A. (1974). *Business and Politics in India.* Berkeley: University of California Press.

Korten, David C. (1986). 'Micro-policy reforms: The role of private voluntary agencies', working paper no. 12, The National Association of Schools of Public Administration, Washington, D.C.

Marx, Karl (1983). "Theses on Feuerbach' in Eugene Kamenka (ed.), *The Portable Karl Marx.* New York: Viking.

Mitra, Subrata Kumar (1991). 'Crisis and resilience in Indian democracy', *International Social Science Journal* 43, p. 565.

Pandey, Shashi Ranjan (1991). *Community Action far Social Justice: Grassroots Organisation in India.* New Delhi: Sage Publications.

Patel, Rohini (1995). 'The pressure group role of voluntary associations: A case study of the Ahmedabad's Women's Action Group and the Self-Employed Women's Association' unpublished Ph.D. dissertation, Pennsylvania State University.

Saint, Kishore (1974).'The role of the catalyst institution' in John Sommer, Pratima Kale and Ranjit Gupta (eds), *Rural Development at the Grassroots: The Catalyst Role.* New Delhi: Ford Foundation.

Salisburg, Robert (1969). 'An exchange theory of interest groups', *Midwest Journal* of Political Science 13, no. 1, pp. 1-32.

Sen, K.M. (1961). *Hinduism.* Baltimore: Penguin Books.

Sethi, Harsh (1935). 'Whither voluntary action?', *Seminar,* May, pp. 18-23.

Shah, Dinesh (1985). 'Voluntary agencies in the seventh plan', *Voluntary Action* 27, nos. 9-10, p. 259.

Shah, Ghanshyam and H.R. Chaturvedi (1983). *Gandhian Approach to Rural Development: The Valod Experiment.* New Delhi: Ajanta.

Sharma, S.L. (1992). 'Social action groups as harbingers of silent revolution', *Economic and* Political *Weekly* pp. 2557-61.

Viswanath, Vanita (1991) *Non-governmental Organisations and imen's Development in South Asia: A Comparative Analysis.* Boulder, CO: Westview Press.

CHAPTER 2

NGOs: Characteristic Traits

Voluntary organisations, popularly known as Non-governmental organisations (NGOs) embrace a wide array of agencies within and across different countries of the world. NGOs are simply agencies or groups which are different from government bodies. However, NGOs are distinctive in containing a voluntary component and because they do not operate for profit. Development NGOs are thus a category of NGOs defined by their purpose of providing development assistance. But even in development parlance, the term NGO is used to encompass a whole range of organisations which differ in size, function, and geographical location.

Thus the term can be used to describe small, locally based, and loosely established voluntary and largely grass-roots types of associations, as well as large, national, and even transnational voluntary associations with formal constitutions, employing hundreds of staff.

As the NGOs are basically concerned with development—the term NGDO—non-governmental development organisation—is frequently used to describe the growing numbers of associations whose work is exclusively concerned with broader development concerns. A distinction is also commonly made between NGOs which originated in and have their home-base in the industrial countries, which are referred to as 'northern' or 'international' NGOs, and those which originate in and operate within developing countries, which are termed 'southern' NGOs.

Of late, there has been a rapid growth in the numbers of NGOs involved in development, in the numbers of people working for NGOs, and in the amount of money which flows into voluntary agencies working in relief and development. Perhaps the greatest growth has been in the thousands of new grass-roots organisations which have grown up locally—some extending no further than one or two villages. However, there has also been a rapid growth in larger indigenous NGOs in the south, as well as in the numbers of northern NGOs. During this period, a number of the older NGOs have changed their role, the most common change being a shift from an exclusive concern with relief and emergency work to a focus which embraces, or sometimes is exclusively concerned with, broader development issues (Korten, 1990b). These trends, and closer examination of the characteristics of different groups, have led to a distinction that is now commonly made between intermediary, or secondary, and primary organisations.

Indeed Carroll (1992), whose work in this field has been particularly influential, distinguishes further between grass-roots support organisations (GSOs) and membership support organisations (MSOs). On occasion this growth has led to a blurring of the differences between governmental and non-governmental, and even between non-profit and for-profit organisations. Thus, in an increasing number of developing countries, it has now become common for government and state agencies or for politicians to set up their own 'non-governmental' organisations, while in industrial countries it is now common practice for governments to channel some of their aid funds to and through NGOs. Similarly, concern with longer-term survival has encouraged some NGOs to raise funds by establishing commercial-type ventures such as shops, stores, and mail-order facilities, while in Italy 'business NGOs' have been formed for the specific purpose of securing aid contracts from the Italian Government.

Northern NGOs

Quantitatively, northern development NGOs has increased rapidly in the 1980s. At the same time, there has been growing diversification and specialisation within the NGO community, reflecting the wide range of activities in which they are now engaged. As a result, it has become increasingly difficult to make generalisations about what northern NGOs do and about the particular role that they see for themselves in development. Within individual industrialised countries, NGOs operate within different legal systems and with different public expectation of their role. In most countries there is a strong church-based link to at least one, and often more, of the major NGOs. Indeed, agencies affiliated to the Protestant and Catholic churches dominate the NGO sector in Denmark and Germany, although most maintain a strict separation between and development work. In Germany, in addition to the large church-based NGOs, there are also the four political foundations which constitute an important element of the NGO community, promoting development within their explicit and different political objectives.

Some important non-denominational NGOs whose interests include work on development were founded in the nineteenth and early twentieth centuries. The British Anti-Slavery Society was established as far back as 1823 and Save the Children Fund in 1919. Others were formed during and after World War II, initially with a focus on relief: Oxfam was founded in 1942 (Black, 1992), CARE (Co-operative Agency for Relief Everywhere) in 1945, War on Want in 1953, NOVIB in 1956, and Misereor in 1958. In the 1960s there was a major expansion in the number of development-focused NGOs, both secular and denominational. In the 1970s and on into the 1980s, new organisations were formed which had a more specific sectoral, technical, or geographical focus. One such in Britain, the Intermediate Technology Development Group, was founded as early as 1965.

Northern NGOs are principally engaged in funding development projects and providing food and other materials for disasters and emergencies. An important distinction is whether they are operational or not: operational agencies implement projects directly in developing countries using their own staff and resources, whereas non-operational agencies finance projects from their headquarters or regional office, often channelling funds through partner organisations with whom special relationships are frequently developed. Large US-based NGOs like CARE, Plan International, and World Vision are all operational, as are ActionAid and Save the Children Fund in the UK. The trend, however, is away from hands-on involvement and towards working directly with indigenous NGOs. In Britain this is now common practice for agencies such as CAFOD (Catholic Fund for Overseas Development) and Christian Aid.

Many NGOs tailor their approach to the situation in particular countries; thus, the non-operational approach is favoured more in South Asia and Latin America, whereas in many parts of Africa northern NGOs continue to be strongly interventionist. Some northern NGOs, such as Oxfam, Save the Children Fund, Misereor, and NOVIB, have in-country offices which liaise with and offer support to indigenous NGOs in the form of training and exchange visits. Others, such as Christian Aid, have made a deliberate decision not to do so (Riddell, 1993), though recent changes have occurred in this policy.

In addition to providing financial support for development projects, many NGOs are involved in development education and advocacy work in their own countries. Indeed, distinct NGOs, like the Centre for World Development Education in England and Wales, have been set up in order to concentrate on such activities. However, emphasis on work in this area varies, and in a number of European countries, where a large share of funds come from the state, advocacy work receives a low priority.

While the statistics are known to be incomplete, OECD data suggest that there were 2,542 NGOs in the twenty-four OECD countries in 1990, compared with 1,603 in 1980 (OECD, 1990a). In addition, almost all NGOs grew in terms of funds and personnel during this period. Between 1980 and 1990, the total flow of private funds sent by northern NGOs to developing countries rose from S2.4bn. to $5.Ibn., rising eventually to $6.3bn. (for recent figures see OECD, 1995: 58). However, a relatively small group of large organisations predominate: some 200 NGOs (less than 10 per cent of the total) account for some three-quarters of the volume of grants to developing countries (*The Courier*, 1987). Absolute numbers and growth trends also conceal significant variation among countries: there are hundreds of NGOs in Canada, the USA, and northern European countries where NGOs have strong historical traditions and thrive on public philanthropy, and comparatively few in Mediterranean countries such as Greece and Portugal.

In Britain, the sector is dominated by a small group of large agencies: out of some 300 development NGOs, twelve account for over 80 per cent of total voluntary income, and seven of these had incomes in excess of £10m. in 1990. Oxfam is the largest in terms of turnover, followed by Save the Children Fund, Christian Aid, the World Wide Fund for Nature, ActionAid, Tear Fund, and CAFOD. Another fail recent development has been the creation of 2 number of specialist NGOs, which focus on specific constituencies, approaches to development, and sectors of activity. These include Water Aid, Health Unlimited, and the Intermediate Technology Development Group, while increased interest in the environment has raised the profile of the World Wide Fund for Nature.

Growth in the number and incomes of development NGOs in the industrialised countries has tended to raise their significance in relation to the total voluntary sector. Thus, in Britain, development NGOs account for approximately one-sixth of the total volume of funds raised by charities in the form of private contributions. There are two main reasons for this growth in size and numbers of northern NGOs. The first has been the increase in media exposure of famine and disasters, together with the more professional manner in which these issues have been presented. Not only has the role of NGOs been highlighted, the NGO BandAid owed its origins to public interest aroused by media coverage of the Ethiopian famine of the mid-1980s. This provided a major stimulus for increased levels of private contributions, which appears to have been sustained into the early 1990s in spite of worries expressed within the NGO movement that a combination of 'aid fatigue' and the media dominance of problems in eastern Europe and the former Soviet Union would lead to a drop in public donations. More recently, however, contributions have begun to fall.

A second set of factors contributing to NGO growth is related more to events outside the world of NGOs. One has been growing disillusion among official aid organisations about their own ability to alleviate poverty through their often large-scale rural development programmes. This has led, in part, to a switch in focus away from small and localised development projects to larger macro-political issues in official aid provision. Another factor has been the increasing prominence given to private initiatives in development. These influences have not only combined to raise the profile and status of the voluntary-sector NGOs in development, but have also led to significant increases in the quantity of public money which government ministries and aid agencies have channelled to and through NGOs. Government funding grew at a faster rate than private contributions daring the 1980s. In the period 1980-8, official contributions increased in real terms by 55 per cent, as compared with 25 per cent for private contributions. By 1988 NGOs in the eighteen DAC member states raised \$4.2bn. from private contributions but received \$2.3bn. from official sources, giving a total of

$6.3bn. By 1992 the total had risen to $8.8bn., though still equivalent to around 15 per cent of total official aid.

In the period from 1970 to 1993, the total non-government funds of NGOs channelled to developing countries rose from $860m. to $6.3bn. Yet as a share of total official aid there was a slight decline over this period—from 12.3 per cent in 1970 to 11 per cent in 1993. The most significant change over the past quarter of a century has been the growth of total NGO income coming from official aid sources. According to the World Bank (World Bank, 1995: 23), in 1970 official donors only provided about 1.5 per cent of total NGO income. But by 1992 the figure had risen to $2.5bn., and to account for some 30 per cent of total NGO income.

The exact proportions vary markedly between individual countries. Though, in some cases, the data are known (by the OECD) to be little more than crude estimates, and it has not been possible for some years to provide comprehensive data for eleven OECD donors, the best available country by country data. For at least four donors, over 20 per cent of all official aid is now channelled to or through NGOs. Of importance, too, the data show that in the case of at least six countries, over 40 per cent of total NGO income comes from official aid sources.

A major cause of this rise in official funds to NGOs has been the rapid expansion of emergency aid and a rising share of this which now passes through NGOs. Thus, whereas less than $1bn. of total official aid went to emergencies and distress relief in the late 1980s, it amounted to over $3bn. by 1993. By the early 1990s, almost 30 per cent of Britain's total official aid allocated by the Overseas Development Administration's (ODA) Disaster and Refugee Units was funnelled through NGOs, compared with less than 1 per cent ten years earlier. For the aid from the European Union the trend has been even greater, with the share of emergency aid chanelled through NGOs rising from less than 1 per cent in the mid-1970s to 40 per cent by the early 1990s (Borton, 1993). In 1993-4, 30 per cent of official Swedish aid going to NGOs was solely for disaster relief (Riddell *et al.*, 1995: 11). Funds are provided to NGOs through five major mechanisms: block grants for which no detailed accounting requirements are stipulated; matching grants for development projects (co-financing); food aid and disaster relief; support for volunteer programmes; and grants for development education. Project co-financing has grown to be the most important of these, with matching grants providing NGOs with from 50 to 100 per cent of total project costs of co-financed projects. Not only do official aid agencies use NGOs to distribute food aid and emergency aid, but some donors now sub-contract specific elements of bilateral aid projects to NGOs for implementation. USAID has relied on this mechanism for some years. Thus in CARE's food-for-work programme in Bangladesh, the NGO assumed responsibility for food distribution and supervision of public works under contract from USAID. Some other donors have since followed suit. For instance, in its 'country-focus' approach, the Canadian Government involves NGOs in the execution, and in some cases the design, of CIDA-financed projects in the main recipient countries.

Besides these different forms of financial support to northern NGOs, some donors provide funds directly to southern NGOs, either bilaterally to individual organisations from aid headquarters or through diplomatic missions. Canada has progressed furthest down this path. In 1987 it provided some S16m. to indigenous NGOs through aid missions in 115 countries. In a variant of this approach, USAID provides umbrella grants through its aid missions for use by US PVO's as well as indigenous NGOs (OECD, 1988: 91-3). The British Government has also started to fund local NGO activities, initially by supporting indigenous NGOs involved in family planning as part of a larger bilateral aid programme in Bangladesh. In 1994 a further new initiative began in east Africa, when ODA began a programme to fund the work of local NGOs directly with an initial budget of £l.'5m. (Riddell and Bebbington, 1995). On the multilateral front, a significant channel for indigenous NGO funding is through the European Community's micro-project schemes, which in many Lome Convention countries are administered by an official paid for by the Community. Overall, however, this channel covers only a minor proportion of official aid allocated to NGOs. Both resistance on the part of some northern NGOs and the limited capacity of most aid missions to monitor small project grants have worked against any major shift in favour of direct funding.

Southern NGOs and Grass-Roots Organisations

While there has been a steady growth in the number and size of northern NGOs in the 1980s, there has been an explosion in the number of southern NGOs. For instance, there are now several thousand NGOs in India engaged in rural development, 550 in Bangladesh, and over 200 in Zimbabwe. In Kenya the number of NGOs active in development doubled from 70 in 1970 to 140 by 1980, with a further increase to some 250 by the late 1980s; the number would expand to many thousands if local women's and other grass-roots organisations were included.

This rapid growth has been spurred by the more positive attitude on the part of donors and many host governments towards the NGO sector, and by the increased availability of funds from foreign donors, both NGOs and governments. It has also been facilitated by the retreat of government provision in many developing countries, manifest in a much reduced role in welfare services as a result of public expenditure cutbacks and a weakening of its legitimacy in the face of pressures for democratisation, which have in turn widened the potential for non-state initiatives (Robinson, 1995).

Some southern NGOs now reach very large numbers of poor people: the Grameen Bank in Bangladesh has over 160,000 borrowers, the Working Women's Forum of Madras 38,000 members, and the Self-Employed Women's Association in Ahmedabad 15,000 members (Tendler, 1987: 6). It has been estimated that in the early 1980s NGO activities reached some 100 million people in developing countries: 60 million in Asia, 25 million in Latin America, but only 12 million in Africa, although, with a rapid expansion in NGOs in the 1980s, this figure has probably increased dramatically (Schneider, 1988). By then (and if it were assumed that NGOs work primarily with the poor), NGOs would have reached approximately one in eight of those living in poverty in developing countries. More recently the 1993 *Human Development Report* judged that some 250 million people were being touched by NGOs and that the numbers would rise considerably in the years ahead (UNDP, 1993: 93).

Southern NGOs vary enormously in their approach and orientation, in their size and location of operation, in the physical, financial, and technical resources they have available, in the scale of their interventions, in the degree of support they receive from government, and, last but by no means least, in the socio-political context in which their interventions are located. They range from small localised NGOs working in a handful of villages in a single locality, to large NGOs working at a regional or national level, for the most part with funds from external sources. In addition to these local NGOs, there are also large international NGOs (often working with local representation) providing funding and support to indigenous NGOs.

A typical southern NGO is a small agency with a handful of staff working in a cluster of villages in a particular locality. Relatively few NGOs possess the staff or financial resources to work intensively at regional or national level, although it is these organisations which are the best known in government and donor circles. Most of these NGOs are engaged in promoting self-help activities, service provision, community organisation, and poverty alleviation with funding from foreign NGOs and, in some cases, government sources. In vulnerable areas, it is still far from rare for development projects to be interrupted by the need to address emergency problems, at times resulting in emergency and development programmes running alongside each other. A common characteristic of most NGO interventions is working through groups, although some interventions, most notably emergency-type projects, work with the poor on a one-to-one basis. NGO groups range from informal community-based organisations to formal membership bodies established, for instance, for the purpose of the project, often facilitating credit or service schemes provided by the government, or else initiated by the NGOs themselves. They are bound together by voluntary contributions of time and resources and function for mutual benefit. These traits distinguish them from NGOs which act as service providers or facilitators (Fowler, 1988: 3-5; Verhagen, 1987: 21-4). In Africa these organisations 'draw cohesion and legitimacy by building on existing forms of social organisation and adapting their procedures to traditional norms of reciprocity.' (Bratton, 1990: 92).

In Latin America, and more recently in parts of Asia, it is common for NGOs to promote and work with grass-roots organisations in order to create popular movements which can use their growing power to attempt to modify government legislation in the interests of the poor, and to strengthen democratic participation in the wider society (Korten, 1990a: 123-8; Clark, 1991; Stephen, 1990; Carroll, 1992; Bebbington and Kopp, 1995).

Other differences are there between NGO approaches, notably between the approaches frequently used in Africa and Asia, reflecting differing historical traditions and political environments. In Bangladesh, NGOs pursue remarkably similar approaches to poverty alleviation, centred on the setting up of savings and credit groups which provide the focal point not only for revolving loan schemes, but also for a range of other sectoral activities in the fields of health, education, income generation, social forestry, irrigation, etc.

In this they are strongly influenced by the models promoted by the Bangladesh Rural Advancement Committee (BRAC) and the Grameen Bank.

Amazingly, Indian NGOs generally exhibit a greater diversity of approach. Two main approaches prevail: small-scale integrated rural development on the one hand and social action on the other. The former is premissed on support for specific programmes and projects organised sectorally and implemented through grass-roots organisations (known as *Sangams* in southern India). In contrast, social action groups concentrate on mobilising the poor to demand better services from government, and work for improved working conditions, higher wages, tenurial reform, etc. while the approaches are very different, there has been some convergence in recent years, with the growing belief among some NGOs that material improvements and empowerment are complementary and can reinforce each other.

In many African countries, the churches play a major role in NGO development activities, many having shifted from relief to development work in the past 10 to 15 years. For instance, in Uganda most dioceses have development arms responsible for channelling funds from northern churches and NGOs to grass-roots organisations in rural areas. Similarly, foreign NGOs tend to be operational more in Africa than in Asia, in part because of the relative weakness of indigenous NGOs and the lack of suitably qualified personnel, and in part because of the many areas which government services simply do not reach and where, as a result, any intervention tends to be relatively expensive.

Trends in NGO Activities

Health care and education were prominent among the initial concerns of many NGOs in the 1950s and 1960s. Increasingly, however, NGOs have moved into projects directly targeted at alleviating poverty and attempting to raise the incomes of the poor. Thus, projects aimed at increasing poor farmers' incomes became fashionable in the 1970s, manifest in a growing concern with income generation, the supply of credit, and crop production. These were often accompanied by measures designed to improve the rural infrastructure in the shape of minor irrigation schemes, the construction of schools and community buildings, local roads, etc.

A rather different trend also emerged in the 1970s, where the emphasis was not so much on service delivery or development programmes, but on organising the poor with a view to enabling them to exercise greater influence over decisions affecting their lives. This 'empowerment' approach has its roots in the view that literacy can often become a means by which the poor can reflect on the causes of their poverty and find ways of tackling them, usually by forming activist groups which put pressure on governments to reassess their policies or persuade the rich to redistribute power and resources in favour of the poor.

New concerns came to the fore in the 1980s, such as gender and the environment, with social forestry and soil conservation prominent among environmental concerns. These reflect an increasing concern about how projects affect the wider setting in which the poor live. Part of the reason for this extension of interests comes from another characteristic which NGOs emphasise: innovation. NGOs pride themselves on being innovative, in the sense of introducing new techniques as well as in fostering novel forms of social organisation. As regards the former this has centred on the development of appropriate, low-cost, technologies, which are accessible to the poor. Similarly, as noted above, some NGOs claim to be innovative in their organisational approach, by promoting participation and forging new co-operative alliances among the poor through the formation of grass-roots organisations.

The 1990s have witnessed yet more changes in the nature of NGO activities. Work in the areas of gender and the environment has been widened, deepened, and in many ways integrated under the umbrella of 'sustainable development'. Additionally, some NGOs have focused their efforts in initiatives aimed at strengthening the power and influence of different (poorer) groups in civil society and in a range of projects and programmes striving to build up the capacity of local organisations.

Cutting across these concerns has been a growing interest in sustainability. There are two reasons for this. One stems from a concern with cost recovery, and the desire among NGOs (especially northern NGOs) to transfer the recurrent costs of project management to the community following the withdrawal of the support agency. This is based on the belief that development interventions can be sustained over the longer term only if the community assumes ownership of the project or programme. A second reason for the interest in sustainability is bound up with the desire to avoid promoting dependence on an external agency. This is based in part on NGOs' not wishing to be perceived as benevolent patrons, especially when external dependence simply replaces the influence of locally dominant elites without addressing the structural reasons for such dominance.

NGO Comparative Advantage: Assumptions and Evidence

So much for the development of the different characteristics and modes of operation of both northern and southern NGOs. In this section we focus more specifically on the advantages which NGOs are said to bring to bear on the issue of trying to solve the basic problems of development and poverty. At one time, there was widespread scepticism outside NGO circles about the potential of NGOs in development. This has now diminished, although as Cernea (1988: 17) notes, 'there are many contradictory views about the comparative advantages and weaknesses of NGOs. These views range from quasi-denial of NGO effectiveness to hyperbolic exaggeration.'

It is common (and understandable) that northern NGOs

tend to project a positive image of their work and the projects that they support in developing countries. This is partly because the public has high expectations of what they can achieve, fuelled by media attention in the 1980s. As Clark astutely observes (1991: 51): 'The media project Northern NGOs as virtuous Davids fighting the Goliaths of famine, climate, government inequity, slavery and oppression. Their staff make such great sacrifices . . . their projects allow crops to grow abundantly where previously there was desert.' It is also in part a function of the literature produced by the NGOs themselves, especially that which is directed to fund-raising. There is a pervasive belief among NGOs in the superior quality of their interventions compared with those supported and executed by official donors and governments. But, to quote Clark again (1991: 53):

> there is surprisingly little objective reporting of NGO projects. Northern NGOs' own writing generally concentres on the success stories and, being aimed largely at their supporting publics, serve a propaganda purpose . . . Most contributors have an implicit faith in the 'NGO approach' which they don't want rocked. After all, one doesn't scrutinise magic too closely, otherwise it loses its charm.

One way of assessing the impact and effectiveness of NGO interventions is to attempt to isolate those features of NGOs which, it is argued, place them in a comparatively advantageous position to work with and assist the poor. In an important early analysis, Tendler (1982: 2 ff.) lists some seven 'articles of faith' about the positive nature of private voluntary organisations. These include:

(i) that the poor participate in their projects;
(ii) that PVOs succeed in reaching the poor;
(iii) that emphasis is laid more on the process through which people learn to gain control over their lives rather than in the execution of particular tasks;
(iv) that interventions are characterised by flexibility and experimentation in large measure because they tend to be small-scale;

(v) and that the costs of intervention tend to be lower than more traditional official agency as well as host government interventions.

A similar sort of listing of NGO attributes is given by van der Heijden (1986: 6-7), who argues that the unique features of NGOs, or their 'comparative advantages', are:

> their ability to deliver emergency relief or development services at low cost, to many people, in remote areas; their rapid, innovative and flexible responses to emerging financial and technical assistance needs at the grass roots level; their long-standing familiarity with social sector development and poverty alleviation; their experience with small-scale development projects as well as with those requiring a high degree of involvement by, and familiarity with, the concerned target groups.

These attributes have been confirmed in some of the more recent literature which continues to make similar claims about the role and often the uniqueness of NGOs. Thus, from the World Bank, Williams (1990: 32) writes that 'international NGO have been effective in their ability to work at the grassroots level, and to operate in remote areas or those sectors that did not have efficient development activity'.

Not surprisingly, given their growing involvement in the funding of NGOs, official aid donors have tended to confirm the claims made by the NGOs themselves. Thus, according to a review of NGO projects supported by official aid agencies, Cameron and Cocking state that Canadian NGOs meet their project objectives; Danish NGOs are believed to supplement and complement official aid work; Irish NGOs are effective in meeting their objectives; British NGOs effectively complement official aid; and New Zealand NGOs contribute to the alleviation of poverty in the poorer regions of the world (1991: 18-19). And in the words of a recent overview of NGOs, undertaken by the OECD (1988: 114-15): 'In general, evaluations conducted so far by the official aid agencies of DAC members, many of them relating to rural development and social services, conclude that NGOs have a good record in rural development.' Such a view is likely to have been strongly influenced by a 1986 Canadian International Development Agency study, based on a review of 420 projects sponsored by CIDA and Canadian NGOs. This concluded not only that the vast majority of such interventions were very successful, but that a full one-third of projects appeared to have achieved financial autonomy. Overall, it is argued that the projects showed a strong rural emphasis and a 'clear focus on the poor' (OECD, 1988: 103).

This viewpoint has, however, been increasingly challenged. Indeed, more common are contributions which refine these rather bold assertions, which challenge outright one or more elements of the conventional wisdom, or which highlight what are seen as weaknesses in NGO interventions. These writings are based on a mix of personal experience, surveys of already completed evaluations, and the results of specially commissioned assessments of particular interventions in one or more countries. Among the most serious problems pinpointed are that the management of projects tends to be weak and, in part relatedly, that sustainability is very difficult to achieve (Brown and Korten, 1989). A third problem is that there is little sign of replicability of particular interventions either by the same or by other NGOs. This clearly weakens the overall impact of NGO intervention. A typical critical assessment of the sustainability problem would be the following comment by USAID quoted by Dichter (1988: 1): 'A review of ongoing and completed AID projects in small-scale enterprise credit indicates that most never become self-sustaining even in their pure credit functions. Even more rarely does any project totally cover the costs of its non-financial components.' Indeed, detailed studies tend to suggest that NGO projects invariably founder once outside support is terminated (Cernea, 1988: 19), unless inputs are locally available, beneficiaries are strongly motivated, and the project is compatible smith existing social and economic structures (de Crombrugghe *et al.*, 1985).

On the management issue, Korten (1990a: 12) reflects an increasingly shared view that NGOs are 'characteristically weak on management and planning'. To which Clark adds (1991: 66):

> NGOs are prone to slow response resulting from cumbersome decision making, are susceptible to paralysis arising from power struggles between competing factions, and can evolve conflicting aims as different departments perceive a freedom to interpret their own role without reference to a strongly defined overall mission.

Similarly on the government/NGO contrast, with experience in East Africa, Fowler (1988) maintains that NGOs do not possess an innate comparative advantage over government institutions: rather, they have a potential comparative advantage which can be realised only if they consciously adopt management tools that are appropriate to small-scale development projects in an uncertain external environment.

In some cases, however, it is apparent that management *per se* is sometimes not such a problem, but that, especially in smaller projects, leadership can often be crucial to NGO impact. Indeed, a new article of faith is simply that 'good leadership is essential to project success' (Commonwealth Secretariat, 1987: 10). Conyers and Kaul (1990: 131) even go so far as to maintain that 'local leadership is one of the most important factors contributing to the success of most of the development projects'. Such a view has been confirmed by Tendler who, writing in 1987, drew attention to the significance of charismatic leadership in successful projects, noting that good political connections and a technocratic outlook were instrumental in their success (1987: 21-2). More detailed analysis also suggests that organisations can stagnate when leaders are away for long periods, that they are prone to decay, and that they have little potential for replication and limited capacity for absorbing new ideas. These observations lead Clark to conclude (1991: 66): 'Though leadership is critical to the success of NGOs usually little attention is paid to the development of leadership potential or to management training. And, once in post, leadership skills are rarely fostered because most NGOs are poor at delegation.'

Management and leadership questions lead naturally to the competence of NGO staff to undertake and execute projects and programmes. Although the issue does not feature widely in the published literature, it has been raised in particular by those with experience in the field. Thus Edwards (1989) maintains that he knows of no project in Zambia or Malawi in which inadequate training did not feature as a problem in project implementation (see also Edwards and Hulme, 1992). Highly committed staff are seen as an important element in NGO comparative advantage, although it is also recognised that this may create inflexibility and resistance to new ideas (Clark, 1991: 62).

Moving to the issue of replication, Brodhead and Herbert-Copley (1988: 110) argue that this is the key factor in evaluating success, but that 'the available evidence suggests that NGOs have had at best limited success in ensuring the replication of their work'. For Tendler (1987: v), there is an inherent conflict between small scale and replicability: smallness and social homogeneity often get lost when NGOs expand. She also links the issue of replicability to the leadership question, arguing that, unless the project is replicated by its founder, the chances of success in replication are thin (ibid: 21). Similarly, Cernea (1988: 18) argues that staff intensity and motivation are essential to successful replication.

While one component of the literature highlights these weaknesses of NGO intervention, another goes on to challenge some other articles of faith. Thus, Annis comments (1987: 129): 'In the face of pervasive poverty, for example, "small-scale" can merely be "insignificant"—"Politically-independent" can mean "powerless" or "disconnected"—"Low-cost" can mean "underfinanced" or "poor quality"—

And 'innovative' can mean simply "temporary" or "unsustainable."' What is more, Tendler (1982) contends that in practice many NGO interventions do not reach the lowest 40 per cent of the poor, and that they are neither participatory nor low-cost, although she goes on to argue that projects are not necessarily failures as a result of being burdened with these particular characteristics. Similarly, from a study of NGO projects in two villages in the Indian state of Gujarat, Griffiths (1987: 43) concludes that, despite a systematic attempt at proper identification and targeting, 'the poorest were by and large not identified whatever the circumstances'. Nevertheless, in contrast, Avina (1990) reports that, in his experience, the beneficiaries are among the poorest sectors of society, even if some of the not-so-poor also benefit.

On the cost issue, a series of USAID-sponsored studies on the effectiveness of NGO projects in health, nutrition, water supply, and sanitation, found that the largely voluntary nature of NGO activities, their commitment to use low cost technologies and streamlined services, and low staff costs, enable them to operate efficiently on low budgets' (Cernea, 1988: 18). In contrast, Bowden (1990) maintains that NGO interventions are not low-cost, Brodhead and Herbert-Copley (1988: 100) that low cost is no guarantee of cost-effectiveness, and Korten (1990*a* 12) that the projects are not is cost-effective as the NGOs themselves think. Brodhead hints at an underlying tension between simultaneously achieving the twin goals of reaching the poorest and executing low-cost projects. He draws on work by Chambers (1983) to suggest that projects which effectively reach the poor require a high degree of administrative skill and capability, which means higher costs per beneficiary.

On the question of the innovative nature of NGO activities, Kottack's analysis leads him to conclude that the projects promoted are anything but innovatory (1985: 323). As Tendler is often seen as a critic of the conventional wisdom, her contrasting views on innovation are particularly noteworthy.

In 1982 (1982: 114), she wrote that PVOs seem to be exceptionally innovative in relation to credit to small business, but five years later she maintained, that NGOs often claim they are pioneering a new approach when they are merely reinventing the wheel.

There has been considerable discussion in the literature on the issue of participation and its importance to project impact. The assumption, as Brodhead and Herbert-Copley (1988: 123) point out, is that participation increases the likelihood of attaining the project's objectives and its sustainability, as well as promoting a more equal distribution of project benefits. Their own view is that participation is important but by no means a sufficient condition for project success. This contrasts with the 1986 CIDA study which argued that community participation was one of three factors leading to project success. In strong contrast, Tendler (1982, 1987) maintains that projects which are not participatory but which are top-down and authoritarian can be very successful. Similarly, de Crombrugghe *et al.* (1985: 80) argue that projects may sometimes succeed without the beneficiaries being involved in the identification of needs, even if their evidence also leads them to the view that projects 'almost always fail' if the beneficiaries are excluded in the planning phase.

Moving from the particular to the general issue of the overall impact of NGO interventions, what is noteworthy is that, with only rare exceptions, most substantive analyses based on commissioned studies come to fairly gloomy conclusions about the performance of NGO projects, even though there is considerable reluctance on the part of analysts to be drawn into making overall or general statements about impact— even in cases where opinions are based on the examination of only a limited number of interventions.

The main reasons put forward for this high degree of diffidence are: the lack of data with which assessments can confidently be made, the differing quality of evaluations which have found their way into the public domain, and a reluctance to make broader generalisations from limited evidence. These points are made strongly, for instance, in the writings of Brodhead and Herbert-Copley (1988) and de Crombrugghe *et al.* (1985). A typical comment reflecting this sense of unease would be the following (Smith quoted in Gorman, 1984: 146, 155): 'the unevenness of evaluations of pvo projects does not help to prove pvo claims that they are more effective than governmental agencies in certain areas of development. . . there is insufficient evidence to substantiate these claims solidly . . . The rhetoric is at times great but adequate information is sparse.'

In spite of the reservations, some overall judgements have been made. They usually share the viewpoint that, while the projects selected are frequently those which the NGOs themselves believe are among their better ones, independent assessments frequently come to far less favourable judgements about performance and impact. Not surprisingly, therefore, the overall view of the impact of NGOs in poverty-alleviating and/or income-generating projects is one ranging from, say, mediocre to poor, rather than, say, from acceptable to good. A typical selection illustrates this particular cluster of viewpoints and conclusions.

> eight of the self-selected 17 projects failed to return benefits equivalent to the costs expended. Another study of 19 projects found 40 per cent to be borderline or unsatisfactory (Ellis quoted in Gorman, 1984: 202).
>
> Both Netherlands and FINNIDA evaluations point to a lack of success with income-generating projects (OECD, 1988: 19).
>
> Ford's experience after 10 years examination of income generating projects is that 'there are very few successes to talk about, especially if you look at post-intervention sustainability (Fowler, personal communication, 1989).
>
> Projects which were initially selected on the grounds that they were successful in fact turned out not to satisfy the evaluation criteria outlined in a surprisingly large number of cases ... Of

> the seven micro-projects visited, six exhibited quite serious problems (de Crombrugghe *et al.*, 1985: 18, 48).

These and similar comments from this critical school lead on to the highlighting of a fourth problem, which, it is argued, plays a major contributory role in the low success rate of their projects.[7] This is the vagueness of many of the objectives of projects, leading to the charge that imprecise objectives are bound to be difficult to monitor and evaluate. In this vein, de Crombrugghe *et al.* argued in the mid-1980s that steps needed to be taken to improve the way that projects were identified, prepared, and initially appraised (1985: 36). Nevertheless, towards the end of the decade, there was still 'a widespread need for better project planning' (OECD, 1988: 115).

A number of more recent studies have placed increased emphasis on yet more factors said to influence project performance. Particular emphasis is placed on the importance of the wider environment—the large number of factors external to the project—which, it is argued, not only need to be analysed when initiating and executing particular projects, but which also heip to explain what appears to be the relatively poor-performance of NGO projects. For instance, Tendler (1987: 102) maintains that the success of NGO operations depends upon a complex set of factors including macroeconomic and socio-political environmental factors, many of which are otters beyond the control of the NGOs.

Similarly, Carr *et al.* (1984: 1) contend that a *sine qua non* of any evaluation of performance is a full understanding of the environment in which the project is located; only when this is achieved can one begin to understand the changes which are talking place, and among them the ones which are applicable to project intervention. More dynamic and historical factors are also highlighted.

A discussion of the importance of power, power relations, and empowerment processes in understanding current impact and future prospects is also relevant in this context (see, for example, Marsden and Oakley, 1990). Debate on these issues can be highly specific, relating to elites and interest-group interests that directly impinge upon the project, or it can be very broad and general, focusing on the nature of the state and the manner in which it is possible for agents external to central power structures to meet the objectives of their very different agendas. Usually, however, when discussion of impact takes place within these wider parameters it also tends to veer towards pessimism. Schneider (1988: 139, 202) writes that:

> Although NGOs often work diligently to eliminate the symptoms of poverty, they are not always conscious of its true dimensions and are frequently unaware of the spiralling effect of these factors of impoverishment...
> In the light of the findings of our study, it is obvious that rural development remains essentially a prerogative of government

When discussion is broadened to external factors it usually emphasises the complexity of factors affecting project performance. Some authors have argued that, because the communities with which NGOs work are always changing, if not the objectives then at least the means to achieve these objectives need continually to be re-assessed and altered as circumstances, both internal and external to the project, change. Conyers and Kaul (1990: 132) suggest that this inevitably brings conflict. Yet another layer of complexity is added when it is argued that project success in one time-period could well be the cause of problems in another. This is well illustrated by a recent review of a World Lutheran Federation water project in West Nile Uganda, where clear success in easing the plight of thousands of people whose lives were threatened, contributed to the build-up of future problems. Thus, according to Brett (1989):

> The field director said they had made three errors: of efficiency, of kindness and of expatriate methods. Efficiency had both created widespread dependency and let it be possible for the government to ignore the area. Proving services that were

> subsidised had created a false sense of values among the people; using foreign methods meant it would be more difficult for others to follow. While all this is very true, there were in fact no alternatives (at the time).

It is by no means easy to come to any firm overall conclusions about either the factors which characterise the uniqueness of NGO interventions or the degree to which NGOs have succeeded in their task of helping to alleviate poverty. It is clearly far from simple to judge whether the views of the optimists or the pessimists better reflect reality. There are four main reasons for this. The first is simply a lack of data. For all the claims and counter-claims made and for all the evidence provided, the extent of reliable evidence upon which judgements have been and are made still remains minute in comparison with both the absolute numbers of NGO interventions and the very different types of project embarked upon. The second is that there still seems to be confusion in the eyes of both the general public and the agencies over claims and assertions about the comparative advantage of NGOs and the evidence which is available. The third is the growing realisation that a range of both complex and external factors play a powerful role in influencing the outcome of NGO intervention in very different social, economic, and political contexts. Finally, judging impact is handicapped by the lack of an agreed method of assessing the performance of NGO protects and programmes.

CHAPTER 3

NGOs: Concept and Theories

No doubt, the current international development effort is directed at a variety of organisations and institutions. Social change is seldom achieved by an individual acting alone. Understanding NGOs therefore requires working definitions.

Institutions and Organisations

The most fundamental definition of organisations is that they are purposeful, role-bound social units. They are groups of individuals who allocate tasks between themselves to contribute to a common goal. This simple definition gets very muddled in practice because, for example, not everyone may share the goal to the same degree, or they may be in the organisation for personal reasons which have little or nothing to do with what the organisation wants to achieve. Despite these complications, the two items to bear in mind are: to exist an organisation needs a purpose; and an organisation is made up of people who know what their role is. The significance of purpose, or mission, in organisational life makes this a common starting point for subdivision or classification. A more difficult classification is between organisation and institution, terms which are, incorrectly, used interchangeably.

Where principles or norms of people's behaviour, become a stable, accepted and collectively valued basis on which society works, we can talk of social institutions. However, not all organisations become institutions and not all institutions are made up of organisations, which can be confusing. For example, marriage is a valued social institution which is not made up of organisations. Similarly, money is a valued social institution, but it cannot be equated to the behaviour of all banks, insurance companies or the Treasury. Corruption can also become institutionalised in some societies as the only way of getting things done, but this pattern of behaviour is not typical of one organisation or one place.

Organisations can become institutionalised in the sense that they are a recognised and valued part of society. In the context of Great Britain, Oxfam has become such a household name that it is itself institutionalised. The same can probably be said for the Fundacion Sociale in Colombia, United Way in the USA, the Bangladesh Rural Advancement Committee (BRAC) and the Red Cross. By and large. NGOs seldom make an adequate distinction between development of organisations and social institutions, which means that their strategies and methods are often not optimal, While there is no water tight distinction, an NGO needs to be clear about these two terms, because they are not interchangeable and affect the way things have to be done.

Organisation: Formal and Informal

To proceed, it is necessary to highlight a common short-sightedness in much Western analysis of organisations and institutions; this is the tendency to overlook what is not formally organised and legally recognised by governments. While informal organisations are found across the world, a significant feature of organisational life in countries of the South and East is that they rely on interpersonal networks. These networks are familial and customary rather than enshrined in organisational constitutions, and can be very powerful in shaping how both organisations and institutions work in practice.

There is a rich array of non-legalised forms of organised co-operation that people create to achieve shared goals; these may be formal for those belonging inside them, even if outsiders see them as informal. Age sets are an example common throughout sub-Saharan Africa, as are the *pakikisama* affiliations in the Philippines. As governments retreat, opening space for civic initiatives, the number and density of both informal and legally formal ways of collaborating is growing rapidly. While the merits of non-formalised organising should not be over-idealised, it would be very wrong, especially in the work of people-centred development, to remain unaware of the resource significance and demands which this type of growth makes on the work of all development agencies.

PRINCIPLES OF ORGANISATIONAL SECTORS

Purpose is a common way of differentiating between types of organisations. Past study indicates that the evolution of societies as modern nation-Mates gives rise to institutions and organisations established for three relatively distinct purposes;

(i) to protect, secure and regulate the lives and actions of citizens; for example, to manage how society is defended as well as how it functions and progresses:

(ii) to make a livelihood and create and accumulate wealth, and accumulate wealth; and

(iii) to purse individual interests or tackle personal or social concerns which are separate from gaining a livelihood.

The first set of purposes typically belongs to governments, the second to business and the market, and the third to the self-willed association of citizens. Organisational science uses a shorthand of first, second and third sectors as labels for these purposes.

The sectors themselves can be divided into whether the purpose they serve is private or public. The first sector is concerned with what is called the public realm, that is the common area allotting all citizens in which they have rights and obligations, both of which are enforced by government agencies. The second sector makes up the private realm of people's initiatives to survive and improve economically; the third makes up the private realm for the pursuit of recreational, spiritual, social, cultural, and other personal or collective interests.

The three-way spilt is confused by the fact that private organisations can play a similar role to governments when they are established for public purposes. For example, rais occurs when a voluntary organisation is set up to serve some common good - such as, helping the aged, or assisting people whose rights base been abided. In addition, establishing a business or a non-profit is an act of free will: society does not expect or require any one private organisation to exist or be around for ever: this is not the case with government. Choosing to gain social recognition by formal registration means accepting society's right to oversee that you do what you say you will. In other words, registration is accepting obligations of public accountability which society determines and regulates. An important division within third sector purposes, therefore, is whether the organisation is established to serve others or to benefit those within it.

This distinguishes between third-party public service providers and self-help or mutual-benefit organisations. The former delivers something to others, the latter is there for the benefit of its own members. A charity can be created to provide clean water to poor household (third parties) while an antateur football team or choir provides mutual benefits for the players or singers. Being either a service or mutual benefit organisation affects how they work.

The size and content of the three sectors varies from country to country and each is usually distinguished and regulated by specific legislation. Relative size is primarily determined by the political ideology dominating society, or the regime in power, and is expressed through policy preferences, legislation, and public versus private investment choices. Two examples of different sectoral set-ups. The left-hand side of the figure corresponds to a society which, like the USA, actively limits the role of government while encouraging private enterprise and voluntary initiative. Western Europe would probably exhibit a larger state sector, with other circles being of a more similar size. The right-hand side is more typical of societies where governments dominate; this is often the case in the countries of the South and East, such as Tanzania, Kazakstan and India, where an ideology of public ownership and central planning has made the state the primary force for economic and social development. It should come as no surprise that the intentions and funding conditions of the international aid system are designed to make the organisational pattern of countries of the South and East look more like those of the left.

Actually, there are many overlaps between each sector, which are important when understanding NGDOs today; these are explained below.

Operating Principles

To understanding the organisational dimensions of NGDOs, it is helpful to compare the basic operating principles of these three sectors. This will enable us to identify features which are supposed to make voluntary organisations particularly suited to people-centred development work. Differences of particular interest have to do with:

(i) obtaining required behaviour of people in the organisation;

(ii) the nature of the relationship between the organisation and the outside world, particularly towards those it serves;

(iii) the way of mobilising resources; and feedback on and assessment of performance.

People in Organisations

How do you get people to behave well in their

organisational roles? Studies suggest that people behave the way they need to in organisations either: because they have to, that is. they are coerced; because they have incentives to do so, they are induced: or they are driven to do so by their own internal beliefs and values. At the risk of gross generalisation, each of the three sectors is found to adopt a different way of ensuring that people behave effectively in their roles: governments tend to rely on hierarchy, command and enforcement; businesses provide (or deny) monetary and other rewards as incentives; voluntary organisations rely on personal values, commitment and self-motivation.

While elements of each type of motivation can surely be found in all organisations, an important consequence of self-motivation in third-sector organisations is that individuals feel empowered to behave like co-owners, with a corresponding expectation to be treated in such a way by management; this impacts on organisational culture and decision-making processes. Of course, a person's technical competence, experience, aptitudes, personal situation, and aspirations are also important for fulfilling a role effectively. But the basic way an organisation goes about motivating all these elements within an individual is distinct for each sector.

Relating to the Outside World

Organisations in each sector tend to differ in how they relate to the outside world, particularly towards those they are supposed to serve. Governments, because of their public role and unique position of power, are inclined to be authoritative in their dealings with citizens; this may be tempered by setting standards for and soliciting feedback on the performance of public services. Further, the state-citizen relationship is effectively tied within a permanent set of mutual obligations which are, or should be, negotiated through the political process. Governments are also empowered to legislate and enforce; in this way they create much of the environment in which they operate.

Private businesses seldom have permanent relationships with their owners or customers from birth to death, although banks and insurance companies may get close to it. The relationship between business and their customers is overwhelmingly based on momentary transactions called purchases - the universal process of buying, selling, or bartering. Lacking formal coercive power, businesses try to condition the external world through advertising, by building monopolies and by, occasionally, employing corrupt practices or attempting to coerce customers into buying from them. Without legislative power to contract the environment in which they operate, enterprises try to protect their internal functioning from external disruption - such insulation is particularly necessary for mass production lines and processes which transform physical resources into products. In addition, businesses are concerned to maintain their image of reliability, quality and corporate social responsibility, where advertising and media events play an important role. However, left to their own devices without public controls or incentives, competition naturally inclines businesses to minimise the internal costs and externalise the public costs of their activity -such as environmental degradation or pollution to tax payers.

Voluntary sector organisations do not have the legislative capability and coercive force of the state nor the economic clout of commercial capital and enterprise. What they have, instead is the dynamism and power of self-willed human action, which can encompass very large numbers of people and exert significant influence in society, is seen in civic protests or consumer boycotts. In as far as voluntary organisations are set up by value-driven, self-motivated people to serve a segment of the population unreached by the state or market, there is a strong identification between the organisation and those it is set up for. In NGDO jargon, this is termed solidarity. Groups or classes with particular interests can go so far as to set up non-profit organisations to gain political power - for example, establishing themselves as political parties.

The duration of relationships between voluntary organisations and the individuals they serve differs widely. For member-based institutions, such is organised religion, the relationship is usually permanent. For others, such as social and recreational organisations, membership is unlikely to be permanent but may span a number of years. For historical and legal reasons, non-membership voluntary organisations are usually most active in providing public goods with a social benefit, such as education, health and welfare. Interactions with clients, therefore, tend, on balance, to be more than momentary but seldom permanent, which orients third-sector organisations towards transactions which could last from days to years, but where the idea of eventual separation is understood from the start.

Looking back to the goals and tasks of development, it is clear that NGDOs can hardly be in the business of selling services to those in poverty. If the poor could pay the full cost, the market, in theory, would respond to satisfy their demand. Moreover, the actual process of 'producing' development is rooted within communities themselves, which means that NGDOs must negotiate in order to integrate their work with ongoing external processes. How they can do this well is the subject of other chapters, where we will see that an NGDO's ability to negotiate is related to its attitude or stance, as expressed through the staff who do the negotiating. In its turn, organisational stance depends on the degree to which the voluntary sector has a vibrant presence. It also depends on the ability to mobilise appropriate financial resources, and here again there are sectoral differences.

Resource Mobilisation

Each organisational sector mobilises resources in different ways. They are Governments function from taxes paid by citizens who should receive adequate public-services in exchange. While shareholders and banks provide capital, a business stands or falls on its ability to sell goods and services to customers for an amount sufficiently greatger than their cost; if not, bankruptcy results. By and large, non-membership voluntary organisations do not recover the full cost of what they provide to their clients or beneficiaries; and this is certainly the case for NGDOs who, on an ongoing basis, have to raise finances from other sources, loosely termed donors.

In the case of international development, most NGDOs fulfil an intermediary role in a chain which generates and transfers resources: knowledge, technology, money, information. The NGDO task is to add value to the transfer process. For the present, it is sufficient to point out that being located between donors in one continent and stakeholders in another, or between affluent urban-based financiers and geographically remote, impoverished and socially marginalised beneficiaries, presents particular difficulties for management; these difficulties are further aggravated by the fact that performance is not easy to measure.

Performance and Feedback

What constitutes a 'bottom line for each sector? How can an organisation find out how well it is doing.' What feedback provides such information? For governments, or better said the regime in power, the bottom line is political the level of citizen satisfaction expressed through the ballot box or through civil disobedience, unrest and riots. For example, refusal to pay local government service charges in South Africa was one way that disenfranchised citizens could express dissatisfaction with services to their townships. Imperfect as they may be, existing democratic systems and public feedback - expressed through civic action, constituents' letters, petitions and percentages of the vote - do periodically focus politicians' minds and call them to account.

While arguments are raised to include corporate social responsibility as an element of performance, the bottom line for businesses remains that of profitability. Market indicators, such as share value, price/earnings ratios and market share, while obviously open to differences in interpretation, provide effective and immediate feedback to managers.

In the voluntary sector, when it comes to performance measures and feedback, there is a significant difference between the two kinds of organisation - mutual benefit and service - we identified earlier. In the former, performance measures and feedback can be readily gained from those who should be reaping the benefits. In formal set-ups, this process is usually built into the governance system of annual meetings and members' voting rights, while informal organisations select their own ways to provide information on whether or not members are getting what they want.

For most third-sector service-providing organisations, on the other hand, no straightforward, uncontented performance measures present themselves. The nearest we can come to a bottom line is credibility and legitimacy, measures which must to be 'constructed' from the combined social judgement of the organisation's many "users', including intended beneficiaries, governors, volunteers and staff. This is a complicated way of going about things, lacks the immediacy of the market, is open to dispute because users are seldom of equal weight, and makes comparisons or 'benchmarking' very difficult. The lack of clear performance indicators makes the management of non-profits more complex and difficult than other sectors.

For third-sector service providers in general, and for NGDOs specifically, the most critical line of feedback and measure must come from the primary stakeholder (this term is increasingly used instead of clients, beneficiary or target group), because it is their poverty or deprivation which is used to justify the organisation's existence. Changes in the well being of the primary stakeholders must be reported back to donors. Unfortunately, this line of feedback is usually very weak and is seldom able to influence an NGDO's overall performance; all too often. NGOs prefer to fulfill pre-defined project activities which qualify for further financing. Relative inattention to long-term impact means that feedback on working with communities does not gain equal weight with pressures coming down the aid chain from constituents and donors.

It is commonly assumed, and argued strongly by NGDOs, that their place within the voluntary (third) sector, and the principles which go with it, give them comparative advantages. What are the arguments supporting this view? First, value-driven, committed and self-motivated staff should mure readily identify with and be able to adopt an appropriate stance towards their clients, engendering trust and enhancing authentic participation. In comparison, and irrespective of the individual or their technical function, government staff always carry with them the status of power, limiting their ability to identify with the poor or to be accepted by them. It certainly confines their ability to support empowerment processes when such processes are directed against government itself.

Second, NGDOs do not need the uniformity or standardisation of practices which state bureaucracies apply; as a result, they can adapt more, readily to local contexts and meet the demands of people centred development. They can organise themselves to provide tailored support to a particular disadvantaged group -unmarried mothers, the landless, people with AIDS, the non-credit worthy, or the disabled. In other words, they are better able to target their assistance, which should improve efficiency and effectiveness. Third, while commercial organisations can adapt themselves to their clients' needs, they are not particularly interested in and cannot reach, the really poor in the way NGDOs can because of donor support (which could be called a form of subsidy): such support is only forthcoming because of die trust in their non-profit principles. Fourth. NGDOs are not a public body, giving them the flexibility to stay long enough to help make a difference, but not so long that dependency results Governments, on the other hand, are there for ever. Fifth, in not seeking profits, NGDOs can be less costly than business, while staff self-motivation enables them to function at less than market rates because part of the employee's reward comes from self-fulfilment. Finally, NGDOs can undertake necessary development functions and supporting processes which are not 'services' as such. These functions can entail, for example, providing a channel for information and other types of 'bridges' between different types of organisation, facilitating links, acting as a catalyst and temporarily filling gaps: such activities are effectively impossible to measure and difficult to classify as a service, but important none the less. Because of their principles. NGDOs are less likely to face the accusation of creating work simply to profit owners, a common complaint made against service-contracting companies, such as consultancy firms, which are driven to sell staff time.

While the validity of these arguments may be questioned, in theory at least, applying voluntary sector principles should be positive in terms of development effectiveness. The next step is to trace what happens when organisational theory moves into today's development practice.

NGDO's : AN ESTIMATE

The three sectors described above are imaginary, they are unlikely to be found exactly like this in the real world. But this framework helps to describe NGDOs and why they behave as they do. identifying underlying forces which must he dealt with in practical organisation and management. When the different principles of each sector overlap within an organisation, however problems can result.

Overlapping Sectors

The overall purpose of NGDOs and the typical tasks and critical balances involved in being effective. Attention should now be focused on what happens to people-centred development in an increasingly contract-oriented aid system. In other words, what challenges arise to NGDO management and organisation when they have to operate in the more complicated areas of overlapping principles?

Rather than dealing with mutual benefits and other types of organisations within the voluntary sector, this discussion concentrates on service-providing NGDOs. One observation is that organisations located firmly within the third sector, and consistently applying its principles, are most likely to be supplying welfare-type services. Like the Lions and Rotary clubs, they may be composed of unpaid volunteers, occasionally raising donations from well-wishers, or they may have evolved into more stable charitable institutions, providing homes for destitute children or people with disabilities. While beneficial, this type of activity is not what today's empowering people-centred development is thought to be about and, consequently, such voluntary organisations, although sometimes recipients of aid, are not the focus of this book.

Instead, the third-sector organisations of primary interest are those operating within the framework of objectives and tasks set out. Today, evidence suggests that these voluntary organisations are more likely to be found in areas of overlap 2, 3 and 4 than in V. Why?' The answer is as follows: over a period of 30 years the aid system has become an aid business demanding a high degree of professionalism from NGDOs, displacing moral motivations with more functional concerns of effective delivery. International assistance, furthermore, is increasingly assigned on the basis of project-based competitive contracts. Aid priorities are shifting away from governments, reallocating what were once state responsibilities for public services into the other two sectors; this has lead to more NGDO tax-based funding. Structural adjustment policies have decreased spending on public services, creating a 'moral' pressure on NGDOs to fill the gup and a dilemma on whether or not they should do so. There is a stagnation in the growth of private donations to development work, and the proportion of NGDO funds derived From official aid donors is rapidly increasing. To appreciate what all this means in terms of effects and challenges, we must look at what is likely to happen to the comparative advantages of voluntary development as the different sectoral principles overlap.

Consequences for NGDOs in Development

Overlaps between sectors can work in tuo directions. For example, business can combine its principles with those of the voluntary sector by, for example, creating non-monetary incentives as a motivation for staff. Conversely, in the voluntary sector values of participation and empowerment can be combined with the material rewards common to business in how staff want to be rewarded. Current trends are towards the latter rather than the former, so our concentration is on how government and business principles overlap and affect the management and organisation of NGDOs.

The Government Overlap

What might occur within NGDOs when they provide public services similar to the state (area 2), which many do? For a start, staff may be inclined to behave in directive ways, treating those they serve simply as recipients who should be happy with whatever level of service they get. Put another say, solidarity is an unlikely attitude. The NGDO may start to believe that it has a right to an everlasting place in society, putting its own interests above the continual need to demonstrate its credibility, with staff expecting permanent employment. Arguing that it is doing the government's job, NGDOs will make claims on public funds which - without sufficient care -bring with them conditions and expectations that the organisation will operate in accordance with government standards, practices and political needs. In short, the NGDO functions as a parastatal agency in all but name. This behaviour is observed in India, where the government has allocated large sums of money for NGDOs to assist an implementing the National Development Plan.

The Business Overlap

Where NGDO functions are overlapped by businesses principles, NGDOs may adopt the ethos of entrepreneurs and contractors. Poverty alleviation and humanitarian relief may change from being a moral response to a social problem, turning poor people into a 'product' to be marketed and sold. Market position, in terms of the organisation's share in private and public aid donations, becomes a dominant concern, leading to fund-raising practices which overstate achievements or which, in pursuit of a sympathetic response from donors, distort information or present images which may do an injustice to those for whom the NGDO operates.

Growth and the ability to spend, rather than the profitability of the company, become criteria for measuring success; the legitimate difficulties of performance measurement may be used to hide shortcomings in development impact. Transparency in operations also suffers because failures or set-backs are treated as potentially bad publicity and therefore unwelcome news, instead of a source of learning. As a consequence, internal systems which seek to monitor or evaluate performance are viewed as a contract imposition and their outputs are not made available to the public, which undermines accountability. Increasing market profile and income share is a now a common concern of Northern NGDOs' fund-raising; overstating impact is wide-spread; distortions in fund-raising images are a frequent complaint of NGDOs from the South and East; and the lack of transparency is a source of growing disquiet in development circles and the media.

Commercial companies continually search for ways to reduce costs, especially by applying economics of scale. NGDOs may do the same in order to save donor funds, but at the cost of diseconomies of development processes and wilful ignoring of indirect effects. For example, an NGDO involved in supporting school construction throughout a country in East Africa negotiated with communities that when they had built the walls, the NGDO would provide the roofing materials. To save money, materials were bought in bulk from one supplier. But the centralised purchasing arrangements bore no relationship to the varied stages of interaction with communities. The rains came before materials arrived, and in some cases substantial damage occurred to the new classrooms. Result? Community demotivation and economic waste. Simply put, economies of scale come at the cost of choice and flexibility. NGDOs must therefore be able to make difficult trade-offs setting desirable economic optimisation against effectiveness in complex development processes.

What the business overlap also brings is a greater concern to control costs and ensure sound financial management. As long as these aspects are applied in ways which do not undermine or limit the application of best development practice, they constitute a significant benefit to NGDOs who are often lax in these areas, partly because business approaches have not been seen as consistent with a culture of solidarity. Part of appropriate NGDO professionalism must include attention to costs and benefits and ensuring proper use of financial resources; business can offer useful experience and guidance, but is not necessarily as pre-packaged methods.

Financial incentives are needed to gain professional staff; however, this runs counter to the spirit of voluntarism and self-motivation and the organisational culture which goes with it. The introduction of a competitive culture creates organisational tensions, conflicts of conscience and personal stress, especially for middle managers. For example, it is argued that hierarchy, which is accepted as normal in government and business, increases effective decision-making, while committed staff, who are prepared to forego a market rate for their labour in NGDOs expect democratic decision processes as well as the right to influence policy and practice; this expectation leads to -'paralysis of participation'. How are the two to be balanced? Finally, pressure to compete can sway NGDOs' attentions towards donors as primary stakeholders, rather than towards those who provide their legitimacy. Put another way, the service given to the donor becomes more important than the benefit to those who justify the NGDO's existence.

The Three-Tiered Overlap

It is easy to sec that area 4 is a position of great complexity, calling for NGDOs to juggle with and balance three different sets of principles at once. They must contribute to sustained poverty alleviation and social justice using their voluntary attributes, while functioning as businesses to provide public services. This is obviously not a desirable position, but sometimes it cannot be avoided, particularly in conditions of severe economic decline, ineffectual governments and high levels of national dependency on aid as, for example, in Burundi, Malawi, Mozambique, Mauritania, Nepal and Sierra Leone. In these settings, NGDOs must operate as very complicated hybrids, with the potential to suffer from all the tensions and unwelcome effects described above. NGDO organisation and management must actively counter the problems arising from multiple operating principles at the risk of otherwise becoming completely ineffective. Governments and businesses are seldom confronted with such situations and therefore have little to offer in terms of proven solutions.

Overall, while varying in degree between and within continents, opportunistic business and government behaviour continues to confuse the voluntary sector. An entrepreneurial shift in the aid market place leads to the NGDO label being appropriated by a variety of participants. Lip service is paid to voluntarism and solidarity. The overriding concern becomes survival at all costs.

Illustration 1 shows the - often less than Haltering - acronyms used across the world for organisations which claim to be NGDOs but are not inspired by the principles and values of voluntarism. One long-term observer asserts that NGDOs are, in fact, no longer part of the third sector, but belong in the second because their practices show that market, rather than voluntary, values dominate. The question this poses, and a concern of this book, is how can NGDOs reposition themselves to regain and apply the principles of development voluntarism in a commercial world?

Reestablishment of NGDOs

The past five years have seen significant tensions and upheavals occurring within NGDOs as the tectonic plates of voluntary, government and business principles collide with each other. In geology, such collisions result in a new landscape or, in some cases, ongoing instability with occasional earthquakes and eruptions. The NGDO landscape is still tar from suible, but there are signs that without conscious counter measures it will settle, Uphoft has argued, outside the third sector. This would be a misfortune.

Northern NGDOs have tended to adopt two distinct strategies in the struggle to introduce and somehow reconcile different sets of organisational principles. Some have embarked on massive and painful organisation-wide processes of reorientation, commonly labelled restructuring. Others have tried to change organisational culture and practices from above by importing chief executives and senior managers from the business world. Some have done both. There has been a common trend to redirect, streamline and increase the impact of operations by embarking on strategic planning, a still ongoing process for many NGDOs which has seldom been part of their management repertoire.

In the South, NGDOs have also been facing the dual challenge of repositioning themselves in a new aid context, as well as adjusting to the installation of democracy, especially

ILLUSTRATION 1: ACRONYMS FOR NGDO PRETENDERS

BRINGO Briefcase NGO	An NGO which is no more 'than a briefcase carrying a well written proposal
ComeN'GO Come and go NGO	An NGO that appears spasmodically; only used by the owners when the NGO pasture looks greener
CONGO Commercial NGO	NGOs set up by businesses in order to participate in bids, help win contracts, and reduce taxation
CRINGO Criminal NGO	Organisation established for illegal purposes, especially import-export (i.e. smuggling); common in transition economies
DONGO Donor NGO	Created and owned by donors to do their job while shifting overhead costs outside
FANGO Fake NGO	NGO used as a front for something else; not uncommon in Eastern Europe
GONGO Government-Owned NGO	Type of GRINGO used to capture or redirect non-profit funds allocated by the official aid system
GRINGO Government-Run and Initiated NGO	Variation of a Quango, but with the function of countering the actions of real NGDOs; common in Africa
MANGO Mafia NGO	A criminal NGO providing services of the money laundering, enforcement and protection variety; prevalent in Eastern Europe
MONGO My Own NGO	An NGO which is the personal property of an individual, often dominated by his or her ego
NGI Non-Governmental Individual	A person who operates as if he or she is an NGO but without an organisational affiliation
PANGO Party NGO	An aspiring, defeated or banned political party or politician dressed as an NGO; species of Central Asia and Indo-China
PHANGO Phantom NGO	NGO existing only in the mind of the speaker; used to bolster an argument
PONGO Politician's NGO	Established to capture or direct NGO funding to the home constituency as a defence against incursion by opponents
QUANGO Quasi NGO	Para-state body set up by government as an NGO, often to enable better conditions of service or create political distance

in Latin America, sub-Saharan Africa and the old Communist block. The responses have been steered by ideology, donor pressure and local opportunities. Soul-searching internal reviews, accompanied by difficult dialogues with Northern counterparts, have been undertaken by many of the larger organisations, such as IBASE in Brazil, DESCO in Peru and by the sound of it, almost all within the NGDO community in Chile. Repositioning through strategic planning is becoming a preoccupation with Southern NGOs, partly as a consequence of the strategic choices made by Northern supporters; these will be examined later.

In the East, local NGDOs are a recent organisational arrival; there is often confusion about their legal standing, especially if the regimes in power are unsure of what autonomy they can or want to tolerate. An example is Kazakstan, where recent constitutional amendments have curtailed possible areas of NGDO activity. The major challenge to NGDOs in finding a social position in Eastern countries is not the pressure that arises from overlapping sectors. Rather, difficulties arise in forming a socially recognised, stable third sector in post-authoritarian states - in a context where long-term support from the North is uncertain and inadequate. However, despite differences within and between continents, one agenda that is emerging for some NGDOs of the South and East which rely on aid looks for long-term strategies which tie NGDOs more firmly to their own economies.

All in all, NGDOs are in the midst of a severe identity crisis. The issue is to determine how NGDOs can emerge from this period so that voluntary values, principles and development advantages co-exist with, but are not made subordinate to, those of business and the market. Some would argue that it is too late; NGDOs as we knew them have already lost their soul. The immediate task is to examine what, in organisational and management terms, can be done to re-establish a position which embodies voluntarism in practice as well as in name.

Regaining Identity within Voluntarism

Retaining a position somewhere within the voluntary sector means ensuring that voluntary values and principles remain dominant in the context of a non-profit market place. Making this happen will depend on the nature and strength of an NGDO's identity, which in its rum is determined by consistency in the beliefs of those who govern its organisational values. Simply put, identity is determined by power over organisational philosophy and its translation into action.

The Importance of Values, Beliefs and Development Philosophy

Examining values and power in NGDOs is not straightforward because the first is highly abstract and the second seldom transparent. We will start with the most fundamental element of NGDO identity, its beliefs. Beliefs are the foundation for organisational values and philosophy of action. Together, beliefs, values and development philosophy form the reference point for what an NGDO is and stands for. They are the measure against which the organisation must judge itself and be judged by others.

Surprisingly, and unfortunately for the security of NGDO positioning, values and beliefs are seldom if ever explicitly talked about or clearly stated. A handful of NGDOs have recently attempted to do just this (see Illustration 2), but in the vast majority of eases we can only deduce what an NGDO believes in from its statements of purpose and the memoes it employs.

ILLUSTRATION 2: AN EXAMPLE OF NGDO BELIEFS

We believe that all people are of equal value and have the same rights, but are born into inequality of circumstance and opportunity; this can be changed.

We believe in the fundamental equality of human dignity which goes beyond the essential inequality of possessions, skills and circumstances.

We believe that poverty is an injustice which is caused, and can be changed by, human action.

A few NGDOs express their beliefs through statements about their analysis of development — for instance, their views on the causes of poverty and strategies for change. A sample of poverty and strategies for change. A sample of NGDO statements about development analysis are shown in Illustration 3.

ILLUSTRATION 3 : NGDO DEVELOPMENT ANALYSIS

Poverty is a result of inequity in the structure of national and international economic systems.

Neglect and abuse of children's rights results from a breakdown in national and family values.

Global environmental degradation is due to overconsumption in the North and the necessary survival strategics of poor people in the Third World.

The positive point about making beliefs and analysis more explicit is that it enables staff to better decide whether or not they belong in the organisation and to identify with the views which underlie its culture. In other cases, clues about what NGDOs might believe in or the values they hold are to be found in their statements of vision, purpose, mission and actions.

Formulating these types, of (mission) statements is also a relatively new endeavour for the majority of NGDOs. Consequently, the most frequent source of information about NGDO identity are simply the statements they make in fliers and information sheets about either the problem being addressed or the activities they are carrying out.

Here, the lowest common denominator is that some individuals cared enough about some aspect of society to form an organisation to change things. For NGDOs which think no further than what they do, identity is equal to activity. In the aid system, this means that an organisation is no more than the project it runs. In other words, what the NGDO does equals what it is. In organisational and management terms, clear values and a philosophy are essential for effectiveness because they link an NGDO's purpose, policies, strategic aims and operational choices (discussed in the next chapter). Beliefs, vision and values are at the top of a hierarchy of organisational features which need to be in place if lower levels of organisational activity are to be done well. Without these 'foundations', serious inconsistencies between policies and real-life practices can and do arise. For example, while an NGDO believes that war veterans have a right to national respect and adequate economic support, their actual activities amount to little more than distributing hand outs, such as food and blankets. The inconsistency between the is not seen or is simply accepted for reasons organisational survival.

Is it chance that so few NGDOs have clear statements of the beliefs which inform their values and purpose? Not really. Most NGDOs are adverse to reaching this level of agreement; if such a statement is made, it appears that a creed must be followed. Better to leave things implicit than face contention and futile debate. This pragmatic view has, however, the drawback of avoiding issues which are critical to interpreting events and making consistent choices in unpredicted circumstances. One of the most important negative consequences is that a lack of shared beliefs and values reduces internal trust, leading to top-down, control-orientation which lessens an NGDOs ability to respond rapidly, to adapt to diversity or to adopt the truly participatory practices needed in interaction with primary stakeholders.

Other Sources of NGDO Identity

In addition to beliefs, the origins of NGDOs are important to their identity and with similarities and difference; between North, South and East. Northern NGDOs have arisen:

(i) from the motivations of social groupings;

(ii) from personal inspiration.

(iii) to support similar organisations;
(iv) to tackle specific issues, such as the environment;
(v) to advance technological solutions to problems;
(vi) from political affiliations;
(vii) for the promotion;
(viii) to promote particular ideologies;

In their many combinations, these different origins lead to a wide diversity in organisations giving each a unique identity as well as a tendenry to ensure that their individuality is maintained.

A similar list of origins applies to Southern NGDOs, but with added historical and social dimensions. For Southern NGDOs, an important additional feature contributing to thyeir identity is past domination by foreign powers, which is still to be found in new guises. Hussein Adam has identified three common identity-shaping responses, of Southern NGDOs to their colonial histories which he terms, 'return to the past', 'seize the future' and "transmission belt'. The first, exemplified by the Six-S movement in West Africa and the Savadoya movement in Sri Lanka, seeks to rehabilitate and build upon the cultural or religious norms which were negated by colonisers and to use them as the well-spring of people-centred development action. Identity is closely associated with indigenous values. 'Seize the future' NGDOs react against past and present exploitation within and between countries. NGDOs within the anti-*dependencia* movement of Latin America, such as IBASE in Brazil, and others associated with communist movements in Asia, such as the People's Organisation for Participation (POP) in Thāiland, find identity, amongst others, from their structural analysis of continuing domination, exploitation and denial of fundamental rights within their society and beyond. Identity is essentially defined in terms of an ideological position. As the name implies, 'transmission belts" provide that function through the transfer of aid resources. Identity derives from their role somewhere in the aid chain and the services they deliver. In other words, who they are is what they do.

In addition to colonial exploitation and injustice; NGDOs in the South and East can arise from struggles against internal oppression such as military or civilian dictators. Often informed by ideologies from the left (including theological interpretations of the Catholic church) and allied to revolt by peasants and farmers, NGDOs have been established by individuals and groups who may have been driven underground, or adopted other forms of resistance. Examples may be readily found in South East Asia and Latin America. But in response to such threats, in order to show that they are concerned about the plight of the poor, dictatorial regimes have been known to form, allow or promote certain NGDOs too. In either case, NGDO origins arise from, and mirror, a context of indigenous oppression. All in all it is not safe to look at the identity of NGDOs devoid of context or history.

NGDO Governance

The mix of values, philosophy and origins described above all contribute to the content of NGDO identity, but not necessarily to its strength or stability under pressure. Resilience in identity depends on how widely and consistently beliefs, values, development philosophy and organisational principles are shared between key groups.

A crude division governing identity can be made between an NGDO's formal 'owners': those recognised as accountable in law; its constituency: the organisation's social base; the leadership: the chief executive and senior management; and the staff at different levels. All groups exert power in their own way and to a different degree. Where significantly different perceptions about beliefs, purpose or principles arise, identity can become fragmented. For example, splits within the NGDO community and within an NGDO like the Philippines Peasant Institute can partly be attributed to widening differences in the political interpretation of the function and identity of NGDOs in the post-Marcos, post-Cold War era. Whether or not splits occur depends on the balance of power between the groups, the type of governing structure, and personalities and communication - where the chief executive's role is often pivotal.

There are three common governing structures: self-regulated, with or without membership: self-selected oligarchy; and constituent based. Much of Latin America conforms to the first type. The civic code under which NGDOs register creates a governing body composed of staff representatives, which can be expanded to include outsiders but this does not have to occur. In this sense, the staff who make up the organisation also own it; in effect, they own themselves and lack a social constituency with formal power. While differences in opinion can exist, in this set-up communication between owners and staff should not pose a problem. Organisational identity is likely to be strong and coherent, unless confidence is lost in the leadership. The drawbacks of this circular or incestuous set-up for public accountability and for dealing with contentious organisational change, such as reducing staff, are examined later.

In the rest of the world a more common structure is a governing board which is self-selected in perpetuity - an oligarchy. Staff and volunteers can be allocated places, but the majority of power rests with outsiders chosen by each other for their social position, political links, expertise, representative status or other beneficial attributes. In these circumstances, significant differences arising between board, leadership and staff on how to respond to pressures on voluntary principles can lead to public wrangling, long-term instability, demotivation and seriously reduced effectiveness. Less frequent, but not uncommon, are constituency-governed NGDOs. Constituency is an umbrella term for identifiable political and economic group(s) in society which the organisation stems from and relates to strongly. In the North, secular NGDOs with constituent assemblies are MS in

Denmark and NOVIB in the Netherlands, the overseas development arms of trade unions to be found in Canada, and Amnesty International. NGDOs funded through child sponsorship, such as Plan International, ACTIONAID, World Vision, Christian Children's Funds and the Save the Children Funds, can readily point to a constituency or social base, but are not governed by them. With slight variations, these NGDOs have self-selected boards and only one includes representatives from countries of operation. which means the South and East are not formally represented; this can give an imbalance in interests served towards funders.

If the system of governance allows them to do so, NGDOs with a broadly-based, clearly definable constituency are more likely to be held to their founding principles and voluntary values than those which do not; members will have to be persuaded that the convictions they adhere to no longer hold. However, constituents' ability to exercise control in practice is largely determined by the information made available to inform their position. And here, leadership and staff usually have the upper hand, which can, and often docs, reduce any governing body to a rubber stamp. What one commonly observes is NGDO leaders and staff shaping and shifting identity.Too frequently boards end up taking remedial rather than preventive action.

How NGDOs go about re-establishing organisational identity when it becomes confused, contested or lost is dealt with in the next chapter. The point to conclude with here is that irrespective of the formal systems of governance, identity boris down to the integrity and honesty with which leaders and staff adhere to voluntary values and founding principles.

CHARACTERISTICS OF NGDOs

What the approach illustrates is that it is possible to describe these organisations in positive ways without having to resort to the double negatives of non-profit and non-governmental. But what does this tell us about the essential characteristics of third-sector organisations and of the organisational and management features of development-oriented agencies?

Non-Governmental Organisations

The formal organisations making up the third sector differ from governments and businesses in that:

- They are not required nor prevented from existing by law, but result from people's self-chosen voluntary initiative to pursue a shared interest or concern.
- Registration means that the founders wish to have social recognition; this calls for some degree of formalisation and the principle of social accountability acceptance.
- Formed by private initiative, they are independent, in that they are not part of government nor controlled by a public body.
- Within the terms of whatever legislation they choose to register themselves, they also govern themselves.

Apparently, these basic criteria cover a vast array of organisations in any society, ranging from the Ku Klux Klan, through churches, amateur football teams, societies for the blind and physically handicapped, foundations for cancer research, ethnic welfare associations, the Ramblers Association, and the Salvation Army. In addition, there is a socially significant set of third-sector organisations which do not seek recognition in a formal sense, but may nevertheless be developmentally important.

Non-Governmental Development Organisations

NGDOs are a subset of organisations within the five voluntary sector criteria listed above, but do not necessarily operate solely on the basis of voluntary sector principles. In terms of their particular characteristics:

1. NGDOs are predominantly hybrid in nature, operating on the basis of multiple, partially conflicting, partially

re-enforcing organisational principles.

2. Realising effective sustainable development is critically dependent on NGDOs retainingvoluntary values and principles as the primary force in their way of working.
3. By and large, NGOs act as intermediaries, providing support to those who legitimise them; they are not mutual benefit organisations or associations
4. Within the framework of international cooperation. NGDOs are legitimised by the existence of the world's poor and powerless and by the circumstances and injustices they experience.

NGOs may face a particular set of challenges which require appropriate organisation and skilled management if they are to be competent agents of development.

NGOs and Organisational and Management Balances

The organisational trade-offs and balances which NGDOs must achieve to be effective can be grouped under three main headings: the nature of voluntarism; the dynamics of the development scene, and the nature of social change in a world becoming dominated by market-driven economics and liberal political systems. As with development work, balancing does not mean equalising, but continually adjusting and managing the mix of internal and external forces to ensure that, overall, voluntarism overlaps government and business principles.

Voluntarism: The Nature

When maintaining voluntary principles, NGDOs will have to:

1. Balance staff participation and empowerment with directive decision-making.
2. Balance and ensure consistency between potentially conflicting claims on organisational ownership and values.

3. Balance a third-sector governance style with market-oriented standards.
4. Balance between trust versus control in the allocation and application of authority.
5. Balance an organisational culture of voluntarism with that of competitive contracting and public service.
6. Balance volunteer and staff self-motivation and commitment with market-related incentives and expectations.

The Development Scene

While operating in the system of international development co-operation, NGDO's will require to:

1. Balance the resource mix to ensure retention of autonomy in decision-making.
2. Balance market-related and development-related performance criteria and demands.
3. Balance individual identity with NGDO collective interests and collaboration with other sectors.
4. Balance accountability to primary stakeholders with credibility towards constituency and contributors.

Social Change

When pursuing processes of social change, NGDOs will have to:

1. Balance operating within market forces with changing how the market operates.
2. Balance competencies in service provision with competencies which cause structural change in society.

It is always easier to state what NGDOs should do than how they can do what is needed. .

CHAPTER 4

What Are NGOs?

The last quarter of the 20th century, specially, have been a difficult period for development practitioners. Leakage of development funds of the government, scams, scandals, corruption and blatant misappropriation of resources have contributed to a gradual erosion of public confidence in the agents of development. This has compelled social and political activists to demand accountability and transparency. The recent movement in Rajasthan since late 1994, for the right to information, especially about funds meant for poverty alleviation and rural development, has changed the texture of the debate. The on-going struggle for people's right to access information about programmes, projects and schemes meant for the poor and the response of the government and other agents of development, are pointers to the deepening crisis in our society.

Despite the fact that all political parties publicly support people's right to information and agree that greater accountability alone will prevent corruption, they have resisted giving ordinary people access to information on muster rolls of rural employment schemes, allocation of government funds for various projects, and accounts of poverty alleviation programmes. It is popularly believed that the bureaucracy too is opposing the move as such transparency cuts at the root of its power. Responding to the demand for right to information, the-then chief secretary of the Government of Rajasthan said in June 1997 that they would be more sympathetic to the demand if a similar mechanism was also evolved for the non-government sector. Naming a few large organisations in the state, he said that while social activists and non-government organisations demanded greater transparency in government, organisations receiving large grants from donors in the name of poverty alleviation and development were themselves not transparent. Workers in many non-government organisations, he said, did not have any rights, leave alone the right to information. There was, he argued, greater transparency in government than in the voluntary sector.

Most people would agree that corruption and misutilisation of resources in government structures and procedures have been responsible for the dismal state of the country' today a lesser number of people are willing to explore the world of non-governmental organisations. Commentators on the development sector agree that there is little visible impact of years of development assistance to voluntary organisations. Request for impact assessment of the voluntary sector is seldom welcomed by agencies or donors. Accountability and transparency are not always the guiding principles of most organisations across the country. In the last 10 years, many bilateral donors have been forced to institute special audits and surprise checks. Some of them have also blacklisted organisations that siphoned off crores of rupees taken as grants for rural development, women's development, literacy and so on.

The development sector is a microcosm of the society we live in. It mirrors the priorities of the elite juxtaposed against the needs of the poor. It also reflects the general decline in our moral fabric. Notwithstanding this dismal picture, it is indeed gratifying to note that despite the erosion of fundamental values, there are many organisations and groups that remain steadfast to their ideals and continue to make a difference. In the ultimate analysis 'development' is about people and expanding their range of choices and enhancing their ability to negotiate this hostile world from a position of strength. 'The realities of poor people are local, complex, diverse and dynamic. Income poverty, though important, is only one aspect of deprivation. Disadvantage and ill-being, as people experience them, include social inferiority, physical weakness, vulnerability, seasonal deprivation, powerlessness, humiliation and isolation'. Coping and survival strategics adopted by the poor are diverse and complex. They invariably rely on non-commodity goods — examples range from collection of minor forest produce, to scavenging, gathering, accessing common property resources and so on. They use the labour of children, migrate in search of work, pledge their children/young adults to money-lenders, landlords, weavers and traders (and even pimps linked to urban sex trade), split their families, mortgage and resort to begging, theft and triage.

Whether it is possible for development practitioners to evolve strategies for the reduction/abolition of deprivation and the provision of sustainable livelihoods.

> Development professionals have more power to change the world for the better than is normally realised. To grasp and use that power requires questioning conventional concepts and realities, exploring and embracing a new paradigm, adopting a new professionalism, empowering the poor to analyse and express their reality, and then putting that reality first.... Professionals, whether in NGOs, government departments, training institutes and universities or donor agencies, have been slow to see that the fine words of 'partnership', 'ownership' and 'empowerment' by and for the poor, demand institutional changes 'by us'. Participation 'by them' will not be sustainable or strong unless we too are participatory. 'Ownership' by them means non-ownership by us. 'Empowerment' for them means disempowerment for us. In consequence, management cultures, styles of personal interaction and procedures all have to change (Chambers, 1995).

Many commentators have argued for a more inclusive view of economic development: one which accommodates the diverse strategies adopted by the poor to stay alive. Adopting such a view permits us to see development as a means to expand human capacity. Their notion of capability is essentially one of freedom — the range of options before a person about the kind of life to be led. Poverty of life lies not merely in the impoverished state of living, but also in the lack of real opportunity, given by social constraints as well as personal circumstances, to choose other types of living. 'Poverty is, thus, ultimately a matter of "capability deprivation", and note has to be taken of that basic connection not just at the conceptual level, but also in economic investigations and in social or political analysis'(Dreze and Sen, 1995). The role of voluntary organisations in social change has to be assessed in this context.

The Changing Face of Voluntary Organisations

India has had a long and chequered history of voluntary work. In the early years after Independence many social workers went into rural areas to live and work among the people. Many of them not only responded to Gandhiji's call but were inspired by ideals of socialism, social and religious reform, and communism. The country was dotted with small groups involved in genuinely voluntary welfare and reform work.

> By the end of the sixties, it was reasonably clear, that the state initiated development welfare thrusts, or the pressure of the 'popular protest movements' had, together or separately, not been able to attack the problems of poverty, inequality, or injustice, as faced by vast sections of the populace. But the range of protest movements, though often unsuccessful in their political objectives, at least served the purpose of stripping the 'official' jargon—democracy, development, participation—of its remaining halo. It was in the context of a certain 'weariness' with existing institutional arrangements and strategies, that attention once again, began to be focused on the more rooted, participative experiments at 'grassroots mobilisation for social change (Sethi, 1987).

The late 1970s, popularly referred to as the post-emergency era, saw a sudden spurt of social activism. Mrs Indira Gandhi's electoral defeat and the restoration of democratic processes signalled the beginning of a new era. There was widespread recognition of the need for legitimate space and forum for protest and social mobilisation. This was also a period when discussions about the need for a committed bureaucracy and judiciary gained legitimacy.

> The euphoria of the restoration of democracy, the need for political parties to accommodate the concerns of the poor, the recognition that the State alone cannot deliver and that the market is iniquitous —all these led to a mushrooming of new organisations and new activities involving new actors working with new issues. To traditional concerns of welfare, relief, charity and development were added concerns about gender, environment and human rights aimed much more at securing entitlements through organisation and empowerment. Along with growing numbers, funding and actors has also come a drive towards professionalisations. Thus the political tendency of reaching downwards and actively involving the poor has been combined with activities like research, training, communication, advocacy, using public interest law and networking, across space and greater spaces for citizens' initiative in development (Sethi, 1997).

The early 1980s saw the emergence of a wide range of organisations that positioned themselves between pure research on the one hand and social activism on the other. Widespread disillusionment with mainstream structures and institutions and the increasing alienation of socially committed researchers, lawyers and scientists led to the spurt of intermediary organisations. During this period government resources and foreign aid to voluntary groups increased significantly. Notwithstanding efforts to control the flow of foreign funds, many bilateral donors, foundations and international NGOs in the business of grant-making opened offices in India and started disbursing funds for development work. Similarly, the governments also initiated special grants-in-aid programmes in adult education, rural technology, rural development, women's development, and family welfare. Around the same time political activists who had become disillusioned with their parties and with 'armed struggles' started rural groups which focussed on mobilisation instead of development projects.

However, by the time we reached the late 1980s, the picture started changing again. While some groups consolidated their work and grew into large well-funded organisations, others, mainly small groups, faced enormous problems. Overtly political groups with an agenda of mobilisation distanced themselves from those involved in contractual development work. The international development climate and growing professionalism created a demand for organisations that could provide professional support to grassroots groups. As a result, the new genre of agencies specialising in training, documentation, research, evaluation, and other forms of resource support became more popular. Some donors found it difficult to deal with a large number of small groups and felt it would be more economical to deal with intermediary agencies. Some other donors were happier making a few large grants instead of many small ones. Organisations were encouraged to upscale their work. Those with the capacity to absorb and manage enormous resources and a wide basket of activities grew at a fast pace. Having created a large infrastructure with many workers, many organisations had no option but to take on large development projects in order to maintain their relationship with the people. Many of them could not participate in popular struggles and became alienated from the very people who were their strength.

As a result, non-governmental organisations today are under tremendous pressure to become service providers over a wide terrain. In order to do so, they have to either form networks or expand their scale of operation. Those who respond to the changing scenario gradually lose their ability to be in touch with the people. Territorial expansion, coupled with diversification into multiple sectors in order to survive frequent change in donor priorities, have robbed many-NGOs of their unique selling proposition: accountability, quality, cost-effectiveness, and closeness to the ground. They also fall prey to the danger of being over-funded. As 'success' is measured by size and scale, they gradually become big and hierarchical.

Reflecting on the trap they are in, a respected NGO leader known for his personal-commitment and incorruptibility said:

> Acquisition of organisational assets, creating infrastructure and staff liability is a trap. Once you are in it you cannot get out. We are now accountable to donors for every penny we receive. All my time is spent filling out innumerable forms, hosting evaluations and reviews. As they change their priorities, we have to learn new buzzwords and submit new proposals. Today every donor wants to support self-help groups on reproductive health. What option do I have? If I do not change with the times, how will I support two hundred families who are dependent on my organisation for livelihood. In a backward region like ours, I cannot shrug off my responsibility. This dependency syndrome was created by us. I can personally move out and another colleague could run the show. This does not change anything, the show must go on. We are linked to the global market now, I am no longer an independent player, I am a contractor. A development contractor who can either accept and move with the times or opt out. My choices have not been widened, they have shrunk? (The concerned NGO leader would like to remain anonymous; Ramachandran, 1996).

Struggling with Accountability

What does all this do to accountability systems and internal democracy? Talking about the early years of struggle, many organisational heads agree that their group was far more democratic when they were struggling to survive. There was a sense of togetherness. Many of them sacrificed personal comforts and family life for the cause. As organisations grew in size, the personal factor got diluted and by and by the iron law of oligarchy started asserting itself. Comrades and fellow-travellers (except for the original group) gave way to employees who were hired for a job. The gap between the middle-class urban professionals and the fieldworkers increased. Many organisations became extensions of the leader's personality, leading to splits, resignations and expulsions. The leader's ability to mobilise funds and network with donors, government officials and politicians placed him/ her above the rest. Survival demanded aggressive networking, publicity, and establishing national and international contacts. Gradually, survival became the key objective. This was not all. Some organisations became family enterprises, with leadership passing from parent to offspring. Organisational assets, patronage networks, and power became an end in itself in many cases. Some leaders became power centres in their own right, moving out of one area to establish patronage networks in others.

Those groups which consciously decided to steer clear of the development trap remained small. One well-known activist who made a conscious decision not to become a development contractor tried to combine mobilisation work with the daily grind of earning his livelihood—*kaam aur kamai* (payment only for work) was his motto. His was one of the most popular groups in the 1970s. Many students from premier institutions came to live with him to gain first-hand experience in a development programme that was striving to be self-sufficient. This activist did fascinating work mapping natural resources and environmental degradation. However, by the mid,1980s, his group found it difficult to sustain its work. After many years of struggle to keep its head above water, the group gradually faded out. Many small groups committed to mobilisation for social change also met a similar fate.

The current scepticism notwithstanding, to the extent that voluntary organisations concentrate on the problems of the poor and neglected communities, they remain important institutions for ensuring equitable development in the country. Close involvement and a long-term commitment to the local community gives them a good understanding of the circumstances dominating the lives of the poor. In the process they acquire knowledge and experience that is useful in facilitating bottom-up planning processes that respond to the needs of the people. Groups involved in such work tend to be flexible and innovative in their approaches to problem solving. They make conscious efforts to involve the local community in whatever programmes they initiate and undertake. Given the diversity and size of the country, and the limitations of the government machinery and programmes to reach the fringes, it is this quality that sets them apart from the government.

However, many of the positive elements of voluntary organisations are sometimes undermined by factors that limit the efficacy and effectiveness of their activities. Many of them find themselves short of qualified and trained personnel who can effectively deal with the multiple demands of the community and also organise activities in a variety of sectors. All too often they have to operate in a fire-fighting mode, leaving little time for reflection on the broader good and impact of their interventions. Voluntary groups themselves feel the need for a greater, analysis of their work to learn about their successes and failures. Documentation of their experiences remains poor and the sharing, of lessons limited. Consequently, policy-makers have very limited information on the cumulative impact of social movements and developmental work in India to improve the well-being of the poor, the cost-effectiveness of their operations, their long-term sustainability and so on. As a result, feeding lessons of NGO experiences into the policy formulation and programming initiatives of government has not been very successful.

New Strains

While the above is representative of the general situation, we need to be cognizant of the recent shifts in the environment. Under the new liberalisation and structural adjustment thrust, there are serious apprehensions about severe cut-backs in official funding for the social sector. Opening out hitherto restricted areas to both domestic and foreign private capital, and the focus on global competitiveness and profits, has also put additional pressure on common property resources, a key resource in the survival strategies of the poor. A wide variety of struggles that have broken out in the country are indicative of the trend. As survival pressures mount on communities, grassroots organisations are likely to face a deteriorating environment, particularly, if they are involved in mobilising the poor. Conflict with the government too is likely to increase, particularly at the local level. This is also likely to affect the support organisations involved in advocacy and networking, since their discourse tends to be increasingly critical of the recent shifts in policy.

At another level, the moral fabric of our society is under stress. As outlined here, innumerable scams involving development resources in the government and the non-government sector, failure of our judicial system to punish the culprits, legitimacy and acceptance of 'scamsters' by our society, lack of employment opportunities for the middle-class, and the acceptance of development work as viable career path as also a route to secure employment in international and multilateral organisations—all these have altered the very face of development. Mediators who interface between foreign aid and grassroots have gained recognition, power, resources and legitimacy. It is commonly believed that almost 30 to 40 per cent of funds meant for development are utilised for administration, consultant fees, overheads of donors and so on. Out of the funds which actually reach the voluntary organisation, another 20 to 30 per cent are spent on their infrastructural overheads. There is considerable anecdotal evidence from donors which suggests that barely 20 per cent of the funds actually reach the intended beneficiaries. The rest are absorbed by the superstructure, including soft activities like workshops, conferences, documentation, publication, foreign travel and the like. Given the wide range of actors involved in this at different levels, it has not been easy to make an accurate estimate.

While the situation may be grim, there is however a silver lining. Many possibilities have opened up as a result of the recent 73rd and 74th amendments to the Constitution devolving greater resources and authority to local government. This opening up, if utilised creatively, can deepen the process of democratic decentralisation and bring 'development' closer to the people, thus increasing transparency. Donor agencies have been trying to associate voluntary organisations, and through them community-based organisations, in a wide array of training and capacity-building programmes. In some parts of the country, voluntary and support (or intermediary) organisations have been struggling for the *de jure* devolution of authority and responsibility. This new phenomenon creates an opening for intervention, albeit a mixed one.

Government views voluntary agencies only as mobilizers and delivery agents, in the post-panchayat elections scenario in February-March 1994, many voluntary agencies were invited to organise training programmes to enhance the capability of the elected representatives to deal with new challenges. The focus has been on administration and monitoring of government schemes and programmes. Many state governments speak the language of people's power, but in reality the greatest hurdles faced by grassroots groups have been posed by the local officials who fear loss of power and subsequent marginalisation in the district. The struggle to involve communities and groups at all stages and levels of these programmes.

Where does this leave us? For any significant, sustainable, and meaningful social change, the desire for change, the motivation for action, and the resources for it have to be generated from within. Working in a 'project' mode, jumping from one project to another, and following an externally determined agenda is likely to be counterproductive. Experience of successful initiatives has shown that identification of the key actors with the struggle (that too outside the conventional 'project' mode) in the elimination of usurious money-lending, exploitative trading channels managed by middlemen, and controlling the siphoning-off of valuable resources meant for the poor by agents of development—all create a positive climate for empowerment and development.

All this demands transparency in work, and a close identification with people's struggles (including appreciation of their apprehensions and fears). Devising strategies to reduce consciously the dependence on the voluntary organisation and/or change agents generates momentum for people-centred development. Such movements not only attack the skewed asset distribution and the monopoly utilisation of scarce resources, but also create alternative power structures which ensure the continuous participation and involvement of the poor in decisions regarding their own future.

There is today in literature some scepticism about the claims of NGOs about cost-effectiveness, closeness to the poor, innovativeness and creativity, particularly when programmes are scaled up. Questions have also been raised about NGOs as representative and democratic organisations. These questions have to be addressed in the larger context where there is a contradiction between economic and political agendas of the State. Large-scale provision of services demands structures that can handle large funding, ensure speedy decision making, etc., while democratisation requires organisational independence, closeness and successful institutional development. The time-frame of donors and governments alike is roughly three to five years. Very few donors are willing to give grassroots groups and movements more time.

Many young dynamic NGO leaders want to make a mark in different areas at the same time. As members of networks they get involved in high profile advocacy; simultaneously, they want to sensitise the media through activist-based news features. Some of them shoot into prominence through high profile campaigns against dams, felling of trees, etc. There are some who are seized with the mission to revitalise and revive age-old movements and institutions. It is not uncommon to hear that a charismatic NGO leader has awakened and mobilised a long-oppressed and marginalised community, not unlike Krishna in his divine form! People love to read about the whirlwind change agents and the media loves to build them up. In the last 10 years we have been witness to many such media heroes. This phenomenon has gripped donors and governments alike. Grassroots groups and organisations planning a steady long-term strategy are seen as being old-fashioned and ineffective. The buzzword today is not sustainable development but 'dazzling' development.

Today ther is an apprehension that this new fashion may result in distorting the accountability of NGOs upwards and overemphasise linear approaches to performance measurement. This has a damaging effect on the ability of NGOs to be catalysts in social change. In the ultimate analysis, it is the quality of relationships between people's organisations, NGOs, donors, and the government that will determine whether patterns of funding and accountability promote or impede wider goals of social transformation. One may need to rethink the new contract culture and the trend towards development showbiz. The public image of NGOs is still mixed; collective memory of exceptional work as well as of scams in the sector is short.

REFERENCES

Chambers, Robert (1995). *Poverty and livelihood: Whose reality counts,* IDS discussion paper, Sussex, December.

Dreze, Jean and Amartya Sen ,(1995). *India: Economic Development and Social Opportunity,* Delhi: Oxford University Press.

Ramachandran, Vimala (1996). 'NGOs in the time of globalisation', *Seminar,* November.

Sethi, Harsh (1987). *Refocussing Praxis.* New Delhi: SETU-Lokayan.

CHAPTER 5

NGOs and Protection of Children's Rights

The UN Convention of the Rights of the Child advocates measures for the protection, natural development of the children, their survival and participation. But that is an ideal which only a few nations have achieved so far.

The Government of India had realised the pitiable plight of the child much earlier and had enacted laws for the protection and welfare of the child, it is rather painful to know that more than seventeen million children of independent India under the age of 14 are working in most inhuman conditions. No proper food, no sanitation, no medical aid and no education. The laws are there, but they are not implemented. These children do not know what childhood is. They do not even know what games in the open air one could enjoy playing. My personal observation of children working in the carpet industry, bangle making factories and bidi factories makes me feel most depressed. These children are working for long hours on very low wages. The parents are obliged to send them to the employers to work under these inhuman conditions for the survival of the family, as the income of the head of the family is too low to meet the basic requirements of the family. Ironically, on one hand we feel concerned about the fast growing unemployment, on the other hand we put the children to work which creates unemployment for the grown ups.

Child labour must be discouraged. Statutory minimum wages fixed for men-women must be paid and here the

NGOs can play the role of watchdogs. Not only this, they can also bring about awareness among people, motivate the parents not to allow their children to work, rather put them in school. They must be made literate, and trained to be able to look after their needs later in life.

The NGOs can approach industries with governmental support to prevent employment of children under 14. They can also help to ensure that adults get their minimum stipulated wages. Where workers have to live in industrial complexes, the children's schooling should be made compulsory in the factory area.

Facilities for primary education have grown more on paper and in name than in reality. Children come, and finding the school closed, loiter about and go back home. At the end of the year there is bargaining between the parents of the child and the school. The child gets promoted in exchange for money. This results in total illiteracy inspite of the existence of primary schools. Here too the NGOs can play the watchdog's role, report to the concerned departments and improve the system. The problem is that the authorities concerned show little interest in taking action. Interaction between NGOs and the concerned department is a prerequisite. It has to be cordial and constructive.

Rural children hardly get any medical help. In remote areas of our rural India we can do something to help and save the life of many children who die for want of medical aid. If there is some rapport between NGOs and the health department, the welfare organisation can do much to save many young lives. We all know that many children die before the age of six and before that many die during the teething period. Proper nutrition and proper medicine is the right of every child. Here too the NGOs can play an important part by creating awareness among the parents and also by insisting that the father and mother must not be deprived of minimum fixed wages, which can enable them to save the situation.

Children are used by boot leggers and drug peddlers. An innocent soul is put on the most hideous type of work. Children are trained for pickpocketing. They are made use of in thefts. These practices have been going on unchecked. Hardly any police help has been available. NGOs can definitely play an important role with the help of the police to check such evils. Many unfortunate children are abducted and made to beg by gangs which have made this into a money making industry. In some cases the child's limb or eye is purposely damaged to make him look helpless and pitiable so that he can fetch more money from begging. Gang hideouts can be detected by NGOs with the help of the police. In female prisons some time we have seen young children staying with mothers under the most undesirable atmosphere and under inhuman conditions. In Calcutta, Bombay and Lucknow our convenors have succeeded in getting the children released from jails and they are then rehabilitated. The NGOs can help the innocent child by getting him out of the criminal surroundings of the jail where he is kept with the mother. Here too we need the sympathetic cooperation from the jail authorities. In short everywhere, in every problem of the child, NGOs can do some constructive work. But for this, interaction with the Government and the concerned authorities is a necessary precondition. Because of its helplessness and vulnerability the child is the worst sufferer in spite of all the "National Plans for the Health, Happiness and Survival of the Child". Let us all: the concerned Government departments, the police and the NGOs and Welfare Organisations join together to protect the Child and its Rights.

The children of a country are its most valuable asset. No nation on this globe can ignore the responsibility to ensure the proper growth and development of children as the future of the country lies with them. However, as a voiceless section of the society, the children have suffered throughout the ages at the hands of those who are supposed to provide them with security and love. It is not uncommon to find children who have been subjected to abuse, torture or exploitation and who are denied their basic rights. Children are the worst sufferers of wars, natural disasters, unemployment, poverty etc. It would be worthwhile here to cite few startling facts. According to the Human Development Report (1994), in developing countries, more than two million children die annually of preventable infectious diseases and 192 million are malnourished. The report also reveals the Human Development Cost of Arms imports. According to the report, India ordered 20 MIG-29 fighter aircraft from Russia at a cost that could have provided basic education to all the 15 million girls out of school. Thus, increased expenditure on defence results in denial of the basic rights to the defenceless section of the society, i.e. children.

The fact that the children are physically and mentally immature necessitates special rights for their nurture, protection and fulfilment of unique needs. The rights of the child should be a matter of great concern to one and all as the children constitute one of the most vulnerable sections of the society. A deprived child may belong to any religious, ethnic, linguistic, socio-economic category and hence universal acceptance and promotion of child rights needs greater emphasis than the rights of other deprived sections of the society.

The Constitution of India under the directive principles of State Policy has laid stress on formulation of policy by the State towards prevention of abuse of children, provision of opportunities and facilities for healthy development and protection of children against exploitation and moral and material abandonment. The Indian Government has also in pursuance of its policy, made continuous efforts in the direction of ensuring fair and just rights to children through enactment of legislation, framing appropriate policies and providing special services to the children. In spite of these initiatives, there is little achievement to our credit. According to 1981 census, the number of orphan children below 14 years of age was 37.59 million. The Government of India estimates of working children show that there are around 18 million working children in India whereas a study conducted by ORG estimated the number of child workers at 44 million. About 90 per cent of working children live in rural areas. Thus India has yet to do a lot to ensure prevention of deprivation. The ratification of UN convention will go a long way in protection and promotion of just and humane rights of children.

Role of NGOs

Non-government organisations, working with children have been the great source of relief especially to the deprived children who live in exceptionally difficult circumstances. NGOs have made untiring efforts to provide for the basic necessities of life to hitherto most vulnerable group not only through custodial care and protection but also through their developmental approach and participation in policy making. Looking at the magnitude of the problem, NGOs, however sincere and committed may their efforts be, have not yet been able to reach all the needy children. The reasons are manifold: scarce resources, inadequate trained manpower, lack of cooperation from government and other bodies etc. However, in the light of the UN Convention on the Rights of Child, NGOs do have to play greater role at different levels. In the present scenario, this would require redefining their roles, change in approach and global thinking. Acknowledging the fact that NGOs, especially working in the field of human rights, have excercised their influence on the content of convention, the implementation of the same can hardly be effective in absence of participation of voluntary sector in the observance of the provisions of the UN Convention.

Redefining Role of NGOs

The NGOs have primarily concentrated on provision of basic amenities to the deprived children while functioning at the grassroot level. Most of the NGOs have made available to the needy children, the services which are better in terms of quality as well as effectiveness. Several NGOs have made effective use of the available resources and with most appropriate methods generated resources on their own. However, besides service delivery, there is also a need for education of the community, particularly at the grassroot level regarding its responsibilities towards children in need of help. Not many NGOs have taken up education of people a grassroot level in an intensive manner. As a result, care and protection of children living in exceptionally difficult circumstances is perceived as the sole responsibility of the NGOs whereas the primary responsibility lies with the family and the community. There seems to be overdependence on NGOs for identification, care, protection and development of deprived children. The NGOs in turn find it difficult to cope up with the ever increasing clientele given the inadequate resources at their disposal. Awareness at grassroot level will bring about increased sensitivity on the part of the society to understand the problems of deprived child and would also help NGOs share its responsibilities with community.

Change in Approach

Here, the NGOs can strive towards achieving what is popularly known as "synergy" through better co-ordination of services at local and regional level. We often come across examples where more than one NGO functions in the same geographical area, with same clientele and provide more or less similiar services. NGOs working for children are no exception to this. A better approach would be to cater to the different clientele or providing different services to the same clientele in a geographical area. This would require local networking through promotion of joint forums. A remarkable example in this regard is the Forum for Disability formed by NGOs working with disabled in Baroda. In respect of NGOs working with children or having children as one of the clientele, such forum will avoid problems of overlapping of its services.

Apart from this, NGOs will have to be prepared for

increased participation in regional/local planning bodies as well as policy formulation with regard to the children. The NGOs, besides being supportive, can also take up advocacy and lobbying for children's rights, particularly at such places where there are increased violations of such rights. Not many NGOs have taken up this as one of the key functional areas. If NGOs are able to pose a united front, they would emerge as a potent force for several initiatives in the area of child welfare and development.

Need for Global Thinking

"Think Globally and Act Locally" has been a popular slogan till now. The problems of children cut across the boundaries of region, nation, caste, creed as well as colour. Although the magnitude as well as nature of the problems may vary from region to region and from country to country, there exists some commonality either in philosophy or future vision. By the end of 1993, 159 countries had either signed the Convention or had become state parties to it by ratification. The NGOs of these countries can interact with greater frequency through international bodies like UNICEF and share their experiences, collaborate with each other on the areas of common concern, transfer the expertise available with each other and thus make the world better place to live for children. The NGOs at present, no doubt, interact internationally at the initiative of International agencies, frequency of such interaction with emphasis of collaborative approach can increase.

The specific areas where NGOs have to intensify efforts also need some attention. The UN Convention on the Rights of the Child draws attention to four sets of civil, political, social, economic and cultural rights of every child. These are in the form of the right to survival, the right to protection, the right to development and the right to participation. The priority areas for NGOs in respect of each of these are discussed below.

The Right to Protection

The right to protection implies prevention of exploitation, abuse and torture which may endanger child's education, health, development or survival. India has a long history of economic exploitation of children who are employed as labourers. Poverty and lack of legislative measures to make primary education compulsory drive the children out of school to work in conditions most unfavourable to their growth and development.

The role of NGOs would therefore be to create awareness among masses against the evils of child labour. Moreover, such awareness should be aimed at building public opinion for elimination of child labour. The crucial task for NGOs therefore would be lobbying and advocacy against exploitation and abuse of children in varied forms.

The Right to Survival

The first and foremost issue that NGOs have to address is dispa ty in boys and girls ratio. According to "the Right to be a Child", a UNICEF India background Paper, there are neatly 4 million "missing girls" in the age-group of 0 to 6 years which is a clear indication of female infanticide—a cause for such adverse sex ratio. Alongwith this, the problem of avoidable child deaths i.e., high infant mortality rate also deserves immediate attention. The present rate of Infant Mortality at 79 and the under-five mortality rate of 124 per 1000 births shows a high prevalence of child deaths due to preventable and environmental causes.

It is an established fact that parental education particularly of women and availability as well as utilisation of health services would bring about remarkable changes in IMR and increase chances of children surviving to a great extent. NGOs can focus attention on the above two areas. Better provision of health-care services can be ensured through active participation of NGOs in health-care delivery system, particularly preventive health-care, especially in the areas where child survival rate is low.

The Right to Participation

The right to participation includes the right of accused children to be treated in just and Humane manner. Although very limited information on juvenile crime and the treatment meted out to such children is available, there is urgency of action in respect of inevitability of adequate resources to provide for legal representation of accused juveniles, facilities for separate custodial care, rehabilitation services etc. The issue of child marriage is also on forefront which demands intervention by NGOs.

The NGOs can work on the core areas by playing the role of educator as well as activist. In order to ensure fair treatment to the children under custodial care, the NGOs may bridge the gap that exists between general public and children under custodial care which would make worthwhile difference not only in terms of nature of care provided but also safeguard interests of the children. With regard to child marriage, NGOs working in the areas where prevalence rate is higher, can take up the issues through public participation in eradication such evil, seeking cooperation of judicial and executive machinery.

Thus, NGOs have vital role to play with regard to basic and just rights of children. No country can fulfil the rights of children without active participation and cooperation from NGOs. The need therefore is to delineate the scope of NGO's functioning and making coordinated and concerted efforts towards ensuring children a bright future.

The UN Convention on the Rights of the Child is the biggest landmark in the sphere of human development at the national and international level. The Convention came into force on 2nd September 1990 and was ratified by India on 12th November 1992.

The Convention had been endorsed by the World Summit on Children. In fact this was the first major global action for the implementation of the Convention. In pursuance of the commitment made at the World Summit, the National Plan of Action for Children thus prepared provides the framework for actualisation of the Convention.

The Government of India is making sincere efforts to meet the provisions stated in the Articles of the Convention to give to the children their rights. Article 42 of the Convention states that State Parties shall undertake to make the principles and provisions of the Convention widely known, by appropriate and active means, to adults and children alike.

NGOs have been a partner to the Government in implementing programmes related to welfare and development of children. It was suggested by the Department of Women and Child Development that NGOs may be actively involved in implementing the Convention. It was felt that for creating awareness and getting inputs from NGOs for this endeavour, workshops may be organised at the state and national levels.

With this in view, UNICEF and the Department of Women and Child Development organised 11 state level workshops in collaboration with ICCW and its state branches and selected NGOs. The objectives of these workshops were to:

(i) orient NGOs on the significance of the Convention on the Rights of the Child;

(ii) identify problems and issues relating to situation of children in general and the girl child in particular;

(iii) analyse problems and suggest solutions for implementing the Convention on the Rights of the Child; and

(iv) identify areas for action which could be undertaken by NGOs.

During these workshops, very useful recommendations were made regarding the implementation of the Convention.

In the present document, Role of NGOs in Implementation of the Convention on the Rights of the Child: Workshop Recommendations, efforts have been made to collate all the recommendations made in the workshops held in Andhra Pradesh, Bihar, Chandigarh, Karnataka, Madhya Pradesh, Maharashtra, Orissa, Rajasthan, Uttar Pradesh and West Bengal. The list of workshops held appears at the end of the recommendations.

The recommendations are grouped under specific areas of action i.e. advocacy, child abuse, child care services, child labour, children in difficult circumstances, community participation, co-ordination and networking, culture, disabled children, disasters and children, education, employment, family, girl child, health, institutional and non-institutional services, juvenile justice system, laws and legislation, monitoring, evaluation and research, nutrition, nutrition and health education, participation by children, plan for implementing rights of the child, policy and planning, pre-school education, recreation, role of media and role of NGOs.

As NGOs have an active role to play in the implementation of the Convention, this document can serve as the basis to initiate action to promote programmes to ensure children the rights related to survival, protection and development and participation.

The Right to Development

Although provision of primary education has been the responsibility of the state, Article 45 of the Directive Principles of State policy as well as the National Policy on Education reflect the firm commitment on the part of state to universalisation of free primary education. There is substantial evidence stating progress in the provisioning of primary education in terms of increase in number of primary schools, school teachers, enrolment but there is paucity of reliable data on quality of education and attendance.

The role of NGOs in this regard would undoubtedly centre around providing supportive services as a result of which *(a)* Girls can avail of the same opportunities as are available to boys *(b)* The dropout rate is reduced particularly among the disadvantaged sections of the society *(c)* assistance to government machinery in better allocation of resources, and *(d)* help in making education a meaningful experience to the children.

Recommendations

Child Labour

A State Level Commission should be set up to work for eradication of child labour. (CHA P8)

There should be an Apex Committee to campaign against child labour at regional as well as State level. (CHA P8)

Children of organised women bidi workers get scholarships/uniform and medical facilities, whereas children of unorganised workers are deprived of such facilities. Therefore, NGOs can organise parents of child labour in their respective regions and make available to them adequate facilities and benefits of various schemes such as Jawahar Rozgar Yojana, Small Scale Industries etc. (MP P9)

For dealing with child labour the relevant Act should be modified to cover all child workers and not only those employed in the organised sector with the ultimate objective of banning child labour. There should be a ban on the use of child labour in households. (WB P4) (AP P22)

Primary education should be made compulsory and the children should be in schools instead of in work places and whatever measures are required must be guaranteed. (WB P4)

Child labour should be banned as soon as possible and families where children are the sole earners should be provided alternate means of income. (UP P47)

Advocacy

NGOs should undertake advocacy and lobbying to defend the rights of the child. (ORI P6)

A Plan of Action for advocacy and dissemination of information regarding the Convention on the Rights of the Child (CRC) should be formulated. (WB P3)

Advocacy efforts to create an action oriented opinion on the CRC is to be operationalised. (WB P5)

NGOs should form pressure groups to motivate the Government to implement CRC. (KAR P4)

Greater attention needs to be paid to advocacy. This should be targeted at policy makers, trade unions, public, legislators, etc. (MAH P8)

Child Abuse

Regarding the issues of physical, sexual and psychological exploitation, the community should be motivated to intervene in cases of such abuse alongwith those meted out to girl children. Community involvement in identification of cases like child marriage, dowry-related abuse and so on should be planned. (WB P4)

Sex education in schools should be initiated and discussions on sexuality and protection from sexual abuse should be encouraged in schools. (WB P4)

NGOs should encourage investigative reports on incidents of child abuse and violation of child rights. (KAR P5)

It is necessary to eradicate various forms of child abuse like child prostitution, child labour, child beggary etc. with the help of laws. Arrangements for rehabilitation of child prostitutes is also very necessary. (UP P46)

All possible measures should be taken for prevention of abuse and exploitation of the institutionalised child by opening up visibility and encouraging interaction of communities and institutions. (AP P24)

Enforcement authorities, NGOs and community at large should be adequately empowered to take all measures to protect children from all forms of physical, mental and sexual abuse and exploitation. (AP P24) (MAH P8)

Child Care Services

The working hours in anganwadi centres and day care centres may be extended to take care to children after 1 p.m. where mothers go for employment in rural areas. (AP P16)

More creches should be opened at work centres of adults. Illiterate parents should be discouraged from giving sedatives like opium, etc. to infants. (AP P21)

Community Participation

To achieve the goals set forth in the Convention on the Rights of the Child, Mandals should be formed involving:

— Children

— Youth : Boys and Girls (Yuva and Yuvati Samoohs)

— Women (Manila Samoohs)

(RAJ P31)

Community organisations should be formed to ensure the enforcement of rights related to child protection. They should be given identity cards and necessarily authorised to work for protection of child rights. (UP P46)

Children in Difficult Circumstances

In the case of a child liberated from difficult

circumstances, proper care has to be bestowed on creating alternative schemes and support systems for the child to see that he/she does not go back to the same or end up in a worse situation. (KAR P4)

Adoption services, foster homes, residential institutions etc. may be started for children born outside wedlock, abandoned children and children who have lost contact with parents in natural calamities, disasters etc. (AP P15)

Co-ordination and Networking

There should be a common platform for addressing common issues and guiding direction about work. (CHA P8)

There should be close coordination between various Government Departments and NGOs and accountability to each other with concurrent monitoring and evaluation to achieve the Mid Decade (1995) and the Decadal Goals (2000) already set by the State and Central Government. NGOs may play a more active role in monitoring and reporting. (BIH P40) (AP P23) (MAH P8)

Donor agencies should fund NGOs directly for small projects not exceeding Rs. five lakhs and undertake monitoring and evaluation directly. (BIH P30)

There should be direct relationship between NGOs and UNICEF for programme implementation. (BIH P45)

Coordination between all agencies working in related areas of rights of children is essential, including groups/ NGOs working with women and Dalits. (MP P11) (KAR PS)

Different Government committees working for children should have NGO representation. (WB P4)

There should be a Suggestion Cell where NGOs can put forth their problems and suggestions. (WB P4)

Links should be established with prominent members of the village for example Gram Sevaks, ANM, AWW, Teachers, Dais, Panch, Sarpanch, influential men and women of the villages and NGOs in the villages. Links should also be established at the block level e.g. with BDO, Government Officials at district and state levels. (RAJ P31, 32) (KAR P5)

A Coordination Committee organised by NGOs should be formed at the district level. In this Committee all NGOs with good contacts should be involved. (RAJ P32)

A Resource Team should be formed so that training can be organised in the villages for village workers, the coordinating group and the pressure group. This team should identify methods, agencies and government organisations. Information may also be given on how to start dialogues with children, their understanding of things etc. (RAJ P32)

Disabled Children

Special attention should be given to handicapped children and children belonging to special categories. (UP P45)

More hostels need to be set up for disabled children in proportion to their numbers. (AP P17)

Specific budget component should be alloted for disabled children. (AP P17)

Disasters and Children

There should be a special department to deal with the protection of children in special circumstances like manmade disasters such as riots, terrorist activities, wars etc. and natural calamities like floods, earthquakes, famines etc. and these functionaries should be trained to deal with all aspects of such situations. (UP P46)

Culture

The syllabus in schools should include lessons on the composite culture of the country. (AP P20)

Teachers should be trained and made culture conscious at the state or central level. (AP P20)

Education

Primary education should be made compulsory by law and available free to all. (WB P4) (AP P13, 22) (UP P44)

Free and compulsory school education for all children upto the age of 18 years in pursuance of the CRC is the need of the hour. Relevant quality education for all children, including the physically and socially handicapped must be ensured. (AP P24) (MAH P8)

The Government may provide some incentives to school going children such as hostels, free food, clothes and books. Families in need may be provided monetary assistance/scholarships for their children. (AP P13) (UP P44).

To ensure cent per cent enrolment and retention, the Mid-day Meal Scheme should be implemented in rural, tribal and urban slum areas. (AP P19)

Timely and adequate supply of educational materials should be made to children living in hostels so that they do not face hardships or punishment for not doing their work. (AP P17)

Quality of education should be improved by providing adequate training to all teachers. Regular and periodic orientation courses should be organised for the teachers. especially in the rural areas. (BIH P25) (AP P19)

Special training should be given to teachers of private schools and recognition accorded to neighbourhood schools so that children continue to get education in the formal system. (BIH P25)

Concentrated efforts need to be made in hilly and tribal areas to reach education to the unreached. (BIH P25)

There is need to develop a cadre of voluntary teachers and barefoot teachers to reach remote and inaccessible pockets. NGOs can streamline such activities by paying a small honorarium to such teachers who carry education to the doorsteps of the unreached. (BIH P25)

Curriculum should be redesigned and learning environment made enjoyable to make education attractive to children, parents and teachers. The syllabus should be more relevant and must prepare the children for real life situations. (BIH P25) (AP P13, 18) (UP P45)

Education should not be linked only with employment. It should be accepted as a means for overall development of the child and for improving the quality of life. (BIH P25)

At present education is considered as Government's programme and responsibility. The focus should be reoriented making education as people's programme. (BIH P25)

Educational arrangements in villages and towns should be such that schools are situated at a walking distance for children. (MP P9)

Schools should also have creches as many children stay back at home to look after their younger siblings. (MP P9)

Adequate teaching staff and teaching facilities should be provided. In addition, facilities like toilet, clean potable water and playground should be made available in schools. (MP P9)

School curricula should include provisions of laws relating to the protection of children's rights. (MP P11) (MAH P8)

Measures must be taken to ensure that school discipline is administered in a manner consistent with the child's human dignity and conformity with the present convention. (AP P13)

Education should develop the physical, spiritual, mental and behavioural personality of the child and his inherent talents. (UP P4S)

At the State level, the budget allocation for expenditure on education should be increased. It needs to be given top priority to achieve Education for All by 2000 A.D. Expansion of social welfare hostels to accommodate motivated children is needed. (UP P4S) (AP P24)

Family

In any programme concerning children's welfare or empowerment, the child should never be looked at in isolation, but as an integral part of the family. (KAR P4)

In the school syllabus, the role of parents and other members of the family in the changing social set up may be depicted appropriately at a suitable level. (AP P15)

For children of prostitutes and children whose parents are undergoing imprisonment or chronic patients, efforts should be made to re-establish family ties so that at a later stage the child can have an identity and support of the family. (AP P15)

Children from battered and violent families are likely to have disturbed and stunted growth and acquire deviant behaviour patterns, hence family counselling centres may be increased in number and run by Government or NGOs with qualified and skilled counsellors so that couples can seek guidance in case of disharmony in the family situation. (AP P15)

To ensure a congenial family environment for the healthy

growth and development of children, pre-marital counselling centres need to be opened. (AP P15)

Employment

After a minimum of 14 years, children can be trained in life skills. In this area, Government can replicate some successful NGO models. (KAR P4)

Fifteen to 18-year-old children should be provided vocational training so that they can earn their livelihood in future by self-employment or in some vocation. The trades taught in Vocational and Guidance Centres should be relevant to the needs, aspirations and requirements of the local area.

Girl Child

An integrated approach for the empowerment of girl child should be adopted through a single window delivery system and not through segregated interventions for health, education and income generation. (BIH P45)

Coordination committees at every important administrative level like Block, District and Division of the Government and NGOs should be formed for effective planning and implementation of the girl child's welfare programmes. (BIH P45)

Sports and karate needs to be encouraged especially for girls, the latter may also help in self-defence. (AP P17)

More facilities should be provided for education of girls. (UP P45)

Girl children in 14-18 years age group should be given vocational education and value oriented education. (BIH P45)

Appropriate legislation should be adopted for effective protection of the girl child. (BIH P45)

Sex related discrimination should be prevented and the practice of sex determination tests should he banned. (WB P4) (UP P44)

Role of Media

There is a need for increased awareness and sensitisation campaign on child rights through media for reaching out to people. Media must play an active role in promoting CRC. NGOs and the media must interact positively to highlight violations of children's rights. (CHA P8) (WB P5) (KAR P4) (MAH P8)

Mass media must play a key role in educating parents and children and make them aware of the importance of education. (AP P13)

Haats (village markets), fairs and festivals should be used effectively for awareness creation and dissemination of messages. (BIH P23)

Success stories should be highlighted through media for recognition and motivation. (BIH P25)

Experiences may be shared regarding what worked and what failed. (RAJ P33)

Parents and children should be educated and informed about rights of children. A simplified version of CRC for children should be prepared and disseminated. (BIH P28) (MAH P7)

Director AIR Patna suggested that NGOs may organise group listening at village level on specified programmes on CRC and give regular feedback to AIR. (BIH P30) (MAH P7)

Appropriate communication materials for information and education should be developed and duplicated in large numbers for field use. This includes scripts for drama, songs, posters, hand bills and portable exhibition kits. Government and UNICEF should jointly develop these materials and NGOs should use them in the field. (BIH P30)

Animators and volunteers are to be trained in effective communication for organising exhibitions, communication campaigns and field publicity activities. (BIH P30)

Monitoring and evaluation should be in-built in the system to study the usefulness and impact of these efforts in communication. (BIH P30)

NGOs should win the confidence of the community and make the public more aware of the rights of children using media like audio-visual aids, films, radio, theatre, folklore, folk dance, street plays, puppet shows, etc. to get rid of the evil of child labour. (MP P9)

Information regarding all the provisions related to rights of children should be disseminated through all available media, specially to organisations working in the field of child welfare such as Anganwadi Workers Training Centres, Bal Sevika Training Centres, Montessori Training Centres, Basic Training Centres and Non-formal Education Centres. (MP P11)

Institutional and Non-institutional Services

Infrastructurel support in the form of Homes and better living conditions within these Homes should be ensured. For such infrastructural support there should be the provision of a Child Budget. (WB P5)

Common procedure may be evolved for all children's institutions run by any Government Department or voluntary organisation whereby food is provided according to scales determined in consultation with the National Institute of Nutrition and other requirements like plates, mugs, clothing, bedding, soap, etc. are issued according to needs without any monetary limit. Sufficiently adequate budget allotment to meet the minimum needs of children, i.e. food, shelter, clothing, education, water and electricity should be allotted to institutions. (AP P14, 16)

Non-institutional approach for child rehabilitation should be given priority over institutionalisation of the child. (AP P24)

Positive cases of child care in institutions should be highlighted. (AP P24)

Health

There is a need for improving referral services. (CHA P8)

Success programmes, such as Medical Melas, i.e., catch up round for immunisation and for comprehensive health care, should be implemented in all districts using district level NGOs. (BIH P22)

Preventive and promotive aspects of health services should involve NGOs in a big way and effective manner by identifying some nodal NGOs in every region of Bihar. (BIH P45)

Well operationalised surveys on immunisation status of children should be conducted by UNICEF through various NGOs all over West Bengal. (WB P4)

Health department and NGO cooperation should be introduced in all programmes like MCH, family welfare and primary health care in rural and urban areas. Mobile Health Care Units too should be introduced. (WB P4)

It should be ensured that health services are available to people, specially the weaker sections, at their doorstep free of cost through improved Public Health Delivery System. (UP P44) (MAH P8)

Mobile vans should be provided to conduct health check up at every school atleast once a month. (AP P17)

Measures should be introduced to regulate birth rate. (WB P4)

Juvenile Justice System

Officials of the Judiciary and Police are to be oriented and updated on the Articles and obligations of the Convention on the Rights of the Child. (B1H P28) (UP P46)

Sustained efforts should be made to disseminate the importance of CRC with the general public to mobilise community support (BIH P28)

Anti-social elements, gangs and groups who induce children to commit crimes should be brought under law and punished. (BIH P28)

Juvenile Courts should be established in each district under Juvenile Justice Act 1986 and a full time judge should be appointed. (MP P11)

Children can avoid the traumatic experience of going through the court procedure if the stipulated number of Juvenile Courts, Juvenile Welfare Board and Family Courts as provided in the Juvenile Justice Act 1986 are set up. (AP P15)

Orientation training for all persons engaged in the field of rights of children should be organised compulsorily. (MP P11) (UP P46) (MAH P8)

There is a need to set up a Monitoring Cell which will coordinate the activities of the Legislative bodies, the Judiciary and Police. This Cell would also hold these different sectors accountable for any breach of duty. (WB P3)

Together with raising awareness on the CRC among the law makers and enforcers, it was also necessary to disseminate information to the public alongwith orientation and training of judiciary and police to deal with child offenders in a better manner. The Juvenile

Justice System needs to be reviewed and revised to make it child friendly. (WB P3) (MAH P6, 8)

For children in conflict with the law there should be efforts to solve minor offences at the community level without going to the Courts for trial. (WB P4)

Juvenile Courts should take the help of NGOs in investigating and deciding cases and the police too should be sensitised and made aware of the techniques of dealing with children. (WB P4)

There is a need for greater awareness on the provisions of the existing laws and their effective implementation. (WB P5)

The composition of the Juvenile Board should be carefully planned so that both the members and magistrates have special knowledge and orientation to child psychology. (WB P5)

Compulsory Legal Aid to child offenders should be provided and a separate panel of advocates supported by social workers to assist and defend children should be constituted. (WB P5)

Mobile Juvenile Courts should be instituted to decrease the delay in the trial process. (WB P5)

A special trained police force with an investigation agency should be provided so that the police are capable of responding sensitively to child offenders. (WB P5)

A Monitoring Committee should be formed at district level with Judiciary, Police, Executives and NGOs for monitoring ongoing cases in court. (WB P5)

More Child Guidance Bureaus may be started by Government Departments and NGOs in rural and urban areas as the provide healthy alternatives to family care. They should also undertake the responsibility of education, training and rehabilitating vagrants, beggars and street children. (AP P14)

Monitoring, Evaluation & Research

For effective evaluation and monitoring of the programmes 'Progress Indicators' may be developed which promote unbiased results. For example, the Infant Mortality Rate, School Retention and Child Labour Status could be the indicators for the Rights to Survival, Development and Protection respectively. (WB PS)

NGOs should monitor the Government's programmes for effective implementation of CRC. (KAR P4)

Studies pertaining to the status of health, education, child labour, children in difficult circumstances should be undertaken to collect the baseline data to identify focus areas and to work for the implementation of CRC on a needbased strategy. (BIH P19)

Studies related to amniocentesis should be undertaken to understand the real situation of the girl child in Bihar. (BIH P19)

We do not have realistic baseline data on subjects like child labour, child abuse and drawbacks in the legal system particularly in juvenile justice. Studies should be undertaken to collect data in specific areas identifying problems and target areas. (BIH P28)

A self monitoring system should be developed. (RAJ P34)

Nutrition

It should be ensured that nutritious food is available cheaply and easily from various centres providing nutrition services keeping in view its importance and need during different seasons. (UP P44)

Greater emphasis should be given to the effective implementation of nutrition schemes for children, especially in tribal areas. (MAH P8)

Nutrition and Health Education

NGOs have individual image and credibility with the community. Right type of NGOs should be identified and their services utilised effectively for NHE by giving proper training, guidance and continued support. (BIH P22)

Health education, including water and sanitation, should be included in the school curriculum and a systematic School Health Education programme should be implemented using the services of NGOs. (BIH P22)

People should be provided extensive education on nutrition and health education in local language. This work could be undertaken by educational institutions, media, other centres/ institutions and organised industries/trades. (UP P44)

Participation by Children

State Parties shall assure the child the right to express his/her views freely in all matters affecting the child and ensure respect for the opinion of the child. Their views may be given due weight in accordance with the age and maturity of the child, especially for victims of natural disasters, girls for consent before marriage, etc. (AP P13)

Children's Development Councils comprising only children below the age of 18 years may be formed at district and state levels with the District Collector and the Commissioner of Women Welfare and Child Development as the Chairman and Convenor respectively. Official recognition should be accorded to such councils. These councils may serve as Advisory, Monitory and Supervisory bodies with regard to policy and programmes concerning children especially in institutions. (AP P24)

In issues concerning children and their rights, the government should seek children's active participation at all stages of planning, discussion and consultation. (KAR P4)

There should be orientation and training programmes specially for decision makers and the children themselves. (WB P5)

Children should be given the opportunity and provided with a platform to express their thoughts, feelings and opinions using plays, games, paintings, essays, etc. (WB P5) (MAH P7)

Children should form their own associations to get their rights. (KAR P5)

There should be child-to-child inputs on information regarding child rights. (KAR P5)

In matters concerning children, children should demand for their participation at all levels, from planning, discussion to decision-making. (KAR P5)

Laws and Legislation

Definition of age of child varies from 12 to 18 years under different Acts relating to children. The anomaly of varying age in defining a child needs to be corrected, uniform definition should be adopted and one comprehensive state legislation on issue of child labour needs to be enacted. (AP P13, 23)

Close monitoring may be undertaken by NGOs regarding the implementation of laws for protection of child rights. (BIH P28)

Like consumer forum, legal cells should be formed to protect children from cruelty and abuse. (BIH P28)

NGOs should function as Pressure Groups for effective implementation of laws protecting children. (BIH P28)

For the protection of rights of children, a state level committee should be constituted which consists of Judges, Police, NGOs, Government and other related people. (MP P11)

A single Court should be set up for disposing of all the cases concerning children registered under various acts. (MP P11)

Arrangements should be made for effective enforcement of laws relating to child prostitution, adoption and child labour. (MP P11)

Cases relating to children and especially those of child molestation or rape may be tried in camera and decided within a stipulated period of six months. (AP P15)

An act should be promulgated to take drastic action against sexual child abuse. (AP P22)

Arrangement should be made to ensure within stipulated time the implementation of rules framed by the Central and State Governments for the benefit of children. (MP P11)

Laws pertaining to children should be more effective and humane and a procedure introduced for accountability on the part of the law enforcers. (WB P3)

Laws and legislation have to be either amended or strengthened to suit CRC. Existing legislation vis-a-vis children needs to be reviewed and revised to ensure that all the articles in the CRC are justiciable. (KAR P4) (UP P46) (MAH P8)

The need is not to formulate more laws but to ensure better implementation of existing laws with superior infrastructural support and greater awareness. (WB P5) (UP P46)

Awareness of parents, employers, school children, inspectors and the general public need to be increased on the CRC and child related laws. Information about laws related to children should be clear at the national, state, block and village levels. (WB P4) (UP P47)

A National Law may be planned for protection of

children based on the articles of the Rights of the Child. A comprehensive local law should be enacted as International Law will not be taken, into cognisance by Indian Courts and present laws relating to children are difficult to coordinate sectorally. (WB P4) (AP P23)

Plan for Implementing Rights of the Child

A Child Rights Commission at Central and State level should be constituted on the lines of Human Rights Commission with necessary machinery for strict implementation of CRC with investigative powers. (AP P24)

Separate Ministries for child development may be formed at State and Central levels so that the main focus will be on children. (AP P24)

A single department may handle all programmes for women and children instead of the present system of Social Welfare Department and Department of Women, Child and Handicapped Development. This department should also be the nodal department to handle CRC. (MAH P7)

Rights of children in institutions need to be protected as a special area. (AP P24)

The State Plan of Action for Children (SPAC) must be more widely discussed with NGOs all over the state. Workshops should be held at the district level in Marathi to ensure better outreach. (MAH P4)

Training and sensitisation of officials at all levels in the fields of law, police, labour, medicine, education and in relevant government departments on the CRC should be done. A child-sensitive approach should be used. (MAH P8)

Increased allocation of budget must be made in social sectors, i.e., Department of Women, Child and Handicapped Development, Education, Health, Social Welfare. (MAH P8)

The Government must strive to create more awareness among the public on the Convention on the Rights of the Child. (KAR P3)

There is a need for setting up a Northern Region Committee on the Rights of the Child. (CHA P8)

There should be regional work plan for achieving the rights of the child. (CHA P8)

Government, NGOs and community should work together to grant the children their childhood. (BIH P28)

Benefits of programmes like vocational training, tribal hostel or Ashram facilities, non-formal education centres, etc. should reach the beneficiaries. Meaningful efforts should be made to remove any discrepancies in such schemes. In case the schemes need modifications, NGOs and Government officers/employees should propose reforms in an organised manner to ensure successful implementation of schemes and enjoyment of rights and opportunities by children. (MP P9)

Panchayats and other NGOs should play a prominent role in publicising rights of children. (MP P11)

Basic needs of children should be identified and measures taken to meet them. (RAJ P33)

A timetable of activities for an year should be chalked out and also the use of all methods including marches, exhibitions, slogans, puppet shows. (RAJ P33)

Pre-school Education

More number of pre-primary centres should be established in the rural areas. The criteria for establishing anganwadi centres should be further relaxed. One centre for every 30 children should be started. (AP P18)

NGOs should be encouraged to start more pre-schools. (AP P18).

Recreation

Children's film festivals and film shows should be organised regularly for their entertainment. (WB P4)

Recreation should be given equal importance in schools in addition to the academic requirements. (BIH P25)

Arrangements should be made for recreation centres, libraries and museums, etc. for children in each area which would increase their knowledge, provide entertainment and develop their mental faculties and talents. (UP P4S)

It should be ensured that proper films and television programmes are shown which leave a positive impression on the child's mind. Vulgarity on public media should be banned. (UP P45)

Holidays should be used productively by organising education tours, SUPW, shramdans in rural areas, etc. (AP P20)

Extra-curricular activities should be identified and made compulsory in schools. Scouts and guides programme and other programmes may be introduced. (AP 20)

Policy and Planning

There is a need for induction of action groups in policy and planning process. (CHA P8)

Representatives of NGOs, experts and regional functionaries from all levels should be involved in the formulation and evaluation of state plans. (UP P47)

Television

1. Prior intimation of programmes related to rights of children should be given from time to time, specially in between popular programmes such as Teer Kaman, Bal Jagat, Chitrahar, Film Shows, etc.
2. Time slot should be such that children, their parents and other viewers in large numbers get to see such programmes. (MP P10)

3. Information concerning the rights of children should be disseminated through programmes like cartoon films, puppet shows, plays, folklore, folk dances, interviews, discussions, etc.
4. Adequate time and coverage should be given to news concerning children and their rights.

Radio

(i) Regular contact should be maintained by NGOs and other Government institutions with AIR stations to broadcast the message of child's rights through plays, folklore, stories, talks in local dialect. (MP P10)

(ii) Time slots allotted for these programmes should be such that children, parents and the public may get benefit of the programme. (MP P10)

(iii) Thoughts, experiences and interviews of children should go on the air through short stories, plays, dialogues, jokes, etc. (MP P10)

(iv) Prior intimation regarding these programmes should be given through radio and newspapers. (MP P10)

(v) The villagers should be encouraged through Panchayats to listen to such radio programmes. (MP P10)

Newspapers

1. In addition to their regular columns on children like Phulwari, Bacchon ki Duniya, articles, stories, Nanhi Duniya, etc. newspapers should also accord priority and importance to publication of articles on child labour and related problems.
2. Outstation programmes for editors and correspondents of newspapers should be organised so that they can carry out their responsibilities in a proper way by publishing prominently news related to child labour and rights of the child in the newspaper.

3. In order to create awareness amongst the public they should carry news related to schemes for beneficiaries and important events in an attractive manner.

Local Programmes

Information relating to rights of children should be disseminated by organising programmes like street plays, puppet shows, seminars, theatre, dance, etc. at various places through Kala Mandalis. Children fairs, games, cultural programmes, debate competitions should also be organised. Exhibitions, children campaigns, parent campaigns and rallies, should be organised to oppose injustice being meted out to children.

The media can play a pivotal role in disseminating awareness about development issues in general and children's rights in particular. (WB P3)

The media also has a very important role in monitoring the implementation of programmes related to the rights of the child. (WB P3) (MAH P6)

NGOs should develop a Special Media Cell to enhance the above process of monitoring implementation of children's rights. Such Cells should be headed by a Coordinator who will be responsible to ensure mutual cooperation and dialogue between the media and the NGOs. (WB P3)

The media may play a 'supportive' role complementing the efforts of NGOs, but the onus is on the NGOs to ensure the media give them enough coverage. As the audio visual medium is usually a more effective vehicle for carrying public messages more effort should be given for their utilisation. (WB P3)

Sensitisation of the media too is required. For this purpose orientation of journalists till the district level should be planned. (WB P3) (MAH P6)

For children to have access to information on their rights, they should be addressed through the school curriculum. Child-to-child communication among children can help them transmit knowledge to their peers. (WB PS)

Schools, anganwadis, children's organisations, NGOs and mothers' organisations should be approached with Information, Education and Communication packages on the Rights of the Child. (WB P5)

Awareness may be created in the community using audio visual and other methods e.g. Prabhat Pheri, Sandhya Pheri, Theatre, Street Plays, Puppet Shows, Cultural Shows, New Games, TV Channels, Video Films, Audio Cassettes. Cultural aspects should be kept in view. (RAJ P31)

Workshops should be organised on rights of the child. Girls should specifically be involved and Bal Mela and Children's Day could be effectively organised. (RAJ P31)

Schools and parents should be contacted and made aware of the effect of our attitude towards children. (RAJ P32)

To increase awareness in the community, a march or Padyatra could be held. (RAJ P32)

Slogans on child's rights should be made and written all over in the villages. (RAJ P32)

A Resource Centre should be created where there are books and material on Rights of the Child. (RAJ P32)

There should be a time slot on radio and TV when children could be called and talks may be given. Culturally oriented songs may be used for messages. (RAJ P33)

UNICEF should produce material on mass scale e.g.

posters (designed by Safdar Hashmi), songs, slogans. (RAJ P33)

Newspaper should be contacted for giving wide publicity to the rights of the child. (RAJ P33)

Media should highlight those experiences which are positive in any community e.g. in some tribal areas, gender discrimination is less. (RAJ P33)

The print media are still very important and must be cultivated to increase awareness. The vernacular media must be given greater importance as their influence is large and continues to grow. (MAH P6)

28. Role of NGOs

NGOs should function as pressure groups in improving the quality of services by creating a demand for them and by motivating the community for active participation. (BIH P23)

NGOs have a key role to play in planning, implementation, monitoring and evaluation of the process of implementing the rights of the child. The state level task force on CRC implementation already formed should have adequate NGO representation. (BIH P19) (UP P47) (AP P23)

NGOs should send their recommendations to the task force which is set up to look into the discrepancies that exist between the Constitution and the Convention. (KAR P4)

To protect the rights of the child, NGOs should undertake the following:

1. Undertake welfare activities for specific target group among the children. (ORI P6)

2. Raise public awareness on various national and international laws on Rights of the Child. (ORI P6)

3. Undertake advocacy and lobbying to defend the rights of the child. (ORI P6)
4. Protest against the policies and programmes hampering the interests of the children. (ORI P6)

Interaction with local NGOs to highlight the situation of children in institutions is important. (AP P17)

NGOs should organise awareness and training programmes for policy makers as well as individuals at the grassroot level. (WB P4)

Periodic monitoring of programmes should be done through NGO networks and other systems of assessment. (WB PS)

NGOs should provide more and better information to the media. They should be oriented on developing competence in communication, i.e. on giving items of news value to the media. (MAH P6, 8)

List of Workshops/Seminars on Rights of the Child Conducted in the States/Union Territories:

1. Uttar Pradesh Council for Child Welfare and UNICEF (UP). State Level Seminar on Child Rights: Potentialities and Possibilities, 1994, Jul 21-23, Lucknow. Lucknow, the author, 1994. (UP)
2. Vihaan & UNICEF (Rajasthan). Workshop on Creating Awareness on Rights of the Child in Rajasthan, 1994, Jan 24-25, Jaipur. Jaipur, the author, 1994. (RAJ).
3. Campaign Against Child Labour. Report of the Workshop on Rights of the Child and State Level Convention on Child Labour, 1994, Apr. 28-30, Angul (Orissa). Angul (Orissa), the author, 1994. (ORI)
4. Concerned for Working Children, Karnataka, Department of Women and Child Development & UNICEF (AP). UN Convention on the Rights of the Child : State Level Workshop : a report, 1994, Sep. 19-20, Bangalore. Bangalore, the author, 1994. (KAR)

5. Bihar State Council for Child Welfare & UNICEF (Bihar). The Convention on the Rights of the Child: A State Level Workshop for NGOs in Bihar: a report, 1994, Oct. 4-6, Patna. Patna, the author, 1994. (BIH).
6. Institute for Psychological and Educational Research, Government of West Bengal and UNICEF (West Bengal). A Report of the Two Day Workshop on the Rights of the Child, 1994, Jun 21-22, Calcutta. Calcutta, the author, 1994. (WB)
7. Madhya Pradesh Council of Child Welfare and UNICEF (MP). A Report of the Workshop on the Rights of the Child, 1994, Aug. 30-31, Jabalpur (MP). Jabalpur (Madhya Pradesh), the author, 1994 (MP).
8. Maharashtra, Directorate of Women, Child and Handicapped Development and UNICEF (Maharashtra). Maharashtra State Workshop on the Rights of the Child, 1994, Jul 13-14, Pune. Pune, the author, 1994. (MAH)
9. Mahila Dakshata Samithi (AP), Andhra Pradesh, Department of Social Welfare & UNICEF (AP). State Level Workshop on Rights of the Child, 1994, Sep. 27-28, Hyderabad. Hyderabad, the author, 1994. (AP)
10. Rural Centre for Human Interests, Development Support Team & Youth for Unity and Voluntary Action. Workshop on the Rights of the Child, 1994, Sep. 27-28, Chandigarh. Chandigarh, the author, 1994. (CHA)

The UN Convention on the Rights of the Child came into force as an international law on 2 September 1990. The Government of India acceded to and ratified the Convention on 12 November 1992. The Convention comprising 54 articles, is a set of international standards and measures that intends to protect and promote the wellbeing of children in society. It provides the legal basis for initiating action to ensure the children their rights related to survival, protection, development and participation. The World Summit on

Children held on 30 September 1990, strongly endorsed the Convention. Infact, this was the first major global action for the implementation of the Convention. India being a signatory to the World Declaration, has formulated the National Plan of Action for Children, which provides a framework for actualisation of the Convention and a practical agenda to guarantee the rights of the child set forth in the Convention.

Today in India, the situation of children has improved considerably. A child who was earlier considered as dependent in every respect on parents is now emerging with his/her own independent identity and is entitled to rights, including self articulation of development paths and goals. Existing constitutional provisions, policy framework, legislation and above all the commitment at the highest government level gives an impetus to the efforts being made to meet the basic needs of the children. As per UNICEF's State of World Children Report 1995, India has made dramatic progress in protecting the health of children and promoting immunisation and iodisation programmes for them.

Still, all the children in the country do not have equal opportunities and facilities for living and learning. They do not have the same level of social acceptability. About 19-24 million children in the age group 6-14 years are illiterate and only 52 per cent of the enrolled children reach primary school. Malnutrition is still a major area of concern. As per Operational Research Group study (1983), there are 44 million child workers, some are bonded and some are sold in prostitution. Further, it is estimated that there are about 500,000 street children in seven cities of India. Children living in difficult circumstances like street children, destitutes, juveniles, children of prisoners, prostitutes, etc. are nearly deprived of the basic needs. Due to existing social problems like infanticide, child labour, child prostitution, dowry, gender inequality, child marriage etc. many children in the country are missing out on their childhood. It is hoped that with the implementation of the Convention, this may not be the reality in the near future.

The Convention on the Rights of the Child is a landmark document, at the national and international level, which has facilitated conversion of the basic needs of the children into their normative rights. It is as important for tackling the children as the Constitution is for the country. In a sense, it is a means of empowering children and creating an environment in which all children are able to live securely and realise their full potential. While the Convention obligates the Government to ensure observance of its provisions, the responsibility of implementing the Convention lies with all concerned with children. Infact, all the Articles of the Convention do not require the intervention of judiciary or Government delivery system to give the children their rights. Most of them are social and cultural commitments, where the community and the parents have a very important role to play. Therefore, in order to arouse public consciousness and political will in support of the child's rights, it is all the more necessary to raise awareness about the Convention and the provisions made therein.

Article 42 of the Convention states that States Parties undertake to make the principles and provisions of the Convention widely known, by appropriate and active means, to adults and children alike. However, it is felt that the awareness about the rights of the child among children and adults is very limited. It is reported (Maheshwar, 1994) that the percentage of children who assert their rights is negligible and 30 per cent of the children are not even aware of their fundamental rights due to lack of education. Similarly, amongst the adults, 10 per cent are aware of the rights of the child, 15 per cent give this subject a thought and only 7 per cent are engaged in facilitating these rights to them.

The most important task before the government is to initiate a plan for creating awareness and disseminating information contained in the Convention to every citizen of the country in the manner in which he can understand the children's rights as a judicial law. People from various walks of life i.e. policy makers, administrators, teachers, lawyers, professionals, medical practitioners, editors, journalists, social workers, opinion leaders, folk artists, etc. must know the details of the Convention and its implications, so that they can willingly participate in the development programmes for children.

The most appropriate approach for creating awareness and wide dissemination of information about the Convention across the whole section of the society is communication media. Communication media can be a powerful advocate and a tool for awareness creation for the rights of the child. Wilber Schramm is of the opinion that media has the power to initiate, stimulate, provoke and promote social development by providing varied perception, interest, motivations, beliefs, faiths and ideas. It is the media which mediates in the production, consumption and accumulation of goods and services; besides promoting potential, social, psychological and cultural processes.

Communication field has a magnetic effect, and any information regarding the rights of the child disseminated through the media will be readily received by children and adults, provided it is presented in an interesting manner to hold their attention and is delivered at the right time. So the role of media in promoting the rights of the child cannot be undermined.

The role of media in implementing the Convention can be envisaged as that of advocacy and social mobilisation to empower all concerned with children, by creating awareness and transferring knowledge, skills and resources related to the basic needs and rights of the child, so as to promote participatory development and adopt measures which give effect to the rights recognised.

As per the Convention, the major areas of concern related to children which need media support are health, nutrition, education, family environment, gender inequality, child labour, welfare of children in difficult circumstances, etc.

Accordingly, the media interventions for advocacy and awareness creation of the rights of the child are:

1. sensitising administrators, NGOs, police, judiciary, professionals, social workers and the community about the children's rights;
2. bridging information and awareness gaps about the issues related to child's rights to bring about desirable change in the knowledge, attitude and practices of the community;
3. educating parents on the rights of the child and their role;
4. promoting democratic process of participatory development and commitment for ensuring the children their rights
5. informing people of the existing legal provisions, spreading legal literacy and explaining the laws as well as structures and methods of administration of justice in a simplified way;
6. alerting public of the changing situation of children and women and the services available for their welfare and development;
7. making children understand the concept of rights, to know what rights they are entitled to, and to empower them to participate and take action to enjoy these rights;
8. monitoring and protecting the child's rights;

At present, the use of media for the child's rights is very limited. Health related issues of national importance get coverage on electronic media at the prime time. Of late, child labour and gender inequality have caught the attention of media professionals. To use media effectively to promote rights of the child, it is essential to consider the pre-requisites for the use of media like communication infrastructure, communication needs, awareness among media professionals, journalists, editors and folk artists, availability of communication software for all media forms, trained manpower, a system to monitor and supply items of news value to the media, coordination and integration among all concerned with the implementation of child's rights for use of media, and above all the political commitment in favour of media.

If we take stock of the communication infrastructure in the country, we will find that the communication system in the country has steadily expanded and has become one of the largest in the world. Today, the radio reaches 96.2 per cent of the population and the television has a reach of 82.4 per cent. The films produced by the Films Division have an audience of about 5 to 6 crores every week. There are about 30,214 newspapers with circulation of nearly 539 lakh copies in 16 major languages and dialects. This infrastructure comprising various communication channels and media can be used for disseminating practical, target-oriented information about the rights of the child.

Though using this vast communication infrastructure to create awareness and to bring about behavioural change on issues related to child's rights is not an easy task, yet it can be accomplished with proper planning, coordination, and by formulating area-specific and need-based action programmes. Infact, there is a need for a Forum or an Action group to facilitate the use of media for the rights of the child by evolving timebound media strategies for implementing and networking communication activities.

There is a wide variety in traditional and modern media and non-formal communication techniques available. Mass media channels are being used for creating awareness, and imparting knowledge and information, and group and interpersonal communication techniques are used for decision making and behaviour change. Electronic, print and folk media are being extensively used both for entertainment and education. Electronic and print media have better reach in urban areas. Folk media is more acceptable at the grassroot levels, and is being used in remote areas where mass media technology has not fully reached.

All these media forms have their strengths and limitations and differ in terms of credibility, physical and psychological accessibility, reach, and other characteristics. Different messages related to child's rights may call for the use of different media, depending on characteristics of various media, there availability, reach and the target audience. On the whole, communication in support of rights of the child requires an integrated deployment and use of media-mix approach and social marketing techniques.

As per Article 17 of the Convention, mass media has a wider role to play in promoting the social, spiritual and moral well being of children. The Article clearly states that States Parties recognise the important function performed by the mass media and shall ensure that the child has access to information and material from a diversity of national and international sources, especially those aimed at the promotion of his or her social, spiritual and moral well-being and physical and mental health.

Now-a-days the popular mass media forms are electronic and print media. Radio and television, soap operas, prime time television programmes, radio jingles and spots, TV quickies, motion pictures, comics, cartoons, books and popular music are being used for disseminating educational messages related to health and family welfare. The same software of electronic and print media can also be used for creating awareness about rights of the child. At the community level, formation of listnen groups/ radio forums can give regular feedback to AIR/Doordarshan on issues related to child's rights.

The producers and directors of AIR and Doordarshan need to be encouraged to produce programmes for children with focus on the rights of the child in which the children can also participate. Children should be provided with a opportunities to express their feelings and opinion using plays, skits, stories, talks, debates, etc. It is important that these programmes are allotted suitable time slots so that both, children and adults can benefit out of it.

Print media especially the local press can play a key role in publicising the Convention among the literate group. Appropriate target-specific print material has to be produced on all aspects of child's rights for children as well as adults. Infact, the simplified version of the Convention should be prepared and translated in various regional languages for children to understand it. Various forms of print material like posters, charts, flash cards, flipbook, etc. are needed for effective interpersonal communication to promote child's rights.

Traditional/folk media are presently being used by Song and Drama Division and Field Publicity Units of the Ministry of Information and Broadcasting for disseminating health-related messages at the grassroot level. The potential of this media can also be explored for promoting development issues concerning rights of the child in the community. Further, fairs, festivals and haats (village market) can also be used as a forum for creating awareness and disseminating messages related to child's rights.

In our country, the Government controls the principle channels of communication i.e. radio and television. The importance accorded for advocacy of child's rights on these channels depends largely on the priority the government places on child's rights as well as the attitude of media professionals. To harness the public media for rights of the child, it is necessary not only to sensitise policy makers and planners concerned with child welfare and development, but also the media professionals, editors, journalists, folk artists, etc. Joint consultative meets, workshops and orientation courses for media and subject experts can provide a forum for creating awareness and exchanging information about child's rights.

Both electronic and print media can also monitor the progress made in achieving the realisation of the obligations undertaken in the Convention. Infact, media can become the watchdog to protect children's rights by highlighting success stories as well as cases of violation of rights. It is assumed that once the media starts taking interest in the rights of the child, the Government will also start taking the Convention more seriously.

The Government of India is making earnest efforts to create awareness about the rights of the child. During 1994, the theme selected to commemorate the Universal Children's Day on 14 November was, Rights of the Child: A Commitment. On this occasion the Department of Women and Child Development released a document giving in brief, the historical perspective of the rights of the child and situation of children with reference to articles of the Convention in the spheres of health, nutrition, education and related aspects of social support. All the State/UT Departments were instructed to make concerted efforts for advocacy for child's rights on the basis of guidelines issued. In addition, simple and selected messages were developed by the Department on rights related to survival, protection, development and participation of children. These messages received adequate coverage in the leading national newspapers.

The Department of Women and Child Development and UNICEF have also been working with the Ministry of Information and Broadcasting in a number of States to bring child's rights into the forefront. An action plan for publicising the Convention on the Rights of the Child has been prepared and is being implemented. The major activities being proposed under the Plan of Action include orientation/ training of staff, development of print material, and programmes for children on radio and television.

NGOs being nearer to the masses are in a better position to organise the community for ensuring the children their rights. These organisations can play an important role in promoting use of media for advocacy and awareness creation for the rights of the child. Some of the tasks that can be undertaken by NGOs in this direction are as given below:

1. NGOs at the grassroots level can become effective communicators or change ageats, and can mobilise and empower the community for their active participation and commitment to ensure the children their rights.
2. There is a dearth of communication software for both electronic and print media. NGOs can be actively involved in planning and production of software and messages.
3. At the community level, they can also mobilise social and cultural organisations, recreational groups, mahila mandals, etc. for child's rights.
4. NGOs can interact positively with media professionals from all fields to highlight success stories as well as violation of child's rights. They should be oriented on developing competence in giving items of news value to the media.

Conclusion

To the Convention on the Rights of the Child is a landmark document and is the first legally binding global prescription to give to the children the best they deserve. Hence, creating awareness about the Convention, its application and monitoring is a necessity and calls for a joint effort of all concerned with children. Communication media can be a powerful tool for advocacy and awareness creation provided it is used in a planned manner. At present, the use of media is limited for the child's rights. There is a need to set up an Action Group on Media, to promote sustained communication efforts on the issues related to child's rights, sensitise media professionals, train communicators, develop adequate messages and software for electronic and print media, use traditional media effectively, involve children in advocacy programmes and coordinate with all the Government Departments, NGOs, professionals, subject experts, etc. working for children. NGOs can play an important role in the use of media.

REFERENCES

Dua, M. R. and Gupta V. S. (Ed.) *Media and Development: Theories in Communication and Extension.* New Delhi, Har-Anand Publication, 1994.

India, Ministry of Human Resource Development, Department of Women and Child Development. Universal Children's Day 14 Nov. 1994, Rights of the Child: A Commitment. New Delhi, the author, 1994.

India, Ministry of Information and Broadcasting. *India 1993: A Reference Manual.* New Delhi, Ministry of Information and Broadcasting, Publication Division, 1994.

Maheshwar, Madan Lal. Role of Media in Creating Awareness for Children Rights in *A Report of the Workshop on the Rights of the Child,* 1994 August 30-31, Jabalpur, M.P.

Mahila Dakshata Samithi. *State Level Workshop on Rights of the Child: A Report.* 1994, Sep. 27-28, Hyderabad. Hyderabad, the author, 1994.

Mathur, Kanwar B. *Communication for Development and Social Change.* New Delhi, Allied Publishers, 1994.

CHAPTER 6

NGOs and Development: An Assessment

It has been noticed that, after the first three decades of planning for development by the government, there was a widespread realisation that the government systems were too rigid and standardised to evolve plans that would meet the varied requirements of this vast country. The government's implementing instrument, the bureaucracy, was too self-centred to attend to people's needs. Both the higher echelons of government and the observers of ground reality felt that government in India was emerging as monolithic, inefficient, highly bureaucratic and corrupt. A new approach and style of working seemed necessary to help in evolving programmes and implementing them in a participatory manner to meet the requirements of the local people with more accountability and transparency, and better quality of development and service delivery. Though the government was committed to people's participation from the beginning of planning in India, such participation had remained confined only to rhetoric; the system had no clue what it meant in practice. Finding that community development was not working as intended, in the early 1960s, the country adopted the model of Panchayati Raj, as if self-government would automatically make development people-oriented.

Since 1970s, and more so in the 1980s, many development NGOs came on the scene; they were distinct, on the one hand, from the government agencies and, on the other, from philanthropic organisations. By 1997, about 14,000 NGOs were registered with the Home Ministry under the Foreign Currency Regulation Act (FCRA) and many more were registered as societies under the Societies Registration Act, 1860. The development NGOs appear to have made some impact. The government as well as other funding organisations have begun to insist on the involvement of NGOs in planning and implementing the development projects and programmes. It is obvious, however, that even thousands of NGOs cannot replace the role of the government. What role and contribution should then be expected of the development NGOs? How do they influence the development scenario beyond the areas they serve? This chapter attempts to explore some of these issues. Its findings are based largely on the personal experiences and understanding of the authors of working of the NGOs. The chapter also presents a short case study of an NGO which has achieved notable success in implementing a participatory watershed development project funded by the Government of India in about 35 villages in Savarkundla *taluka*, of Bhavnagar district, Gujarat.

Issues in NGOs' Contribution

The achievements of the NGO are by no means negligible, but juxtaposed against the work done by government agencies, they pale into insignificance. What then is the import of the AKRSP's contribution or of similar NGOs, whose work looks small when compared to that done by the government agencies? This question cropped up in 1985 when the AKRSP had completed a lift irrigation project an,d built a percolation tank in a very short time with actual cost being less than that estimated by the government. The quality of work looked very impressive, and in fact, has continued to remain so all these years. When the NGO was asked about the special value of the structures, it proudly pointed to the quality and cost-effectiveness. Government could not have done it through its run of contractors. A well-wisher of the NGO sector asked, 'Are you then a good contractor for the government?'

'Certainly not; our motive was not profit. It was good work for the benefit of the people', was the pet reply. Not fully satisfied, the well-wisher asked, 'Are you then a contractor for the people?' The response was that the AKRSP was a people's supporter. It raised a very relevant question: What is the role of an NGO in a programme which the government has been implementing for decades? It was obvious that, even after expansion in the not so distant future, the AKRSP was no match for the magnitude of the government's programme. It was then realised that the contribution of development NGOs such as the AKRSP should be judged not in quantitative but in qualitative terms. However, in order to judge the quality, some standard and comparable parameters have to be evolved. In projects and programmes that have to be implemented with active community/people's participation, the following parameters may be considered:

(i) cost-effectiveness;
(ii) technical excellence;
(iii) People's participation;
(iv) accountability/transparency.
(v) institutional, financial, and environmental sustainability;
(vi) equity-concern for the deprived, and for women;

The AKRSP has always strived to achieve these quality parameters in its programmes. None of its percolation tanks or check dams has burst. Utilisation of the potential of the canals, in which people have taken over the management under the guidance of the AKRSP, is dose to 80 per cent and recovery of water charges is almost 100 per cent. Survival rate of its saplings and plantations is over 70 per cent, and more than 85 per cent of the biogas plants are working satisfactorily. The strength of the development NGOs, therefore, lies in the qualitative aspects of their work. There has been a conscious effort on the part of the NGOs to ensure quality, cost-effectiveness, and accountability in whatever they try to do.

The mission statement of another NGO, the Development Support Centre (DSC), says:

> Development Support Centre is established to provide support to people-centred organisations, programmes and policies in natural resource development with an emphasis on participation, equity, efficiency, cost effectiveness, honesty and transparency.

However, even if the performance of NGOs is good compared with that of projects and programmes implemented by the government agencies, a question may be asked, 'So what?' If the government remains a much larger actor in the development programmes, what exactly is the value of NGOs' contribution? Is it limited to the villages they work in? The AKRSP, for instance, hardly works in more than two per cent of the villages in Gujarat. Fortunately, the efforts of development NGOs to improve the quality of programmes do not remain limited to the villages or the areas where they work; there are also a lot of spread effects. Let us examine a few of them.

Pressurising the Government to Improve Performance

People in villages served by NGOs start comparing similar work done by government agencies and then demand an improvement in quality. For instance, village leaders of Dhandhalpur in Sayla *taluka* (Surendranagar district), one of the three project areas of the AKRSP, approached the district administration to improve the quality of a check dam being constructed by a contractor which was obviously inferior to the check dams constructed by the AKRSP. The government contractor had to improve his work. Thus, quality work by reputed and credible NGOs generates pressure on the government systems and some positive response from the government may follow as illustrated. The AKRSP's biogas programme in Junagadh district, the programme of Sadguru Water Development Foundation to promote lift irrigation and social forestry in Panchmahals district and artificial insemination services run by the Bharatiya Agro Industries Foundation in several districts, have the potential, by virtue of their quality, to create pressure on the government to improve its performance in the same field. With some initiative and efforts the 'islands of success could spread to a larger area'.

Institutionalising Changes in Systems and Procedures

NGOs, particularly those in the area of natural resource development, have to interact closely with government agencies to obtain official permissions at various steps and, often, funding assistance. Of the Rs 1,766 lakhs spent up to 1997, by the AKRSP on their programmes, government funding accounted for about one-third. For certain programmes, such as biogas production, the share was much higher. Close interaction with the government on financial and procedural matters often leads to appreciation by government agencies of the quality work being done by the NGOs. Thus, when they agree to provide support to NGOs, the government agencies have to modify their own systems and procedures to make them more flexible and locally relevant. Interestingly, when NGOs participate in government programmes, they bring up issues which have not been previously considered by government officials. For example, since the early 1970s, the Government of India has adopted the command area development programme which concentrates on only the on-farm development below the outlets and that too only on the sites of major and medium irrigation works. Interestingly, the issue of the inappropriateness of such a restricted approach was brought up by Anil C. Shah in the Working Group on Participatory Irrigation Management (PIM) set up by the Planning Commission for the Ninth Five Year Plan. The government was persuaded to broaden its improvement strategy to include minor irrigation works and the irrigation systems above the outlets. The AKRSP has successfully carried out the rehabilitation of structures in the minor irrigation sector. Influenced by the experiments, the Gujarat Government has already agreed to make PIM all-encompassing.

Strengthening Participation

The greatest strength of NGOs is their approach and method for enlisting people's participation. Working informally in a friendly manner, they do not undertake development as government agencies generally do, with the primary concern being the achievement of a certain target irrespective of the needs and priorities of the people. They do not confine themselves merely to consultation as government agencies sometimes do, but they work for popular participation in planning, implementation and management of local resources. The NGOs increasingly play a supportive role rather than become implementing bodies themselves. Adoption of the Participatory Rural Appraisal (PRA) technique since 1987 has proved extremely valuable for development NGOs as it helps them to go beyond the traditional leadership of the village, usually the elderly males, and reach out to ordinary women and men working on their farms or at home to learn from them about their problems and the possible solutions. PRA also helps to determine people's priorities and what responsibility they can accept if appropriate development schemes come up. The NGOs have readily accepted the principle of people's contribution as they could recognise its value as, to use World Bank terminology, 'a litmus test' to ensure genuine participation in and acceptance of a programme. Following the efforts of Anil C. Shah the principle of contribution was incorporated in PIM in Gujarat and in the recommendations of the Working Group for the Ninth Five Year Plan, 1997-2002. When the officials of the Gujarat Land Development Corporation (a government agency), have visited the villages where NGOs have carried out watershed programmes, they have been embarrassed to learn that the government works were of poor quality, easily damaged in a short time, and not maintained by the people— because they were not works 'of the people'. On the other hand, people considered the works promoted by NGOs as 'their own' and maintained them. Government officers visiting these programmes could not but appreciate the sustainability of programmes where people were genuinely involved in their development. Such demonstration effect has led government agencies, particularly at the higher level in central and state governments, to appreciate the need to integrate the participatory approach in their development schemes. The work done in Ralegan Siddhi, and by MYRADA, AKRSP, and KRIBHCO has helped the Ministry of Rural Development to formulate its watershed development programme, launched in October 1994, on the participation principle. Similarly, the impact of the AKRSP's participatory canal management in Bharuch district has persuaded the Government of Gujarat to adopt participatory irrigation management.

NGOs, which by and large steer clear of electoral and party politics seek to influence public policies and practices on the strength of their close collaboration with the people. This may not be an agenda for reforming political institutions and political processes (Bhatt, 1995) but it certainly aims to reform public systems. The central element in these two approaches of seeking to influence public policy and reforming political institutions is that of appropriate and adequate assessment of ground realities and community needs.

Promoting Sustainability

Sustainability is not merely sturdy structures and their good maintenance, although these are necessary conditions for the success of development projects; they raise the production potential of factors of production. The most important aspect is the sustainability of people's institutions which are expected to create and manage schemes that are developed with substantial financial assistance from the government. NGOs have understood the sustainability aspect better and continue to spread the message through their efforts. For instance, to ensure institutional sustainability

Anil C. Shah, in 1992 as chief executive of the AKRSP, persuaded the irrigation minister of the government of Gujarat that the canal irrigation cooperatives should be obliged to charge 'not less than' the government rates rather than 'not more than' the government rates. Since a good number of lift irrigation and canal schemes are managed by farmers, with NGO support, in a financially sustainable manner without government assistance for operation and maintenance (O&M), the government should be encouraged to charge water rates that cover at least O&M costs. Thus, some NGOs support reduction of subsidies which perpetuate dependence on government.

The approach to strengthening institutional sustainability, which implicitly ensures technical and financial sustainability, also strengthens environmental sustainability. Broad-based participation of the village communities helps in starting debates on the best possible use of natural resources (such as land and water) which have competing public *vs.* private, men *vs.* women, rich *vs.* poor) and alternative (domestic *vs.* irrigation) uses. The NGOs are generally in a better position to both comprehend people's perspective at the local level and share with people the changing perspective at the global level. In this sense they 'act locally and think globally'.

Government—NGO Collaboration

In a number of schemes, particularly those promoted by the Government of India, where cooperation and participation of people are considered essential, collaboration of NGOs is welcomed. For instance, in the area of development and management of natural resources, for such schemes as Joint Forest Management, Participatory Irrigation Management, and Watershed Development, government agencies have been seeking collaboration with NGOs. Fruitful relationships emerge when NGOs respond positively, appreciating that the government is to remain the major actor in rural development and collaborative efforts will better serve the common cause of helping the people. In the process, NGOs also get opportunities to 'upscale NGO intervention without a substantial increase in staff and operations' (Fernandez, 1996). The collaborative arrangements also help to identify issues that need to be addressed to evolve healthy and efficient working relations on various fronts. Some of these issues are listed next:

(a) To enable the NGOs to participate with ease and dignity, there is a need to simplify the government systems and procedures. This can be attempted by an NGO such as the DSC which can draw upon the experience of government systems and also has a firsthand knowledge of the special requirements of NGOs and people's organisations.

(b) NGOs have found in scheme after scheme that it is much easier to work with the Government of India than with the state governments and, similarly, with senior officers rather than with officials at the district, block and village levels, in that order. The lower level functionaries perceive NGOs as an 'encroachment on their territory[3] (Arya, 1996). There is a need for organised fora where policy and operations issues can be brought up and resolved. State-level working groups with multi-source membership of government officers, NGOs, and academics have proved a convenient mechanism in Gujarat for programmes of PIM and JFM. Similarly, there is a need for coordination committees with multi-source membership at regional and district levels where problems of implementation can be sorted out. After a study of government/NGO collaboration in Rajasthan, it was found that 'delinked autonomous structures' are better suited to promote a healthy relationship. At the same time, depending solely on government funding creates dependency, leading to gratuitous compromises (Gulati, 1996). However, experience has also shown that merely setting up such working groups and coordination committees does not guarantee their regular and satisfactory working. Usually, NGOs have to cake the initiative to ensure their active functioning. It would be much better if a reputed NGO leader headed such fora. Such an arrangement is not uncommon with the Government of India, although rare in the states.

(c) Government agencies collaborating with the NGOs usually expect the latter to take the responsibility of creating awareness and motivation amongst the people about development schemes. The actual implementation, they assume, should be done by the government agencies which have technical competence and their 'own' resources. However, experience has shown that just bringing people to the government agencies does not lead to participatory development. The NGOs must remain involved in implementation to ensure that people's knowledge, skills and needs are properly integrated. Knowing that there are elements of reluctance in government/NGO partnership (Ferrington and Babington, 1993), it is possible to attempt organisational designs for optimum drawing of relative strengths in this partnership. This may be termed as 'joining of strengths'. The DSC has tried to work out, for each step of planning, implementation, and management, the contribution each partner should make depending upon its relative strength. The comparative advantage of the government is large resources and spread of technical manpower, while the strength of NGOs lies in their commitment to reaching difficult areas and deprived sections. 'Joining of strengths' is more easily understood and agreed upon when both partners fully realise that their common goal is to develop the capability of the people and their institutions to take maximum responsibility for their own development, through a strong sense of 'ownership', framing of rules and enforcing discipline, transparency in operation, and sound financial management (Fernandez, 1996). However, admittedly, only development NGOs aim at such 'joining of strengths' and not the 'action NGOs', because the latter have a different and perhaps larger agenda of transforming social and political conditions in favour of the poor (Pandey, 1991). Indeed, the action groups may, at a later date, desire to collaborate with the government, at which time the theme of 'joining of strengths' would apply.

(d) With increasing demand for contribution by NGOs in government schemes, it has been found that there is a dearth of suitable NGOs particularly in the area of natural resource development. The DSC has, therefore, taken the initiative to encourage and support new voluntary organisations and those working in traditional voluntary sectors, such as health and education, to facilitate their entry into the area of natural resource development. The emerging issue, then, is one of laying down the criteria and then activating the process of NGO selection. It has been possible to bring in several such voluntary organisations to work as implementing agencies for the watershed programme. The DSC is offering support to such new entrants to develop their capability in organisational, technical, and management areas. The DSC's experience, so far, has been that many voluntary organisations find it difficult to appreciate that natural resource management requires technical and organisational inputs which are new for them, and that participatory development demands skills different from those required for inservice delivery activities. For most of the existing voluntary organisations, it is a steep climb, requiring unloading of past baggage to become a learning organisation, readily engaging with their staff, without status barriers, into open sharing and critical reflection. Of course, there are some voluntary organisations that have developed their capability quite rapidly with support of this kind.

The five major areas identified here cover the most vital aspects related to the working of the NGOs and their immediate and larger contribution to the development process. The following section, briefly reviews the experience of an NGO which has, since October 1994, planned and implemented a land and water resource development project with people's participation. The NGO was provided technical and professional support by the DSC. Interestingly, although the NGO had had a long experience of more than 50 years, it was receptive to outside professional support and was willing to try out new approaches in planning and implementing.

The Case of Kundla Taluka Gram Sewa Mandal (KTGSM)

The Kundla Taluka Gram Sewa Mandal (KTGSM) has its roots in Gandhian ideology. Three of the founding members of the Mandal had actively participated in the freedom struggle. Interestingly, each had his special interest in a different area and each pursued work in his respective area of interest. The economic programme of the then informal Mandal was initiated way back in 1936. However, the Mandal was formally registered as a society in 1955. Deeply influenced by the Gandhian idea of *'Gram Swaraj'*, establishment of Khadi and village industries for generating non-farm employment in villages emerged as the main programme of the Mandal. The Mandal also opened primary and secondary schools in a few villages on the lines of 'Buniyadi Talim' (basic education).

The villages in Savarkundla are inhabited mainly by patels, rajputs, kolis, ahirs, harijans, rabaris, and Muslims. The socio-economic status of patels and rajputs is generally better, and among kolis and ahirs some have been able to improve their conditions. However, kolis, ahirs, harijans, rabaris, and Muslims have remained socially backward. The *taluka* receives low and irregular rainfall ranging between 400 to 650 mm, more than 90 per cent of it during June to August. It is covered under the government's Drought Prone Areas Programme (DPAP). There is acute water shortage both for agriculture and drinking and domestic purposes in years when rainfall is below normal. According to the 1991 Census, the percentage of irrigated to total cultivated area was 9.9 per cent, which was lower than in many other *talukas* in Bhavnagar district and also in comparison with the district and state averages of 23 and 27 per cent, respectively.

The Khadi enterprise with its headquarters in Savarkundla has a national marketing network and supports more than 2,000 families. The spindles, yarn, and other accessories are supplied through 22 sub-centres in the programme area. During the 1990s, average annual sale of Khadi has been valued at over Rs 17 million. Besides Khadi, the Mandal also manages dyeing and printing, an oil milling unit, condiment units, and manufacture of soap from inedible oils.

A residential educational centre was developed in Khadasali, a village about 25 kilometres away from Savarkundla, the *taluka* headquarters. From a very modest beginning in the late 1940s, the campus now has developed schooling facilities up to the higher secondary level. Agriculture and animal husbandry are special vocational subjects. There is a separate hostel for girls. Use of hybrid seeds, biochemical inputs, and agro-mechanical devices is taught and students and teachers carry out extension activities in the neighbouring villages.

In 1982, a cyclone struck the area and rains ravaged crops and settlements. With financial aid from OXFAM, the Mandal carried out relief operations and as a part of rehabilitation organised vegetable growing in the river bed into a co-operative. The Mandal helped in regularising the tenurial rights of the landless and small cultivators.

In 1984, the Christian Children Fund (CCF), an American donor agency, supporting the children from poor families for their total development, agreed to fund a project in the villages where the KTGSM operated. By 1997, more than 700 children from about 570 families had been provided support for schooling, better nutrition and personality development. Interestingly, the village-level workers who identify poor families and eligible children therein, have themselves benefited from the programme during their childhood. Besides supporting individual children, the programme provides for community building, such as pre-school child care arrangement (running *Balwadis),* mother and child health care clinics and support for the housing and vocational guidance of high school children.

The programme also supports creation of community assets to raise income generating capacities of poor families. Under a project taken up in the early 1990s, four check dams were constructed in a row on a small rivulet to impound rain water. Deep cuts and erosions were also plugged. The project had a very positive impact. The recharge in wells improved so much that wells which otherwise used to go dry by February had water the following summer. Encouraged by this experiment, the Mandal planned more projects under another government scheme, the Sarvodaya Yojna. In 1992-93, the Mandal supported about 50 *bandharas* (earthen bunds) in which farmers had to contribute 50 per cent of the total cost.

The *bandharas* and check dams caught the imagination of the people quickly mainly because in almost all the villages the water table had been going down rapidly. Since early 1980s, and particularly after 1987 (a year of severe drought), digging of wells and bore wells had picked up. The topography of the *taluka* is not suitable for any canal irrigation projects because the *taluka* is almost divided into two parts by a hilly ridge known as Lamdhar. Rain water runs off on both sides of the ridge and farmers rely exclusively on ground water sources for irrigation.

The Project

Encouraged by the results of *bandharas* and check dams, the KTGSM wanted to launch a similar project on a larger scale if only funds were available. It had identified the development of agriculture in the drought-prone *taluka* of Savarkundla as the key area for its intervention. Incidentally, the Department of Rural Development, Ministry of Rural Areas, Government of India, was keen to finance some innovative projects under the third stream of Jawahar Rojgar Yojna (JRY), an employment-generation programme for rural areas (named after the first prime minister of India, Jawaharlal Nehru). With the help of the Development Support Centre, the KTGSM prepared a proposal for scientific development of watersheds. The project, covering 35 villages of Savarkundla *taluka*, had two components: It was proposed to build water harvesting structures on farmlands and adjoining public land to increase the rainfall retention for augmenting water supply for irrigation and drinking purposes and second, a land development programme was to be initiated in five identified micro watersheds.

The project was estimated to cost Rs 30 million over three years. In all, 12 percolation tanks, 14 check dams and 760 gully/*nalla* plugs or *bandharas* were to be constructed, an area of about 3,500 ha. was to be treated, and 300,000 trees were to be planted. An estimated 890,000 person-days of employment were to be generated to benefit more than 7,000 families.

The Objective

The objective of the project was to develop not only physical infrastructure but also management systems and village institutions through participatory processes for sustainable development and use of water resources to improve the income generating capacity and quality of life of the rural communities in the *taluka.*

Implementation

The project was sanctioned in September 1994. It was executed by a relatively small team of 15 members including the project co-ordinator and four engineers. The estimated total administrative cost was 7.5 per cent of the cost of works. The project activities were planned and executed between September 1994 and June 1998 because monsoon sets in around June end, after which no work is possible. Since most of the work was over by the first year itself, second year onwards the activities slowed down. Performance in terms of the construction of the physical structures was spectacular.

During the second year, planning for land shaping also began. Initially, eight villages, where construction of water conservation structures was complete, were selected. The actual work of land shaping started in the third year and by June 1998, a total of 3,711 ha. were covered by contour bunding and trenches for drains; 121,800 saplings were planted to improve tree cover. Approximately, Rs 25 million were spent on all these works. Compared to any similar government programme, this achievement was indeed spectacular.

The water conservation structures were designed to impound more than 100 MCFt of water. More than 1,900 wells are to be recharged. A total of about 9,786 ha. of land will be brought under assured irrigation. After the first year, there was significant improvement in the area under cotton, which is the most paying crop in the region, followed by groundnut. There are significant inter-village and intra-village differences in the yield of cotton owing to various factors. However, assured irrigation has improved the yield by half, on an average. This increase in yield may be attributed to timely and adequate supply of water which was possible because of recharged wells. The output of other *kharif* cereal crops such as *jowar* and *bajra* was also stabilised with support irrigation. The KTGSM has tried to collect some information on area and output of crops in project villages, but there are some methodological problems and, hence, it is not possible to quantify the impact of the project with a fair degree of precision. Indirect evidence, however, suggests that the income of farmers rose in most of the villages. In Mitiyala, for instance, for the first time in the history of the village, a contribution of Rs 28,000 was collected for a socio-religious function, 'Tulsi Vivaha', in which even the Muslim households participated. It was a result of good income earned by farmers from irrigated cotton (farmers in Mitiyala have built a check dam, 4 percolation tanks and 95 *bandharas* to recharge their wells).

Participation Process

Information about the project was disseminated to all the 35 project villages by the project team including the project co-ordinator. The latter is a very senior member of the KTGSM's core team and enjoys high credibility among the villagers. The villagers were asked to identify sites on or near their fields where water courses could be bunded or dammed. Once the sites were identified, farmers had to notify the project office in Savarkundla. One of the engineers then visited the selected sites, inspected them, consulted the leader of potential beneficiaries and gave technical clearance. The engineer came back and prepared a plan and cost estimate for the proposed work. The farmer leader was then informed about the estimate and was asked to deposit five per cent of the cost towards a maintenance fund to be maintained by the project office. When the amount was deposited a work order was issued to the farmer. The farmer was then to execute the work under the technical supervision of the project engineer. Upon completion of the work, the engineer measured the quantum of work done and estimated the actual cost. Eighty per cent of the measured cost was reimbursed to the farmer or the group of farmers who constructed the check dam/*bandhara*/percolation tank. This ensured people's contribution of 20 per cent towards the work.

Under the project procedure the KTGSM motivated and organised people for the work. During the first year, execution of work assumed priority. During the second year, village committees were formed in all the 35 villages. The DSC has provided continuous critical feedback on participation processes and a methodology to measure it. An important contribution of the DSC has been the introduction of Participatory Rural Appraisal (PRA), first to analyze the village situation, to identify sites for water conservation structures and finally to encourage involvement of the people in the activity. PRA encouraged many usually silent persons to speak up. In all the project villages, at least one PRA exercise was conducted. Interestingly, the village committee members showed keen interest in the concept, planning, and implementation of water conservation structures. The usual run-of-the-mill political leaders were generally relegated to the back seat. In a number of villages new leadership emerged. The village committee comprised eight-to-ten members drawn from all castes and classes. Their main function was to visit and approve the sites suggested by farmers. Most of the committees were active during the planning and construction stage. In each village, at least one committee member took active interest in the project and assumed the entire responsibility of contacting farmers, visiting sites, obtaining consent from the group of beneficiaries, and helping to collect the five per cent contribution. Some enthusiastic committee members also helped the beneficiary farmers in the construction process without any personal gain. Similarly, neighbouring farmers also helped by supplying water at the construction sites (without any charge for electricity or diesel oil used to pump it). In some instances, farmers also permitted submergence of a part of their farm to facilitate the construction of a structure, especially in the case of percolation tanks.

Individual farmers had to assume responsibility for land shaping activity on their own farms. The farmers had to contribute 50 per cent of the total cost of land shaping, the upper limit of which was Rs 4,000 per ha. A farmer received a maximum subsidy of Rs 2,000 per ha.for his work, and had to contribute the rest. The implementation procedure was the same as was followed for water conservation structures. The project engineers visited fields, provided guidance regarding the location of contour bunds, and prepared cost estimates. Farmers then built the contour bunds and the engineer measured the work done. In 13 villages where the water conservation structures were completed, an area of 3,711 ha.was brought under land shaping.

Is the Performance of NGOs Better than Government's?

It was argued earlier that the contribution of NGOs to the process of development has been through quality work and its impact on other processes. The KTGSM story confirms this thesis. Let us look at the evidence.

Quality of Work

Over a period of two-and-a-half years, a total of more than 850 water conservation structures were constructed by the people including 97 check dams and percolation tanks. Most of these structures have withstood at least one monsoon, and some have withstood two. None of the check dams and percolation tanks has been damaged. In case of *nalla* plugs or *bandharas,* only 56 out of the 826 built were damaged. Most of them were rebuilt by the farmers and interestingly the entire repairing expenditure was borne by them. Some initial inexperience was probably responsible for the damage. A retired chief engineer of the Government of Gujarat, engaged as a consultant by the DSC, visited a large number of sites and besides suggesting additional engineering inputs, he also recorded his appreciation of the quality of construction by the farmers. The fact that the structures were not built by contractors seems to explain the excellent quality of construction.

Cost-Effectiveness

The works executed by the KTGSM and the people of Savarkundla *taluka* were cost-effective partly because the administrative cost of the project was only 7.5 per cent of the total, as compared to the usual 20 per cent when handled by government departments. The compensation to staff in voluntary agencies is much lower than that given by the government. The KTGSM was no exception. The project co-ordinator accepted an honorarium of only Rs 3,000 per month, and that too, after the first year. Project engineers were paid between Rs 2,500 to Rs 4,500 per month, and the rest of the staff was paid Rs 1,200 to 2,000 per month. In a way the NGO sector provides subsidised service to society by accepting lower remuneration than offered in government departments (the latter is more than the opportunity cost if [eft to market forces). A pertinent question is whether the NGO sector should underpay its staff, all of whom may not share the voluntary spirit. Looking at the quality and quantity of work accomplished by the NGO sector, payment of market-based remuneration to its staff could become an added incentive for an expansion of its activities, if the requisite resources can be raised.

Second, no government department could have accomplished in two-and a half years as much as KTGSM. It took less than a week to prepare the plans and estimates for check dams and percolation tanks. In the case of *nalla* plugs, they were prepared within a day or two. Such speed is inconceivable in a departmental framework. It would have taken months to design and technically approve the same number of structures by a government department. Obviously, such speed raises cost-effectiveness. The KTGSM engineers did not have all the skills necessary for conducting technical surveys and preparing plans and estimates at the beginning and the DSC provided frequent guidance in the field as well as in the office. The project engineers were also trained in special training workshops. On the basis of its field experience, the DSC standardised certain designs and related calculations and put them on the computer to make them easily accessible to the KTGSM computers. The standardised formats were then installed in the KTGSM computers. This input from the DSC added significantly to speed and accuracy in designing, calculations, and billing. Further, the estimates were prepared on the basis of the 'Schedule of Rates (SOR)' approved by the government. The people contributed 20 per cent of the estimated cost of the structure in cash, kind, or through labour; but the total cost of most of the works was less than the initial estimates. In effect there was a saving of resources. Generally, in drought-prone areas, the contractors quote above the tender rates which are computed using the SOR, and the government approves such higher quotations. Had the government tried to implement the same project in Savarkundla by itself, several contracts would have been awarded at significantly higher rates.

Sustainability

As noted earlier the structures are technically sound. Since farmers have themselves built them to augment the water supply in their own wells, they undoubtedly take good care of them. In a few instances where the structures were damaged, the farmers and the members of the team reached the site and tried to repair the damages as soon as possible. In fact, the farmers have realised that there is hardly any effective alternative to the managing of natural resources than the one suggested to them by the KTGSM. Hence, the probability of sustaining the current method of resource conservation and management in the area is quite high. The land shaping work will help reduce soil erosion in the fields and the *bandharas*, check dams and percolation tanks will raise the water table.

Participation by the people has been fairly good. Women are yet to participate actively in decision-making processes; however, their participation by way of providing family labour and as hired labour for building the structures was substantial. As stated earlier, the project has brought about a change in the leadership in many villages, and because the new leaders are attracted towards development, it is likely that the interest in project activities will survive in the long run.

Conclusion

The cited case study reveals positively that the NGOs in case was a credible NGO with appropriate and adequate professional inputs and training (through the DSC in this case) can plan and execute a government programme that has been languishing for decades, and achieve a sustainable impact. Watershed development is not a new programme for the government. It has existed for a long time in one form or another, with various departments. However, the government programme has not been able to make much of an impact. In fact, obtaining consent for land shaping and creating small surface water conservation structures with the help of the village community has always proved difficult.

REFERENCES

Bhatt, Anil (1995). 'Voluntary action in India', *Economic and Political Weekly*, Vol. 30, No. 16, pp 870-76.

Fernandez, Aloysius P. (1996). *Working with Government*. Bangalore: MYRADA (Mysore Resettlement and Development Agency).

Ferrington, John and Anthony Babington (1993). *Reluctant Partners*. New York: Routledge.

Gulati, Ravi and Kaval Gulati (1996). *Strengthening Voluntary Action in India*. Delhi: Konark.

CHAPTER 7

Towards Accountability

Accountability, a virtue by nature, is neglected in all spheres of life—whether govt. in action or individuals. Indian affairs are badly hit by non-accountability. Mushroom growth of NGOs has proved futile. Ar NGOs only meant for amasing the funds? Despite statutory provisions, who will look to enforce accountability? Now voices are being raised demanding accountability. Here are some excepts.

On July 11 1997, *The Hindu* carried the following report:

The Social Work and Research Centre (SWRC)—better known as Tilonia by the name of the village where it is located—has volunteered to disclose its accounts and provide details of its funds and activities before a public gathering which would include the people's representatives from the area to set an example to the much maligned non-governmental organisations (NGOs) in the country.

The *Jan Sunwai* (public hearing) is scheduled for July 13, 1997 at Buhura, a village seven kilometers from Tilonia in Ajmer district. Perhaps this is for the first time a NGO of the stature of SWRC is taking such an initiative in the whole country. Though the director of SWRC, Mr Sanjit (Bunker) Roy, has been contemplating a public hearing of its accounts and activities for quite some time, the immediate provocation is believed to be allegations of misuse of funds levelled against it.

In 1985, as consultant to the Planning Commission on voluntary agencies, Bunker Roy was responsible for initiating a move to formulate a Draft Code of Conduct for Rural Voluntary Agencies. At that time, many of the major NGOs and their associated forums, decried this move as sinister, as an effort by the government to tighten control over a sector and agencies widely believed to be at the cutting edge of developmental and social action. It may be recalled that the decade from the mid-1970s to the mid-1980s had witnessed traumatic processes—the Emergency, the defeat of Mrs Indira Gandhi and the rule of the first non-Congress regime at the centre, its subsequent collapse and the re-emergence of Mrs Gandhi's rule, militancy in Punjab and the tragic assassination of Indira Gandhi, resulting finally in a Congress Party victory with the largest ever mandate given to a political party.

During this period both the bureaucracy and political parties were seen with increasing scepticism, if not hostility, by a large spectrum of articulate opinion. Most important, both nationally and globally, there was a discernible excitement about voluntary groups —not just as agents of service delivery, but as key players to resuscitate civil society, empower the poor and impose new standards of accountability. Expectedly, this led to a major infusion of funding into the voluntary sector with most development schemes being designed to encourage voluntary sector participation.

Why was the move for a code of conduct initiated by Bunker Roy greeted with such hostility? Was it because of the quasi-official source of the move? Was it because of the alleged proximity of the initiator to the then prime minister, Mr Rajiv Gandhi? Or was it because, as Bunker Roy charged, the major opposition was orchestrated by foreign donor agencies and their partner organisations, wary about public questioning of their assets, activities and lifestyles? Intriguingly enough, around the same time, the Communist Party of India (Marxist) too launched a campaign against NGOs receiving foreign funds, characterising them as agents of neo-imperialism.

Eventually, the move to evolve a code of conduct was quietly shelved. But today, a dozen years later, the situation has not changed. As recently as November 1996, Bunker Roy described many of his compatriots in the NGO sector as 'non-gazetted officers, with minds like habus, selfish to the core and careful to say the right thing? He went on to call them 'power brokers, who live entirely off foreign money with no independent source, who would like to have all the money for themselves and then dish some of it out to others as patronage, using foreign money as a means to co-opt, control, discipline and dump'. He compared them to touts — 'Uriah Heeps — hypocrites who perform activist roles with no activists present, graphically relate stories of struggles, campaigns, rape and state brutality to show how close they are to the grassroots, thus fixing trips abroad to workshops and conferences'. He not only called these voluntary sector power brokers 'scum'; he even wrote an open letter to the union home minister demanding a more stringent application of the Foreign Contribution Regulation Act (FCRA).

Such descriptions of NGOs from a leading exemplar of the sector are both disturbing and shocking. Political parties, particularly those of the Left, only arrack NGOs, particularly those receiving foreign funding, as 'a new factor in imperialist strategy'. And here too, the focus is primarily on the relatively new, urban-based, professional NGOs that normally specialise in intermediary functions like training, research, documentation, advocacy, film-making, networking and so on, and not the many small groups who work in villages and slums and actually dirty their hands.

To come back for a moment to the SWRC, Tilonia '*jan sunwai* was indeed unique in the range of documents about itself that it made public — complete financial audits, detailed reports on all programmes, salary and asset statements of all employees, even details of foreign trips undertaken including who paid for the tickets and who picked up hotel bills. Clearly, such details are never provided by our political parties. Admittedly, however, the Tilonia example has remained a one-off. To date, no other NGO has sought to emulate it, far less improve on the methodology of public audits. Further, both at the time of the debate on the code of conduct and now, NGOs have, as a rule, remained hostile to public scrutiny. They claim that as field-based practitioners, they know best, that evaluations while sometimes unavoidable, are at best an irritant and at worst mechanisms for introducing external control.

The wheel for Bunker Roy, and SWRC, Tilonia, may have come a full circle. But in my view, the general proposition holds. Activists in the field (howsoever defined) are rarely excited about the prospects of an external evaluation. It is not just that they are anti-theoretical, see little value in academic papers and reports, or that they are fundamentally secretive and look at all such intervention as intrusive. It is also not that they are only seeking affirmation and validation, though who does not love praise. Rather, it is their deep distrust of general and universal criteria of assessment. If everything is relative and contextual, then evaluations can at best be sensitive descriptions, reflective more of the power position occupied by the researcher/ evaluator than any effort at presenting objective pictures.

Any researcher who has been engaged in preparing case-studies of NGO efforts has faced a latent hostility from the 'subject' organisation. And if perchance the evaluation is linked to a donor agency, irrespective of who actually 'commissioned' the work, and the 'conclusions' turn out to be even mildly critical, the usual response of the subject organisation is that the work is shoddy, that insufficient time was spent in the field, that the research team was biased, and so on. Such, at least, has been my experience in the three situations when I was invited to be part of an evaluation team (in ail cases, not by the donors, but by the subject organisation). And one of them happened to be the SWRC, Tilonia.

The Current Context of Voluntary Action in India

The praxis of accountability has become contentious because quite unlike the early social reformers, the church-based or Gandhian institutions, even some of the efforts initiated by the political parties, the modern NGO phenomenon (at least a significant section of it) locates itself in an explicit critique of the state and political parties, particularly their relative inability to respond meaningfully to the survival and dignity issues of the poor and the excluded. This is even more true of support NGOs (middle class and mainly urban) who seek to work, not directly with base communities, but field organisations involved in an effort to improve their efficacy, individually and collectively.

Much of this orientation evolved in a phase when donor organisations, official or otherwise, national or foreign, started stressing the inefficacy of working through official structures to tackle widespread but local issues of oppression and survival. From the formal recognition granted to NGOs in the Seventh Eve Year Plan to the shift in the priorities of multilateral, bilateral and private co-financing agencies, the period from the late 1970s has witnessed a massive escalation of both support and funding to NGO formations.

Not unexpectedly, this change in environment led to a major explosion in the number of NGOs. While a large part of this munificence was channelised towards conventional charity and developmental organisations, a large residual market was simultaneously created for NGOs working with a political orientation. Thus new groups, whether working directly with the concerned populace in the field, or as support organisations mediating between micro social action groups, or between them and the state, through a diverse set of activities earlier unknown in the NGO world, acquired a new presence. Through seminars and workshops, theatre and films, newsletters and journals, lobbying and networking, these new groupings with specialised skills attempted to reach out to both the grassroots and the policy-makers. Central to this new enterprise were new ideological debates — on human rights, ecology, feminism and the law — efforts at reconstituting the epistemological universe in which meanings are ascribed to political and developmental activity.

At one level, this proliferation and diversity in the NGO sector and discourse about it has contributed to the difficulty in making sense of this activity. Second, the stakes of the game have become considerably higher, given particularly the centrality of the NGOs in development policy formulation and practice. Finally, with grassroots and social movement studies more focused on NGO activism than political parries and movements or organisations of workers and peasants, we have the emergence of a new academic market with considerable funding support.

One interesting implication of all this has been the progressive radicalisation of language and concepts. The shift from the mid- 1970s towards NGOs as a favoured entity for funding support owes much to their 'brand distinction' from official agencies. In relative terms, they were seen as locally rooted and environmentally sensitive, flexible, low-cost and honest, and thus 'proper' instruments to reach the people. However, as criticism grew of top-down, non-participative approaches to development and democracy, much greater stress began to be laid on processes rather than products, particularly those that helped in the conscientisation, mobilisation and organisation of the poor and hitherto excluded.

This heightened radicalism led to a purposive devaluation of the notion of service, of doing good, of helping others in need. Older voluntary formations, albeit of a conventional charity and development type, were made to appear as irrelevant. It also led to a decline in the importance of material interventions in the lives of the poor, since activities like introducing new technologies, focussing on income generation through production, etc., were construed as consolidating the capitalist system, as helping the better-off.

This new political role, accompanied by radical rhetoric, has generated new pressures from diverse sources on the NGO sector. As a result of the new expectations that NGOs have generated, there is an overloading of demands from the ground. Networking and coordination, combined with servicing grassroots groups and struggles, is a complex task. The inability to satisfy these expectations has led to the trading of vilificatory charges—that NGOs have become corrupt, lazy, used to an easy lifestyle, distanced from base communities and groups—some of it unfortunately true.

The 'phobia' about the sector emerging as the new dissenting force (a result both of description and self-description) has led to a new alliance of forces arraigned against the sector as also new, official, restrictive conditionalities. Towards the end of the millennium, the India faced a daunting situation. More than seven years of attempts at economic liberalisation, designed more to globally integrate the economy and roll back the State even from its constitutionally mandated role rather than 'free' domestic production and distribution, has created a new stratum of the relatively deprived.

Whatever be one's personal assessment of the reform initiatives, it is difficult to deny the increase in inequality, and this when the masses remain deprived of the basic requirements of a life with dignity. Our formal political structure is in shambles, unable not just to enable stable rule but even to intervene positively in daily life. Many of the protective legislations have been shattered.

Challenges Ahead

The debate about NGOs and community initiatives and formations thus needs to be located in this context. Issues of accountability and modes to ensure that the NGOs remain transparent have to be tackled with urgency if we are to re-infuse the sector with a new spirit. Otherwise, notwithstanding greater funding support and glamour, the inflow of dedicated and creative people, particularly the young, is likely to dry up.

This needs a little elaboration. A half century back, the epistemic shift in the voluntary sector was from service to empowerment, development to political action. The drawing edge came from ideological commitment. NGOs, whatever their organisational affiliation—Gandhian, religious or Marxist/Socialist—seemed keen to focus on the poor. As NGOs started offering a viable career option, the social base of their cadres slowly started changing. Given the new activity mix, more so of the intermediary support organisations, the emphasis shifted to skill and efficacy. Our argument is not that the new generation of NGO activists is less concerned about issues related to the poor and deprived. It is that they are, in relative terms, more concerned about themselves and thus relate differently to issues of accountability to their respective organisations as also to the people they work for and with.

[Source: *The Pioneer*, 12 Nov. 1996.]

CHAPTER 8

Social Development and NGOs

> [Then feed on thoughts that Voluntary move
> Harmonious numbers... Thus with the year
> Seasons return but not to me returns
> Day or sweet approach of ev'n or mom
> Or sight of vernal bloom or Summer's rose
> Or flocks or herds or human face divine.
>
> —*Milton*]

India has a very long, ancient and traditional background of voluntary organisations and voluntary leadership, at times even based on elected leadership that sounds very ultra-modern. Before proceeding to discuss the contemporary international scene and the current national situation of voluntary organisations, let me discuss our own past and the institutions inherited by us, almost intact, from times immemorial, which have been either adopted or adapted to suit the needs and requirements of our modern democratic framework.

Terry Allibund in his book *Catalysts of Development—Voluntary Organisations in India, 1983,* reviews briefly India's recent historical record and its past development successes and failures in the field of PVOs, i.e. what be labels as "Private Voluntary Organisations", According to him, from an historical perspective, India's PVOs have provided a valuable series of unplanned (and largely unanalysed) socio-economic change-experiments. Hatch's work with the YMCA in rural Kerala, Elmhirst and Tagore's efforts with Bengali peasants, the early Christian missionary colonies in the North-west region, Bryane's authoritarian approach to change in

Gurgaon District, Gandhiji's programme intended as a model for the rural development of independent India, and Mayer's demonstration of successful social and economic change at Etawah, are all cases that provide one of the richest sources of insight on appropriate and feasible development-methods in India.

Terry Allibund uses the words—"Voluntaryism" and "Volunteerism"—quite distinctly, the former meaning an institutional movement, and the latter pointing out individual initiative. Of the urges that propel people to voluntary action, Rajni Kothari observes: "The process of secularisation of power in place of the traditional ascriptive basis of power has generated two opposite forces: the few groups that were able to enter the political terrain and had the necessary means to retain their new-found position in the secular order have been possessed by a great sense of power and ascendancy, while the large majority of citizens whose aspirations have been aroused by the values of the democratic system but who did not have the necessary means to realise them have been possessed by a sense of inferiority, powerlessness and discontent. This is the great hiatus which divides the Indian people."

Dr. B.G. Verghese has drawn attention to a movement within the Catholic Church in Kerala that interprets true religion as a struggle for bread, human dignity, and social justice. He likens that movement to what he calls "the new awareness within the Gandhian movement", which focusses on "struggle" and on "organising the poor to overthrow the bonds of dead habit and vested interests of every kind". In another context, J. Duncan Derrett has shown the many ways in which a combination of constitutional provisions, public opinion and law, are forcing a number of previously idle Hindu religious endowments to be invested in educational and charitable endeavours that often end up promoting voluntary work with development objectives, such as in the case of the Ramakrishna Mission. Amongst such early endeavours, stand the most notable of such projects headed by Rabindranath Tagore in North Bengal, by Dr. Spencer Hatch at Marthandam in Madras, by F.L.Bryane in Gurgaon, Haryana, and by Sir V.T. Krishnamachari in the old princely state of Baroda. Both the Christian and the Hindu organisations, since Independence, have taken upon themselves the leadership-role in voluntary movements. Swami Sivananda's Divine Life Society spearheaded social and medical programmes. So does the Satya Sai movement all over India. The proceeds of the Indira Gandhi Award for International Understanding were donated by Swami Ranganadananda for tribal welfare programmes in Bastar District of Madhya Pradesh. Government developmental programmes also increasingly came to be implemented by registered voluntary agencies of beneficiaries at the district level. Girijan Development Agency of Srikakulam District of Andhra Pradesh was the first of its kind in this regard for tribal development as a pace-setter as early as 1970.

Most modern Indian social theorists have attempted to find a way to preserve the warmth and intimate social relationships associated with traditional Indian social institutions while introducing greater degrees of equality within and between different groups. This effort is prominently reflected in the Indian Constitution, which as Galanter points out, "sets forth a general programme for the reconstruction of Indian society. It clearly sets out to secure to individuals equality of status and opportunity, to abolish invidious distinctions among groups, to protect the integrity and give free play to voluntary associations, (and to provide) the widest freedom of association to the individual and generally the widest personal freedom compatible with the public good."

The Government of India has taken, a cooperative stance toward voluntary associations, although it has been clear that foreign and international agencies are to operate within the country only under close supervision and monitoring. As observed by Marcus Franda in his *Voluntary Associations and Local Development in India: The Janata Phase,* "Continuity of this policy was confirmed dramatically in June 1978 when eight foreign members of the American-based Institute of Cultural Affairs were asked to leave the country after President Sanjiva Reddy had raised questions about why so many foreigners were participating in a rural development project in Maliwada, Maharashtra. Caution about foreign agencies is in some measure a reflection of India's general nationalist distrust of the activities of outsiders in the country, but it is also a function of Indian leaders' intense conviction that the nation must nourish its own developmental and relief capabilities. This was clearly President Reddy's concern when he visited Maliwada in 1978."

Voluntary organisations in India have also become professionalised because they have built up a corpus of specialised knowledge and experience about what does and does not work in bringing about socio-economic change. Such knowledge is only in small measure the preserve of technicians and scientists— geologists, well-drillers, agronomists, engineers, veterinarians, bankers, doctors and so forth—within these organisations. Much of it lies within the domains of economics, sociology, psychology, anthropology, communications, education, management, political science, law and other "softer" disciplines, all of which are also represented. Needless to say, graduates of professional schools and universities still prefer to go into government work, or into private or public sector industry; but the number who opt for participation in voluntary agencies is increasing.

Realising the above hometruth, successive governments have laid great emphasis on voluntary organisations. From "Family Planning" to "Antyodaya", the conspectus is complete. As Marcus Franda observes, "The fact that both Jawaharlal Nehru and Indira Gandhi have contributed to the, mushroom growth of local initiatives in the rural areas despite their emphasis on heavy industry and capital-intensive development-strategy for the nation as a whole brings home the point that almost everyone in India favours at least some degree of emphasis on Voluntary Organisations for rural growth." Today we have homes for adoption of children, shelter-homes for harassed wives, "Sumaitri Crisis" Centre at New Delhi for counselling, Senior Citizens' Resorts supported by HelpAge, "Sisters of Charity" running a chain of institutions all over India, attracting the young and the old.

There are many who look down upon the so-called "Subsidy-culture" in the field of welfare and rural development. Here one must remember that the Green Revolution would not have been a great success but for the largescale subsidisation of inputs even for the big farmer — particularly the chemical and mechanical inputs — as well as concessional interest on borrowings. Subsidisation of Voluntary Organisations particularly in the field of Weaker Sections' Welfare is very important, provided it is ensured that assistance reaches the target-groups. For this, mass-opinionisation through motivation and campaign is required, and this can be achieved only through Voluntary Organisations. Nevertheless, self-reliance on simple needs and requirements can, be brought about at the local level only through cottage-door education.

Dismally, it is true that the so called "leading villagers" invest their surpluses in cities and *not* at their homes and hamlets, mainly because real estate appreciates much faster in urban centres. Government investment alone cannot clean up and beautify our villages, as our priorities right now, are drinking water, immunisation and nutrition, which can also be promoted by Voluntary Organisations.

There have been different systems of assistance to voluntary organisations in India. The assistance may be advanced by the Central or State Governments concerned either directly or through their undertakings, corporations or autonomous bodies. This may be advanced either to totally private voluntary organisations or such other registered societies that are headed by certain district authorities. With regard to funding from abroad, this may directly go to the voluntary organisations concerned, i.e. those registered with the Home Ministry for receiving such funds under the Reserve Bank surveillance. We have been having a number of programmes of assistance to voluntary organisations right from the mid-fifties such as Freedom-form Hunger Campaign (FFHC), Action for Food Programme (ACFO), People's Action for Development (PADE), and quite recently the Centre for Appropriate Technology (CART). Now, there is only one central and controlling agency of channeling the foreign financial assistance to voluntary organisations all over India, namely the CAPART which has merged both the "Appropriate Technology" and "People's Action".

The CAPART thus becames the sole arbiter of selection of the voluntary organisations. For example, the Indian Red Cross which is a statutory body is considered a voluntary organisation whereas the National Institute of Social Action which comprises 22 non-officials out of the entire 33 -member committee is not considered a voluntary organisation by the CAPART, although both the Red Cross and the NISA have the concerned Governor as the Ex-officio-President. The list of participants, both individual and institutional, would clearly show the totally voluntary and non-governmental nature of the organisation which the CAPART has not considered as "Voluntary". The self-same CAPART considers registered societies headed by the District Collectors as voluntary organisations. Such anomalies could be eliminated if there is proper screening and better understanding of the voluntary nature of the organisations concerned. This article is a step in this direction, bringing together on the same forum hundreds of smaller voluntary organisations under the banner of an apex body called "NISA".

The Kudal Commission urged the Government to make suitable legislative provisions either to stop the entry of foreign funds in the country through voluntary organisations or to regulate their inflow through Government channels only, and keep a close watch over their utilisation. The Commission said that the Government ought to preclude voluntary agencies getting involved in any clandestine and anti-national activities especially in the restricted areas of the country, and that the Government should review its policy pertaining to mapping and surveying of such areas, especially the aerial photography by private individuals or organisations and make relevant statutory provisions to put an end to this practice.

The role of voluntary organisations in the international field has been greatly enlarged during last century. Apart from the International Red Cross in the field of relief and rehabilitation, and the United Nations and its allied international bodies in the field of peacekeeping and development, we have been witnessing a tremendous spurt of international voluntary bodies like the Rotary, the Lions, the Jaycees and so on, not to speak of the time-honoured Free Masons' Lodge. In the field of religion and philosophy, education and philanthropy, trade and commerce, professionalism and journalism, sports and games; there have been an unanimous universal response to voluntary effort and, voluntary participation. The Olympics and the Asiad are examples of this exemplary progress towards voluntary unification of nations and towards a world brotherhood. If only we enumerate names of all organisations under each category mentioned here and their work in their respective fields, it will literally and metaphorically speak volumes of voluntary human organisations spanning a wide variety of human endeavour towards individual and collective human happiness.

CHAPTER 9

Towards Financial Resources

CHARACTERISTICS OF FINANCIAL RESOURCES FOR SUSTAINABLE DEVELOPMENT

In addition to quantity, aid for development has two other characteristics which influence NGDO effectiveness: quality and temperature. These features can show why NGDOs behave as they do, the dilemmas they face, the capacities they need for fund-raising and the risks they run in mixing funds as money supply changes.

The Quality of Aid

At its simplest, quality is the degree to which aid resources match the demands of best practices in participatory development. The greater the constraints on best practice, the lower its development quality. Six factors contribute to the quality of aid funds for NGDOs. These are:

— method of allocation;
— level of administrative burden;
— predictability and reliability;
— conditions and expectations of the giver (especially respect for NGDO autonomy);
— continuity and necessary duration;
— timeliness in disbursement.

This section looks at each. For case, the term 'donors' will be used for professional funders within the aid system, 'contributors' for the general public who voluntarily support NGDO work.

Funding Conditions and Expectations

Most aid comes with conditions and expectations. In technical terms, funds are 'tied' to requirements which can range from loose and open-ended to tight and stringent. Explicit conditions tend to be set by professional funders and are usually written into proposals and funding agreements. Expectations relate more to the general public who are motivated to support an NGDO's work, equivalent to moral rather than written contracts.

The positive impact of conditions is that, when right, they increase effectiveness. But when they are wrong, the opposite occurs. In both cases, donor conditions can cause unwanted organisational effects on NGDO autonomy, identity and capacity. For example, it is very unusual for donor conditions not to compromise independent organisational decision-making to some degree. Setting the right conditions is probably the most critical factor to a donor's professionalism. An ability to match funding conditions to the recipient organisation determines whether or not assistance leads to effective, sustained poverty reduction. When official aid agencies try to apply government-to-government conditional styles and practices to NGDOs, the results are generally disappointing.

Appropriate funding conditions are equivalent to extra capacity in terms of creating a more professional NGDO approach and should be welcomed. However, inappropriate conditions undermine an NGDO's own knowledge and professional capacity. To stop this happening, NGDOs must be secure in, but not arrogant about, their own knowledge and understanding of what is best practice in their situation. This capability comes from a strong identity and an active learning from proven experience. Without these two, NGDOs are in a vulnerable position when negotiating conditions.

Tying' assistance can have a negative effect when the problem an NGDO wants to address can only be seen in terms of the solutions and expertise known and available to the funder. This effectively disempowers the recipient and may result in poor-quality or expensive goods or services. When Southern NGDOs cannot shop around, tied aid acts as a constraint on best performance and typically increases costs.

Donors rightly set conditions on the authenticity and accuracy of financial and narrative reports. Unfortunately, by insisting on their own format, donors complicate an NGDO's system of financial management, making it more costly. Reporting on multiple formats, often over different time periods, is so common a problem for NGDOs that much of their management energy goes into this, at the cost of attention to development. A typical donor assumption is that its wider experience gives it an implicit right to influence, if not dictate, design. Comparative experience gets greater value than local knowledge. In Colombia, CINDE wished to adopt an indirect education-based approach to tackling the problem of empowerment under a military dictatorship. Their Dutch donor would only fund a direct activist, popular mobilisation approach. Only after activists were assassinated did the Northern agency come around to accepting the merits of a more subtle strategy.

In short, finance which comes with strategic, operational, economic and political conditions and assumptions which do not match the situation, or respect the autonomy of local NGDOs, lowers the quality of donor resources.

Contributors' expectations differ from professional donor conditions because they are created by NGDOs as they go about fund-raising. Messages are sent and images are created which lead individual givers to expect certain achievements for their support, an implicit contract which an NGDO must satisfy. For example, in the late 1980s Catholic Relief Services (CRS) in the USA suffered major negative publicity when it was discovered that millions of dollars raised for humanitarian relief in Ethiopia had not yet been spent, but were sitting accruing interest. There were good reasons why CRS was not spending; adopting a development-oriented relief strategy calls for care and time. But this appeared contrary to the public appeal, which stressed the immediate dire need for money: give your gift today. tomorrow may be too late'.

As a result, NGDOs must have the ability to communicate in ways which generate a feeling of personal obligation without creating false expectations which the media might expose. NGDOs which invest in development education have less to tear about, which increases the quality of the funds they raise.

Funding Methods

Project-based finance can seriously reduce the quality of aid funds for people-centred sustainable development. Recognition of the drawbacks to project aid has initiated experimentation with other ways of allocating finance. The most common innovations are programme-funding agreements between governments and Northern donor NGDOs, but less frequently between these NGDOs and their counterparts in the South and East. This type of cooperation increases flexibility as well as an NGDO's control over decision-making.

Programme funding of NGDOs—a block of money allocated within an agreed framework for a known period—is a major step forward which should be expanded, especially North-South, but can also have quality limitations. First, the framework of a programme agreement can import donor-dominated priorities, such as gender, urban development and the environment. Second, an intermediary NGDO can act as a proxy for the donor by taking on responsibilities which do not belong to them. Third, an intermediary is added in the chain, introducing new costs and problems. Fourth, when donors naturally ask for specific performance criteria at the end of the programme period, they impose a demand which they cannot usually satisfy if they do the work themselves. Moreover, in order to generate the necessary performance information, the intermediary must allocate finance on a project-by-projcct basis. In other words, the quality benefits of programme funding are lost as projects reappear further down the chain. Without doubt, greater attention must be paid to performance, but care must be taken on how this is implemented.

Administrative Burdens

Money causes paperwork. Logic would suggest that the better the paper definition at the beginning, the less need there is for further reporting. This does not occur in practice because a highly detailed design generates more herns on which to report. Therefore, as a rule of thumb, the greater the amount of paper required to obtain a grant, the higher the administrative burden. High-quality donors recognise and make few extra demands on the administrative system already in place. (An associated issue is that costs of donor-specific administration are seldom met in full because official aid is generally averse to financing organisational overheads.)

As the amount of paperwork and administrative energy per grant grows, the number of grants that can be given per staff member decreases. Consequently, disbursing the annual financial allocation calls for an increase in the average size of a grant or the introduction of a programme which shins grant-making along the aid chain. In other words, the economics of grant or loan administration push towards big rather then small funding, which does not match most community-based needs. When donors are under pressure to disburse and staff turnover is high—which always seems to be the case—NGDOs face the burden of educating new incumbents. Although the situation is improving, too often official aid agency personnel have little if any exposure to NGDO culture or practices. Satisfying administrative requirements and coping with inexperienced, transient donor staff can be an enormous quality-reducing burden on NGDOs. Moreover, this burden is seldom financed.

Predictability and Reliability of Funding

A precondition for effective development initiatives is that the resources needed during negotiation will be available over the long term. In other words, NGDOs must.be able to operate on the firm assumption that predicted incomes will be raised. Guaranteeing incomes or resources years ahead is never easy. Official aid agencies with tax-based incomes can probably predict for the duration of an electoral cycle, but even that is less certain today. Foundations raising income from prudent investments are probably in the best position in terms of predictability (Black Monday aside).

Predictions on public fund-raising are very difficult. For example, in 1996 Save the Children Fund UK and Oxfam announced income shortfalls of £9 and £5.6 million respectively. Internal solutions designed to increase reliability, such as reserves and contingency funds, are constrained by the fact that contributors expect the money they give will be spent soon and not invested. The financial management skills required by NGDOs dependent on public fund-raising and dealing with fluctuations with many currencies are awesome, and market rates for people with the necessary skills usually put them beyond reach.

Reliable funds are those which remain secure once they have been accessed, depending on where the donor gets them from. Northern NGDOs structurally funded by their governments enjoy pretty reliable funding. This is especially true in Scandinavia, the Benelux and Germany. Child sponsor funds call for substantial initial effort, followed by attention to maintenance. Once the investment in mobilisation has hooked a sponsor, keeping them costs much loss. In all cases, long-term reliability depends on NGDOs' capacity to continually satisfy donor needs through high performance and information.

In sum, high-quality incomes are those which can be predicted for many years to come, are generated in such a way that they can be accessed or paid out when needed, and are reliable. Endowments come close to high quality as do annual bequests from the estates of people who have died. Needless to say, there is not a lot of this type of money around. Unpredictable and unreliable funds are those which, for example, come from specific appeals, and actions, donor fatigue setting in if they occur too often or are too similar. By and large, NGDOs work in the world of unreliable funding.

Continuity and Necessary Duration

Reliability, that is an assurance that donors will have always have access to the funds they give, is different from continuity. Continuity is the ability of the funder to ensure the support an NGDO requires as long as it demonstrates its merits while progressing along an uncertain road. Where decisions about funding are dominated more by internal donor considerations or domestic politics than by NGDO performance, continuity is threatened in a way that the recipient can do little about. Financial resources which are not allocated on the basis of performance but on fashion, self-interest or donor politics are lower in quality than those that have a long-term continuity tied to proven impact.

Project-based funds are typically one—to four year grants. One reason for this convention is so that project performance can be evaluated towards the end while a new project is negotiated. This practice also builds in an exit possibility for unreliable donors. Stakeholders and staff are therefore in a state of insecurity from the word go, which can naturally lead to ambivalence in their commitment. Furthermore, evaluation becomes a threat or a ritual to justify donor decisions already made rather than a tool for learning. For most types of sustainable development work, short-term money without performance-assured continuity is low in quality.

Timeliness in Disbursement

A common lament of NGDOs, especially in the South, is the poor time-keeping of their funders. Delayed disbursements usually have no penalty to the giver, but cause enormous headaches for recipients. Unless recipients have substantial flexible reserves or overdrafts—which is not likely—the solution is to cross-finance from other sources, which upsets auditors. Cross-financing also means reduced transparency and increasing stress for managers who must keep staff motivation high. Donors who cannot deliver payments as agreed are responsible for reducing the their resources' quality.

Development Funding

When mobilising finance, an NGO leaders manager's task is to arrive at the optimum mix of quantity and quality in relation to mission, culture, strategic goals and best practices. This is a difficult task made more complicated by the feet that the quantity/quality landscape is changing fast. In this uncertain situation, another way of working out fund-raising strategies and their likely consequences is to assess an additional characteristic of aid money: its temperature. Basic physics can show what lies ahead as leaders/managers hunt for the right mix. Aid funds get their temperature from the process of giving.

An individual choosing to sponsor a child or responding to an appeal brings individual concern to the funds they give. This is hot money, loaded with personal warmth and expectations. Funds taken from taxes and distributed to an IFI, such as the World Bank, for disbursement—along with other countries' tax income as an official loan running into minions or billions of dollars—has tost personal human attachment. International bureaucrats and national politicians may talk to each other in governing bodies, but the individuals whose labours have generated funds from direct taxation or indirectly though company profits are not involved. Multilateral money is anonymous and impersonal, it is stone cold. Bilateral aid may not be quite as cold because a discernible country and population is involved and must be accounted to.

Hot money impacts both positively and negatively on quality. On the negative side, hot money has to be spent because contributors expect their support to solve an immediate problem. On the positive side, hot money keeps NGDOs in touch with their civic soul and nongovernmental selves. It holds them to a constituency which must be convinced of their legitimacy, potentially enhancing quality by acting as a counter-weight to self-delusion, self-satisfaction, corruption and co-optation. Hot money is a double-edged sword that is much better to have than have not. The official aid system transfers mainly cold money, some US$ 55 billion per year, as soft loans and grants to governments for large-scale investment projects, sector support and rural and urban development programmes.

Cold money is most cost-effectively applied to 'cold' purposes. For example, millions of dollars put into import or commodity support are cost-effective paper transactions between treasuries. But community-level work which embodies highly differentiated primary stakeholders offers few economies of scale suited to large amounts of cold aid.

Sustainable micro-development needs hot money: assistance which is humanised and personalised through authentic participation. So when donors want to apply cold money to sustainable human-development, costs increase because energy has to be applied to get the temperature up to a human level. The official aid system has two primary strategies for heating funds. First are conditions to make cold money more human centred. Aid conditions have always been around, but today's insistence on stakeholder involvement, PRA techniques and emphasis on capacity-building of local people's organisations, are all requirements which should humanise official aid-hence increasing its temperature. Second is a priority to fund hotter organisations such as NGOs. While aid levels are stagnating -dropping by 7.8 per cent between 1992 and 1993 alone—over the period 1990 to 1995, official aid to NGDOs has risen from US$ 2.3 to

$4 billion. Unfortunately, this growing inflow brings drawbacks which have cooling effects on NGDOs. NGDOs have an organisational temperature, determined by their ideology, constituency links, staff motivation, people-centred development approaches, and their resource base. Becoming and staying a hot organisation means making careful choices about the temperature of the resources mobilised and their proportion.

Common values and approaches in authentic North-South/East partnerships 'insulate' hot money as it shifts across the globe and reaches primary stakeholders. Transnational NGDOs—organisations where funds are raised from individuals in the North for individuals in the South or East—also insulate the financial transfer by containing the whole process. These transnational are 'horizontally integrated'.

When hot NGOs mobilise proportionally larger inflows of cold aid money, the laws of physics say that the organisation will get colder. This shows up in more bureaucracy, less flexibility, changing staff attitudes and reduction in NGDOs comparative advantages. Stopping this happening requires an energy input from somewhere, but from where? One avenue is to raise more money from hot sources, but this is not easy because, globally, the proportion of hot volunteered money is dropping and will be at or less than 50 per cent of NGDO income by the next decade. Alternatively, the proportion of funds raised and allocated to internal heating processes can be increased. The difficulty here is that the resources needed for heating processes, such as community negotiation, staff development, more flexible, systems, better monitoring, and learning are (mis)treated as overheads which must be kept low.

The low overheads myth works against allocating additional resources to counter the effects of taking cold funding. There is, however, a financially costless, but vital source of energy to stop an NGDO cooling off. This energy comes from owners and leaders/managers and staff who stay true to founding beliefs, values and voluntary principles. It is their ethos against convenient self-serving compromise that withstands buying into fashionable theories and cold aid interpretations of development. The heating power of personal principle and staff values has no monetary cost, but in today's real-politick is in clangor of being marginalised.

Fortunately, however, the aid system will not herald in a new ice age; instead, official agencies are slowly increasing the temperature of some of their funds, primarily by modifying their practices and conditions based on agency-wide learning. For example, the *Handbook on Social Development* published by the UK, Overseas Development Agency, distils its experience in the form of best practice guidelines and checklists. Previously, the problem of increasing the temperature of official aid agencies used to be one of not learning from experience. Today, evaluation and learning receives much more attention, which shifts the heating problem from a lack of knowledge to translating lessons into agency-wide procedures, practices and culture.

The jury is still out on whether the official aid system will succeed in heating itself—without cooling NGDOs in the process. The official aid system is also drawing more on proven NGDO practices, project negotiations and joint implementation. Learning from NGDOs by funding them has been called the 'reverse agenda' and needs, further support. Heat exchanged from NGDOs to the official aid system is a type of leverage that, in addition to policy advocacy, must become more central in NGDO strategic thinking.

NGDOs and Assessment of the Organisational Implications of Accessing and Mixing Funding Sources

What an NGDO manager leader will look for are ideal funds which:

— are free from stringent, inflexible, imposed conditions;
— are allocated on programme or intervention terms (rather than as projects);
— are not constrained by accounting and administrate requirements which impede best practise;
— can fit into existing financial, administrative and other systems;
— are predictable in terms of where the donor obtains them and reliable in terms of flow;
— will, when based on demonstrated performance, be available throughout all stages of an intervention (continuity is not simply subject to donor interests or politics);
— arrive on time as agreed.

To fund their work, NGDOs can tap into three types of economic surplus: personal giving, the tax base and the market. These types of surplus produce three main funding sources for Northern NGDOs and five for the South and East. Each has distinctive qualities, temperatures and trends; each calls for different responses.

NGDO FINANCING IN THE NORTH

(1) The Gift Economy

The gift economy is the technical term used for funds given voluntarily by an individual, group, civic organisation or business. An economic surplus coming from people's pockets for development can, for example, be in direct response to an NGDO appeal, or a school collecting funds for another school somewhere in the South or East. Gift income can also be generated indirectly. Examples are regular wage deductions to create a development fund, a method employed by some Canadian trade unions, or allocations from national lotteries, which is happening in Britain. Indirect giving reduces personal engagement with development issues, but there is still a clear constituency concerned about what happens to their contributions.

Expectations generated by fund-raising messages can open or restrict freedom, and NGDOs have to decide how far this type of income is tied to a specific purpose or impact. If done properly, the quality can be high without being too hot. Data from the Netherlands indicates that the ability to mobilise gift funds is related to three key NGDO competencies. These are:

— An ability to personalise the recipient. Child sponsorship organisations are obviously at an advantage here.

— An ability to communicate and use the media well. This means being as technically professional as commercial organisations which set the standard for the public's Judgement of what they see and hear.

— Choosing the right issue—one that people relate to because they experience it. For example, leprosy is no longer a very strong message in the North; environmental pollution and child abuse are.

The common area of organisational struggle in Northern NGDOs is between fund-raisers and development professionals. Why? Because the messages needed to raise money in the North—appeals to pity and compassion—are inconsistent with the dignity of the poor and the slow, contextual nature of sustainable development work. False expectations are created which professional developers know cannot he realised. Effective NGDOs ore those capable of internally reconciling the different realities of public fund-raising in the North and sustainable development in the South or East. Another way of looking at this organisational difficulty is to recognise that, to be effective, staff must 'import' the interests, perspectives and values of the major external constituencies they deal with. This means the NGDO must reconcile the contradictions and tensions of poverty in a rich world, brought within the organisation. The task for leaders/ managers is to organise and continually manage these tensions because they cannot be eradicated unless there is a major shift in contributors' understanding. Here is another place where the strength of shared beliefs, values, identity and confidence in the leadership are important. Why? Because they provide the emotional reference points which managers rely on to hold the NGDO together. An overall decline in the Northern public's sense of personal social obligation, is leading to stagnation in the growth of the Northern development gift economy.

In 1989, private giving generated some US$3.4 billion, constituting 65 per cent of total NGDO disbursements of US$ 5.2 billion. Tentative figures for 1995 suggest an unadjusted total NGDO disbursement of some US$8 billion with official aid now contributing almost 50 per cent of the total. Unless Northern NGDOs do something about this, a highly competitive gift economy will not continue to grow for them.

(2) The Tax Base

Northern governments take citizens' and corporate taxes and allocate them to international aid, mainly by using bilateral or multilateral channels. Multilaterals can be divided between the UN grant-making agencies and the (soft-) loan development banks. While the level of difficulty varies, NGDOs in the Ninth ran access tax-derived funds from each of these sources. Data above shows tax-based aid to be a fast-growing source of NGDO funding. It will probably continue to be so, given the aid policies of privatisation and civic strengthening which show little signs of abating. In other words, there will be more and more cold money around.

An OECD study describes the various ways Northern NGDOs access domestic tax-based funds. The coldest funds are commonly allocated on the basis of logically framed projects with targets related to donor priorities and other interests in a particular country. In countries where bilateral or multilateral relations are or were strained, official agencies use Northern NGDOs to gain a presence and potential foothold until times improve. Examples are Myanmar, Nicaragua under the Sandinistas, Cambodia, and South Africa under apartheid. When desired political change occurs, Northern NGDOs are pushed aside, ignored or their work sidelined. NGDO policy-makers must be aware of and deal with the co-optation into foreign policy underlying all funding from official aid. Bilateral funds allocated on a block grant or programme basis -agreed amounts of money to be made available each year—are higher in quality to the extent that they provide the NGDO with flexibility and discretion. The danger of co-optation into foreign policy strategies is also reduced. Accessing funds from the UN system is less coloured by bilateral interests, but NGDOs face complex administrative rituals; the politics associated with recipient governments' co-ownership of UN agencies; and the ambiguity of delegated authority with the UN system.

Despite a shared development vocabulary, basic preconditions for collaboration between NGDOs and UN agencies do not exist—they must be constructed each step of the way. For example, theories of cause and change may differ; decision-making processes are not the same; personal motivations, incentives and rewards are incompatible, diplomatic protection and personal privileges set UN staff apart in the world; access to and relations with governments bear no similarity; organisational performance measures are not the same; and they are positioned and act differently in relation to power in society. Working through these differences calls for significant upfront investment in time and energy for NGDOs, which many lack. NGDOs who have this capacity are likely either to enjoy untied resources or are funded by the UN, which contuses relations from the outset. Both reasons can create an exclusive club of NGDOs able to interact with the multilateral systems to the exclusion of others. This is a divisive effect potentially .

Muitilaterals also interact with NGDOs to have their funds heated up, while NGDOs interact with multilaterals to gain scale and leverage for their work. This apparent mutuality of interest does not readily translate into equality of costs and benefits. In fact, accessing multilateral funds creates costs and structural tensions which NGDOs must be ready and able to deal with. The first is co-optation into strategies, plans and programmes already negotiated with recipient governments. Excluded on the grounds of sovereignty and national security, NGDOs are hired as implemented, having most influence over the least strategic aspects of development decisions. Second, co-optation brings with it a reduction in autonomy and one-way accommodation of relatively small NGDOs compared to relatively massive donors. Third, multilateral have a natural inclination to employ the instruments and terms they apply to governments or contractors. Modifying donor internal procedures is a major struggle requiring a long time. A slow pace of change calls for NGDO patience.

Fortunately, it is not all a one-way street with some NGDOs able to swim against the flow of cold aid, while others are swept away by the current. Although slow to change, the official aid system is adapting to the requirements of working with NGDOs in ways that do not diminish their comparative advantages.

The past many years have seen efforts within the World Bank to educate staff on what participation and constructive collaboration with NGDOs means in operational terms. In addition, steps are being taken to amend bank procedures which work against best practice in sustainable micro-development. Bilaterals are also amending their NGO interface. For example, USAID has a New Partnerships Initiative which incorporates learning from past difficulties, and the Japanese are recognising the role of NGDOs in the analysis of how to achieve development goals. But as in any two-way street,

NGDOs must be capable of understanding and taking on board the modifications needed to work with official aid.

What can be said about the capabilities and characteristics NGDOs need if they want to tap tax-based, cold incomes without cooling off? The key capacities may be summarised as:

- a proven track record;
- clarity of identity and development analysis;
- sufficient untied funds or other sources of capacity to protect autonomy, and to cover the substantial staff time for negotiation and proposal writing;
- an ability to speak on a par with the often highly qualified staff who are not necessarily professionals in terms of micro-development and are often transient;
- an ability to write convincingly and argue through funding proposals;
- good communication and shared understanding between the proposal writer and the operational staff who must provide the real-life data;
- patience.

The third item—access to untied funds—is tricky. Using contributors' funds to obtain official aid can be the trigger to a mine-field which has exploded for more than one NGO. The trip-wire is pulled when a Northern NGDO uses untied gilt economy money to access cold funds, which is not what 'hot' funders were led to expect. Save the Children Fund (SCF) USA were exposed by *Penthouse* for doing precisely this. A substantial proportion of funds raised from the general public were used to cover costs of the SCF-USA office needed to mobilise and run projects funded by official aid agencies.

Currently, NGDOs need flexible resources to engage with the official aid system or to access official aid funds. The risk is diversion of hot gift money to gain cold income and leverage rather than to do direct development work. An alternative source without the drawback of donor expectations and unexploded mines are the high-quality, untied funds raised from the market.

The Market

NGDOs can generate income from the market either by direct activity or indirectly through corporate support . Direct fund generation is of two main types: commercial enterprise or market investment. There are some examples of Northern NGDOs running their own commercial operations. Oxfam UK/I is one of the oldest examples. In 1993, for example, Oxfam shops in the UK generated some £ 17 million on a turnover of £53 million. Sales of Christmas cards is a seasonal, but insecure, way of tapping the market. Sales of handicrafts from Southern artisans, or publications about NGDO work, are not uncommon. NGDOs concerned about fair trade, such as Max Havelaar in Holland and TradeCraft in the UK, generate both their incomes and more equitable terms for primary producers.

Raising income from investment is exemplified by American philanthropic organisations, of which the Fard Foundation is the largest with investments amounting to some US$ 6.3 billion. However, unlike commercial activity, stock market investment offers little opportunity to create a positive public profile and 'capture' buyers in terms of promoting the NGDO development agenda. New market-based variations, such as a percentage of credit card transactions coming to the NGDO, are also starting to appear. But on a global scale, the proportion or funds raised by Northern NGDOs through these means is small, amounting to little more than 2 to 4 per cent of the total. While small in volume, this type of money is probably the highest in terms of quality and development value. Why? Because profits come without strings, they are unconditional. An NGDO is only constrained in using this type of income by its registration as a non-profit organisation—not by the income itself. The temperature of market income can vary. Volunteers in shops, workers in fair trade NGDOs, and others who express a similar commitment give human warmth to these funds, with expectations about how they will be applied. They form one key group which the NGDO must be accountable to if it is to rely on their efforts in the future.

Funds generated by market investment are not warmed at their source, it is the NGDO leaders/managers and staff who must add this element, which leaves significant freedom, together with strong challenges of probity and accountability. Market-based incomes are going to play a critical role in the future NGDO balancing act. Aside from moral dilemmas, the organisational challenge for NGDOs directly engaged in generating market income is how to legally deal with two distinct sets of operating principles and taxation requirements. A common solution is to establish the for-profit business as a separate legal entity, but under the sole ownership of the non-profit board, trustees or whatever the law has designated. Where staff are predominantly volunteers, it may be possible to locate the business arm under the same management as the development organisation. This is the case with Oxfam UK/I. Where staff are not volunteers and competition demands a market rate, it is difficult to bring business and non-profit development under one management as opposed to under one owner.

Terms of service, incentives, culture, management style, reinvestment needs, and tax concerns can all differ too much from the value-orientation and work styles of development to make a happy marriage between the two. Without separation, transparency suffers; subsidising poorly functioning business operations can too easily occur, threatening the viability of both operations.

Collaboration with businesses in support of development

work is receiving a boost from two directions. One is from NGDOs themselves, who see benefits from teaming up with companies and are actively hunting for opportunities. The second push comes from the growing, but disputed, political impetus for corporations to demonstrate greater social responsibility and take sustainability seriously. The hoped-for win-win dimension in corporate fund-raising lies in a positive public image for the business with income for the NGDO.

In other words, it can make good business sense to engage with and support social development -tax incentives included. The word partnership is also being applied to this sort of cross-sector relationship.

From the perspective of NGDO perspective, a threshold choice is the type of business, the products it sells, the level of trust it enjoys with the general public, and the image it wishes to promote. A company manufacturing electric cattle prods, also sold as instruments of torture, may want to improve its image by sponsoring an NGDO's work. Would this be appropriate? Is Shell in Europe today a good company for NGDOs to be associated with?

In terms of competencies and organisational issues, an NGDO seeking to access corporate funding needs:

- an ability to carry out a thorough examination of a prospective corporation in terms of its core business and subsidiaries: (a late discovery that an associated company is involved in exploitive or dubious activities could be a public relations disaster);
- an internal review process to critically vet possible corporate supporters;
- something tangible to offer which is attractive for support because it enhances corporate image or market position;
- reference points for the way in which corporate assistance is 'advertised' at the site of its application—in a village, on a vehicle;

- a system enabling field operations to advise on, and if necessary veto, proposed corporate collaboration;
- resources to enable a fairly long process of development, including exposure to the NGDO's work;
- certainty that collaboration will not unacceptably compromise or limit who is assisted, and how.

Corporate contributions can be warm, but of medium to low quality because of the close tie to image and other interests. This type of income is very small within the total funds disbursed by NGDOs, probably contributing less than 1 per cent of the US$9 billion total. Nevertheless, the ongoing Northern political debate about the social function and responsibilities of corporations is creating a reenforcing environment which NGDOs can capitalise on. But this will be in heavy competition with domestically oriented non-profits who benefit from close proximity in their impact.

NGDO Financing in the South and East

At first sight NGDOs in the South and East appear to be in a better position than their Northern counterparts when it comes to sources of finance—five against three. For reasons of history, socio-economic development and culture, reality does not, however, match this picture. Again, we take a tour around each source; in the next section we analyse critical dynamics between each one which impact on the shape of NGDO communities as well as steer their social and political relationships.

Northern NGDO Funding

Historically, channel 4, has been the dominant source of finance for NGDOs in the South and East. Reliable statistics are not available, but informed guesses suggest that up until the late 1980s funds raised by Northern NGDOs from the three channels described previously probably constituted some 90 per cent of income for Southern NGDOs; Eastern NGDOs were yet to be 'discovered'. Though uneven, the trend today is away from an unparalleled dominance of Northern NGDOs as funders because of growth in direct funding from official aid and greater efforts at local fund-raising.

Many South American countries and South East Asian Tiger economies, such as Thailand and Indonesia, are being placed on the 'fast track' of withdrawal by Northern NGDOs. There are at least three reasons for this shift. First, economic indicators provide less justification for support, fuelling the argument that local NGDOs should access growing, local resources. Second, new opportunities in Indochina and Eastern Europe are attracting attention and diverting funds. Third, a more strategic approach to financing is highlighting irrationality in the existing NGDO assistance spread.

Amalgamation of domestic sources leads to varying temperatures and qualities of Northern NGDOs and their funds. And Northern NGDOs will differentiate themselves more sharply in the future because of their varying capacities to access cold money without cooling off. Some Northern NGDOs will be co-opted, becoming an official aid channel in alt but name. Southern NGDOs already see this happening as their previous 'partners' start to call a new tune of neo-realism with market rules. The implications for Southern and Eastern NGDOs are two-fold. First, authentic partnerships with high-quality Northern NGDO partnerships will become more valuable but more difficult to attain. Second, there may not be much difference in dealing with cold NGDOs and other cold sources. In other words, it may be preferable to deal with official donors directly. Because of direct funding this is possible.

Direct Funding from Official Aid

Direct funding by official aid agencies to Southern and Eastern NGDOs, bypassing she North, is a change on the aid scene which began in the 1980s and is gathering momentum. Justifications for direct funding are grouped around issues of greater efficiency in aid delivery; better governance in terms of supporting and building local NGDOs as stronger civic actors; supporting donor sectoral priorities and donor learning about local conditions: and maintaining legitimacy for aid by better demonstrating impact. In addition, Northern NGDOs have found it very difficult to come up with firm evidence that they do add something to development to justify their costs. This inability makes their reservations sound weak and self-pleading. While seen by some as a mixed blessing or threat, direct funding is generally welcomed by recipients who are disillusioned with the practice of NGO partnerships with the North; are increasingly capable of negotiating in their own right; and have overtaken Northern NGDOs in their development thinking and strategies towards their own countries.

There is, in fact, less difference in dealing with Northern NGDOs channelling aid on essentially official terais and dealing directly with official donors who are slowly interacting with Southern and Eastern NGDOs in more appropriate ways. Harshly put Northern NGDOs who want to stay in the aid game had better make sure that they have, and can demonstrate, their comparative advantages. The capacities Southern and Eastern NGDOs require to directly access official aid are the same as for their Northern counterparts, which pesos difficulties for weaker organisations. However, Southern and Eastern NGDOs face an additional demand.

They must cross a threshold to direct funding by being classed as 'wheat amongst the chaff'. Why? Because NGDOs with no voluntary ethic, understanding or vision are being created by politicians, ex-civil servants and entrepreneurs solely for the purpose of tapping aid flows or building a political base. For them NGDO registration is a strategic convenience. Confined to their offices, official donor staff are too seldom able to verify what they are told. They can be taken in by unsupported but well-formulated proposals, be oversensitive to political name dropping, and may not invest in trusted third-sector links which could provide a third-party opinion—the cocktail party circuit acts as a substitute. Donors often compensate for these weaknesses by recruiting NGDO liaison personnel from the sector. However, local recruitment may import the personal biases and politics of the NGDO community; this cannot be adequately countered because of the high turnover of international supervisory staff, who are generalists anyway. In sum a distinct requirement for local NGDOs wishing to access direct funding is to establish legitimacy and credibility. A reciprocal requirement for official aid agencies is to gain knowledgeable and independent advice.

Despite different donor positions on the merits and pitfalls of direct funding, there is little doubt that in money volume terms this trend is set to continue. If there is not much to separate cold donors and cooled-off Northern NGDOs in terms of aid quality, the expanded choice of funding sources made available by direct funding could strengthen the negotiating position of competent Southern and Eastern NGDOs. Such possibilities should, however, be approached strategically rather than opportunistically because of potential negative effects on local relationship of NGDO.

Funding from Southern and Eastern Governments

Local NGDOs can try and access funds from their governments, both nationally and locally. The funds governments have to give can originate from local taxes or from international aid obtained as grants or loans. In countries with substantial economies, where aid is a small proportion of GDP and NGDO-government relations are positive, there is a potential for NGDOs to access indigenous tax-based funds—South Africa and India provide examples. Even if they had the will, governments in low-income, aid-dependent, resource-poor countries expect NGDOs to bring additional resources into the country, not knock on the door asking for financial support. This is the scenario in most of sub-Saharan

Africa where in extreme cases such as Chad, NGDO finance for health services exceeds that of the government department doing similar work.

Where funds are available from (especially poorer) Southern governments, it is increasingly because the official aid system is pushing for NGDOs to be included in the activities they finance governments to do. For example, the new generation of social development funds in Latin America have, on donor insistence, a strong NGDO element.

Similarly, bilateral onors try to include NGDOs when their finance needs heating up. What happens when official aid is diverted to NGDOs, or ties them to governments, is discussed below. NGDOs in Latin America and South East Asia who are being fast-tracked out of Northern NGDOs because of their countries' economic performance are actively looking at ways of obtaining resources from their governments as a matter of right, not privilege. The argument is that they are contributing to socio-economic development and well-being and, like businesses which benefit from investment incentives, local NGDOs are also entitled to supportive state policies and finance. It is too early to tell how successful this reorientation will be, but the switch from higher- to lower-quality funds, which the move from Northern NGDOs to Southern government money implies, introduces a danger zone of co-optation and decreased ability to adopt a critical stance on issues of social justice and rights. Here, lessons can probably be learned from domestically oriented Northern third-sector organisations because many are financed by government.

In Latin America, Mariano Valderrama describes two types of initiatives, in addition to local NGDOs making demands on government. One is self-finance through the promotion of loan and cooperative funding, such as micro-enterprise credit in Peru and FINCA (Campasino Financing Fund) in Costa Rica. Another is Northern to Southern NGDO finance shifting from a grant to an investment logic by, for example, providing credit guarantees for development loans. Research and Applications for Alternative Development (RAFAD) is an early example of a guarantee approach initially applied in West Africa. For NGDOs in ex-Soviet bloc countries the dynamic differs. These newly independent states are adjusting to imposed political sovereignty, bringing with it both a loss of financial stability and the benefits of integration associated with the rouble zone and incorporation in the Soviet economy. The tenuous financial situation of Eastern states is not a good starting point for NGDO claims on government resources.

In addition, NGDOs are a newly emerged quantity, often existing under inappropriate legislation or in a constitutional limbo. Moreover, they face suspicion from ex-Soviet schooled regimes of being little more than fronts for political interests, or groups out to show up government inadequacies. In the words of a Kazak NGDO leader, dealing with the government calls for 'gritted teeth, keeping your nerve and a lot of patience.'

Eastern NGDOs who owe their existence to external aid face a long uphill battle in fund-raising from the state. The potential for government funding of local NGDOs therefore varies across countries of the South and East, but is generally on the increase, bringing opportunities and dangers. A common drawback with funds from the domestic tax base, or donor funding to governments with an NGDO component, is that both can be used to re-enforce patronage or corruption. The prime capacity required of Southern and Eastern NGDOs, therefore, is to cope with becoming enmeshed in the politics of public finance, followed by competencies to deal with bureaucracies which are perhaps not independent of the regime in power and suffer poor working conditions. Colder aid from Northern NGDOs may reflect self-interest but corruption is less likely.

The Market

The fourth source of funds is from the market. As for the North, this source can be divided into NGDO direct economic activity and corporate support. Direct economic activity can mean commercial operations or income-generating investments. Concern for self-sustainability is leading more and more Southern NGDOs to embark on direct economic activity, usually with finance from the North. With noted exceptions, results have been disappointing because either the concept was not viable to start with, or the organisation could not cope with the dual management demands of for-proftt and non-profit activity under one roof. Sarvadoya's investment in a printing press is an example of the latter. Set against this is the success in commercial income generation of IBASE in Brazil, which raises 44 per cent of its turnover from commercial activity, including the management of an e-mail node.

BRAC in Bangladesh is well known for its local entrepreneurship, running a cold store, a printing press, a chain of handicrafts stores and garment factories. In 1994, 31 per cent of its income came from business operations. Introducing for-profit activity with a development dimension came naturally to BRAC's founder, Fazle Abed, who was originally in business working with Phillips. He established BRAC at the time of the war of independence against Pakistan in 1971. However, becoming commercial was less natural to staff who objected that potato cold stores would benefit richer farmers.

Determining to be commercial and non-profit at the same time has major implications. Factors to be considered include the following:

— It is important to overcome entrenched beliefs that business exploitation and profit-seeking is the cause of poverty and injustice and that NGDOs are simply going to add to this. Distrustful of money and business,

NGDOs have not developed commercial expertise—in fact, there is a fear that doing so will make them lose their 'non-profit virginity'.

— The organisation as a whole must be convinced that income-generation is vital. In other words, instead of complaining about donor conditions and autocratic attitudes, people from bottom to top must realise that repackaging projects and putting even more effort into finding unexplored donor territory is not a viable way ahead.

— Be aware that adding a commercial operation might mean a loss of cohesion and resulting confusion for existing staff and stakeholders. For example, the Grameen Bank's perceived callousness in getting loans repaid is seen by some as a loss of their commitment to the poor rather than a means of instilling a sense of discipline.

— The concern about exploitation, because this is what NGDOs see around them, has to be overcome by recognising that not all for-profits rip-off workers and damage the environment. A further fear to be tackled is the perception of exploiting 'poverty' and packaging the poor as an aid to generating business.

— NGDOs which have been living in the comfort zone of grants need to rebuild the entrepreneurship existing at their inception. But, with backgrounds in politics, activism and the social sciences, most NGDO leaders do not have the experience necessary to manage commercial ventures themselves. Who should they turn to?

— A change in structure is needed to enable two cultures—each with their own objectives, activities and rewards—to operate alongside each other without interference, but with sufficient interaction to ensure that they both push in the same direction.

— A change in mentality is called for, moving from

expenditure budgets, projects and reports to a concern for revenue budgets, profit-and-loss accounts and reinvestment strategies.

— Public suspicion needs to be dealt with, because adding commercial activities can feed a perception that NGDOs are businesses in disguise. In addition, politicians may be less comfortable with an NGDO who enjoys greater financial autonomy than one dependent on external aid which governments can better control.

— Be aware that the legal and tax situation may not cope with for-profits owned for non-profit purposes. NGDOs must be sure that taxes will not render the whole enterprise a waste of time.

— Be aware that governments may be suspicious about loss of tax revenue and unfair market competition because NGDOs have access to grant funds.

NGDOs pay insufficient attention to establishing necessary preconditions when embarking on profit-making enterprise. Too frequently this new step is simply treated as an add-on to the existing organisation, instead of a decision with far-reaching consequences in terms of organisational development.

Gaining income from investments carries with it the concerns listed above, but the organisational implications may be less severe. For example, investing in a building which provides both NGDO offices and space to rent out need not involve the organisation in day-today management this can be contracted to an agent. PRRM in the Philippines has raised US$12 million by selling land donated to them in the 1970s. Some of the funds will be used to obtain new office premises, including rental space for third parties. The remainder will initially be divided between investment brokers to compare their performance before a final allocation is made.

Endowment funds are another form of investment for a recurrent resource, but substantial amounts are needed to generate a reasonable income. For example, an NGDO with a budget of $300,000 a year and 15 per cent overheads would require an endowment of $450,000 generating 10 per cent interest to cover administrative costs. Where inflation runs into double figures, either the returns need to be far above the inflation rate and with substantial reinvestment, or the endowment sum must be much higher.

Investments generating an untied return are most attractive because they produce high-quality funds. They have also been the most difficult for donors to support for reasons ranging from legitimate worries about governance and probity, to a concern to keep hold of the purse strings. Nevertheless, with strategic efforts of foundations such as Synergos and Ford in the USA, and the odd one-off grants by donors, such as USAID in Pakistan, slow progress is being made on the establishment of foundation-like organisations (FLOs) in the South and East, such as the West African Rural Foundation (WARF) and the Mozambique Community Development Foundation (MCDF). However, while a high-quality resource, FLOs are not set to produce significant income compared with current levels of external flows to NGDOs. This is unfortunate, because it is access to this quality of money which will shape the NGDO community in the next millennium.

Southern and Eastern NGDOs can also reach the market through local corporate support. The issues raised and competencies needed are not yet that similar to those of Northern NGDOs. The economic situation of many Southern countries offers opportunities not readily available to the North in terms of international corporations which cannot repatriate funds and possibilities for debt-equity swap arrangements. For example, ORAP in Zimbabwe used its access to foreign aid to help a battery company buy out its multinational owner. In return, ORAP gained 10 per cent of the share holding, a seat on the board and technical expertise. On the other hand, where political and economic power are closely tied, or markets are thin and weak with monopoly players, or state ownership dominates enterprise, there may not be much corporate interest or need to promote a positive public image. For this reason, corporate sponsoring of projects is less likely than other options.

Where markets are strong and free, moral and political motives can encourage business to take the initiative in establishing funds for financing social development directly and through NGDOs. Fundacion Sociale (FS) in Colombia was established 30 years ago by a Jesuit priest in the service of social development and was designed to be self-financing at the outset by running a commercial enterprise. The foundation currently owns 13 companies with a value of US$ 1 billion. Profits are used to run its own development programmes.

In India, corporate philanthropy for social development has a long history. In 1893 J N Tata established an endowment scheme to educate Indians abroad. Other wealthy industrial families followed suit and today there are almost none without a family philanthropic trust. This initiative was complemented by Ghandhi's concept of trusteeship, inspiring the wealthy to start and support schools and hospitals and endow temples. Post-independence government take-over of these facilities and social functions led to a decline in private giving, and family trusts now tend to run their own social development work for populations around the areas where their factories operate. Financing development work as undertaken by foreign-funded NGDOs seldom interests them.

Philippines Business for Social Progress (PBSP), established in 1970 during the Marcos era, was intended to act as a counterweight to ultra-nationalist agitation against what was seen as multinational exploitation. The then chairman of Shell copied a Venezuelan model to set up PBSP and pledged with others an amount of finance, currently set at 1 per cent of net income for social development. Some 0.2 per cent goes to PBSP to utilise as its sees fit, while 0.8 per cent is allocated to social development under the companies' own management. Obviously this is one way that the 180 corporations who are members of PBSP can buy off their social responsibility. Over the years, PBSP established a buffer fund to protect the continuity of its support and now operates with an annual budget of about US$ 6 million. A proven record in development funding has attracted official aid agencies who provide some $4 million of this total.

On balance, accessing the market through corporations in the South and East requires financial insight and acumen, together with an ability to recognise and quickly exploit opportunities while barriers to financial flows are removed and markets expand. Fund-raising from market actors is a dynamic country-specific process which is growing in potential as an NGDO financial source.

The Gift Economy

The gift economy and its potential as a source of NGDO finance in the South and East depends on two primary factors. First is the availability of personal economic surplus. Second is a social morality and social relations which induce a sense of personal obligation towards others and the public good. A prerequisite for contributing to the gift economy is an ability to do so, determined by the level and distribution of affluence and disposable surplus. Simply put, if you do not have the money, you cannot give it away. So the level of wealth in society and the extent to which it is concentrated sets conditions for who is able to give and to what extent. In the South substantial proportions of the population live below the poverty line, with wealth concentrated amongst a few families—so the base for giving is narrow. The East is in such a state of flux and recent impoverishment due to devaluation, inflation and external limits set on government expenditures that its gift economy is, at best, embryonic.

However, an ability to give does not mean that people will do so. Social morals, derived from custom, religion and/or ideology, influence whether or not people believe they have an obligation to assist others or personally contribute to the public good. If they do feel this way, it is the nature of social relations which determines if they provide support directly to the individuals or institutions who deserve it or give indirectly through an intermediary.

In the North, charitable or philanthropic giving has its roots in Christian teaching, while highly individualised social relations have given rise to non-profit intermediary organisations who receive and distribute gifts according to contributors' wishes. In Islamic countries *zakat* is a teaching which has also led to the founding of intermediary organisations. More generally, in the South people are much more likely to give directly to the person or the institution of their choice. Intermediaries are not a common way of expressing social obligation. As Pushpar Sandar says of the Indian situation:

> 'Whereas in the West, individual contributions constitute the bulk of funds available to organised charity, in India this does not appear to be so. This is not to say that individuals are any less charitable in India, but only that individual charity is informal and flows spontaneously to individuals needing help on a one-to-one basis and does not go to organised bodies. The significant non-governmental indigenous funds for welfare and developmental work, then, are those from religious bodies and the business sector....'

The traditional preference to give directly builds bonds of mutual obligation and assistance which form a safety-net in times of hardship. In the South, reciprocity is part of a survival strategy as well as a way of establishing and maintaining social cohesion where inheriting and fulfilling obligations is an expression of status and power. An additional feature of Southern giving is its orientation towards religious and charitable purposes, not towards long-term sustainable development. This is the government's job. Discussions with NGDOs across the world lead to a consistent assessment that, certainly in the short term, it will be difficult to redirect existing patterns of local charitable, welfare and religious giving towards the type of development work funded by the aid system.

The important conclusion for NGDO strategies is that the necessary preconditions for growth in local giving to intermediaries are not necessarily built into the values or practices of societies in the South and East as in the North. While a gift economy exists, it does not fund third-party organisations since direct one-to-one giving is preferred. In other words, there is unlikely to be much local, good-quality, hot money for NGDOs to access for development as opposed to welfare. In the few cases where an affluent middle class grows rapidly and familial ties loosen, as in the Tiger economies of South East Asia, gifts to intermediaries may be on the increase—the Community Chest in Singapore is one example. Other signs of this happening are moves by transnational child sponsorship and other Northern NGDOs to fund-raise and spend on development work within countries such as Hong Kong, Singapore and Malaysia, instead of remitting funds.

Overall, for most countries the gift economy is unlikely to be a substantial source of local NGDO financing, mainly because it will take a long time for socio-economic conditions to create a widely shared surplus, and for social morality of giving to redirect itself towards funding intermediaries.

Issues and Challenges in Today's Resource Trends

The trends identified so far bring two important effects that must also be kept in mind by donors when formulating funding policies and by NGDOs when selecting funding strategies. The first is the response of Southern and Eastern governments towards NGDOs. Second are relationships between NGDOs as civic actors.

Government Attitudes

Aid trends are introducing tensions between Southern and Northern NGDOs as they sort out their new divisions of labour. In addition, shifts in funding are influencing relations between NGDOs and governments. Diverting shrinking levels of official aid to NGDOs means less for local politicians and bureaucrats to control, which is not popular. Insisting that NGDOs are involved in bi—and multilateral-funded programmes may not go down well either. Both policies encroach on sovereignty in terms of deciding how resources are divided and by whom—causing antagonism between Southern and Eastern governments and the NGDO community. Setting up commissions to investigate what NGDOs are up to—in India and Sri Lanka—is one sign of regime discomfort. New NGDO legislation and administrative procedures—adopted in Uganda, Kenya, Zambia and Zimbabwe—are another indication that some Southern governments are not prepared to lose influence over funds which used to come to them.

In the extreme, careless diversion of aid from governments to NGDOs can undermine the functions which state and civil society are supposed to fulfill. Supremacy of national governance is compromised as donor conditions change the roles of local institutions; competent civil servants are enticed away because government cannot match NGDO conditions of service. On the ground, NGDOs deliver more than ministries do, which erodes regime legitimacy; aid-driven NGDO expansion may also provide cover to subversive elements, or corrupt organisations, provoking crackdowns which close space for all civic initiatives. In other words, more official aid to NGDOs can work against good governance and the strengthening of civil society: objectives used to justify increased Northern tax money to NGDOs in the first place. Donor practices can undermine their own goals while making life more difficult for legitimate NGDOs.

For NGDOs, Changing Partners Means Different Dances

NGDOs who decide to follow aid money without paying attention to what this means for identity and long-term relationships between North, South and East risk weakening their contribution to civic development locally and globally. Changing partners means learning new dances, (the contractor waltz), at the cost of forgetting the old ones—such as the solidarity two-step. If NGDOs get seriously out of step in the North, South and East, an influential part of the citizens' sector will be less likely to oversee whatever system of international governance evolves. In turn, weak civic control on governments limits the public's ability to control how transnational markets operate and who wins and loses from how they work.

In deciding strategy, Southern and Eastern NGDOs must look carefully at the costs and benefits of cutting Northern NGDOs out of the aid chain. Instead of switching partners, Northern NGDOs should be pushed harder to deliver on their comparative advantages as intermediaries, which are to:

- help Southern NGDOs retain their autonomy as civic institutions;
- reduce the perception that Southern NGDOs are competing with their governments for aid;
- incorporate appropriate technical assistance that is based on mutual values;
- ensure that aid can be more flexibly applied;
- work against simple substitution of Southern NGDOs for the state in service provision;
- broaden support of Northern constituencies:
- maintain plurality in the aid system;

— strengthen South-North collaboration in policy impacts at the international level by bringing 'testimony' from the lives of poor people and their struggles.

The lower circle is not a realistic representation of the complex NGDO community with sector and interest groups, factions, overlaps and constructed barriers. The different ability of NGDOs to access sources in the South and East may drive more wedges between them. Two splits are reasonably obvious. The first is between NGDOs with the capacity to deal with the official aid system and those that cannot. The second group may be squeezed out and resent it. The second is between transnational with a built-in capability to take learning from one place and apply it in another, both North and South, placing local NGDOs at a disadvantage, leading to nationalist feelings and resentment again. The capability of NGDO co-ordinating structures to mediate and bridge fund-related divides will be critical in years to come.

Managing Deflection and Displacement

The picture looks pretty clear: the future of NGDO funding lies in the hands of the official aid system, with the self-financing development banks playing an increasingly dominant role as bilateral funds shrink over, the longer term. These trends present managers with the challenges of deflection and displacement. Deflection is a redirection of management focus and energy from the founding purpose and civic constituency. Two types of deflection are likely to occur. The first is satisfying the demands of governmental agendas at the cost of attention to civic roots and constituency. Second, when focusing on development banks, NGDOs can lose sight of the fact that it is the borrower rather than the giver who should be at the centre of attention. Improving the quality of a bank's lending conditions may only re-enforce the problem of lack of borrower ownership and responsibility. Again, it is not a question of either/or improving the quality of what IFIs do should be pan of the NGDO agenda, but not at the cost of engaging with the borrowing governments. As a strategic first step, it is the dialogue and interaction between development banks and borrowing governments with which NGDOs need to engage; this is now occurring, for example, in the Philippines in preparation for donor consortium meetings.

Displacement arises when new tasks of engaging with the official aid system are taken on without extra capacity. Inevitably the human capacity in time and effort is withdrawn from elsewhere. Making up for displaced capacity is not easy because the interaction is not a 'project' and therefore calls for high-quality money which is in short supply. Serious attention needs to be paid to making good displaced management capacity if an NGDO's effectiveness is not to suffer. Dealing with displacement will put a particular burden and responsibility on a small group of Northern donor NGDOs.

MANAGING WHILE MOVING AWAY FROM AID

Managing Multiple Donors

Generally, multiple donors are a management burden and an asset at the same time. The burden is essentially one of dealing with low-quality money and individualised demands on time. The blessing is less dependency on any one source, which reduces vulnerability and increases negotiating power. The challenge is to find an optimal number and balance of sources when managing more than one. Conversation with leaders suggests that between five and eight donors is optimum—a few unadventurous and reliable, complemented by others willing to experiment and then perhaps move on. A common way of reducing the disadvantages of multiple donors is to form roundtables or consortia.

Rountables and consortia are structured relationships between an NGDO (often southern) and its donors, where a common set of ground rules are agreed and adhered to by all parties. This structure is used by BRAC and PROSHIKA in

Bangladesh and various councils of churches. The format usually involves the following:

— Support is pledged and provided as a proportion of the whole with agreements on performance criteria, overhead levels and admission of other funders.

— The NGDO prepares a multiyear programme of activity to be funded, which may be made up of distinct related projects, but is treated as a logical, integrated whole.

— A system of periodic monitoring, evaluation and reporting used by all parties, perhaps with joint evaluation teams or other technical support.

Experience suggests that this set-up can work effectively if five conditions are satisfied. These are:

— The NGDO must have the capacity to deliver what it has planned, including the capability to monitor, assess and report on what it has or has not achieved.

— The NGDO must be strong enough to formulate a comprehensive, detailed statement of what it wants to do, where and why, including frank assessments of its strengths and weaknesses.

— Donors need to reassess what they consider to be overhead or indirect costs to ensure that process features and the institutional capacity development of the NGDO are properly valued.

— Donors must relinquish their 'project possession' way of thinking, supporting instead a coherent programme (even if for domestic consumption they stress activities which correspond to their priorities).

— Donors must be able Co accept and work with consolidated reporting, both financial and narrative. Translation to individual formats become the donor's responsibility.

While usually to be recommended if the conditions are met, the drawback for NGDOs, as Sarvadoya and ORAP in Zimbabwe found, is that donors can co-ordinate their support and priorities in such a way that it is equivalent to 'ganging up', severely limiting the NGDO's room for manoeuvre. The chance of this happening is greatly reduced if the NGDO can demonstrate real impact. More often than not, multiple donors do not form consortia or roundtables and so it is left to the leader/manager to do just that: provide leadership and management of diverse donors.

Donor management is seldom found in the curricula of NGDO management training programmes, but is a crucial demand that must be done well. This gap needs to be filled.

Strategic Choices in Funding Sources

Based on the previous analysis, and looking ahead, what conclusions can be made about preferred strategies for NGDO financing? The following six conclusions stand out.

- NGDOs everywhere are well advised to spread their income sources, ranking them according to existing potential and trends in quantity and quality. Each NGDO needs to decide on a strategic mix and develop the necessary capacities.
- Southern and Eastern NGDOs are vulnerable to political aid decision-making in the North, over which they have minimal control or influence. To be viable, autonomous and truly indigenous, resource strategies must be directed at 'rooting' them in their own economies.
- Aid available to NGDOs is getting colder; official funds will start to dominate, allocated on a 'contracting' basis. Avoiding a contractor's role calls for access to (small amounts of) hot funds to protect organisational autonomy.
- High-quality funds generated directly from the market do not carry the complications of public expectations,

together with the risk of not living up to them. In other words, market operation is the preffered source; everything else brings costs and constraints.

— Combining non-profit and for-profit activities must be structured so as to avoid too much of an overlap, but without breaking the relationship between them. Distinct legal entities under separate management, but single ownership, is preferable where the law and the tax situation makes this possible.

For the South and East, the choice between Northern NGDOs and official aid agencies will be less important because their sources, conditions and obligations are beginning to merge. Only those Northern NGDOs with substantial autonomy from the influence of official aid will remain distinctive, offering the highest potential for authentic partnership.

The future of NGDO viability and third-sector identity, therefore, lies in balancing opportunity with find-raising strategy.

Translating Strategy into Practice

Assuming that NGDOs have surveyed the potentials and limitations of different sources, how can they translate their choices into practice? In today's language, how can they mobilise financial alternatives to the aid system? Readings provides useful publications on practical steps.

Santar Datta indicatres that, launching a fund raising programme involves ten sequential steps, which draw on any of these methods. The steps include the following:

— *Define the purpose.* Sort out why you want to fund-raise (the ends) from the activity the money will be used for (the means). For example, the goal of improving education is not the same as teaching children.

— *Analyse funding requirements.* Goals and activities may require different types of money, such as one-off investments, ongoing cover for recurrent costs and expertise.
— *Map the potential sources.* Look at the environment to see who has the type of resource you need.
— *Assess potential contributors.* Analyse a contributor's worth against the costs of persuading them to give and collect donations. For example, a monthly collection of $10 from 1000 people might cost more than a single gift but offers long-term continuity.
— *Define a strategy and plan.* For each contributor, detail how you will approach them, the preparations needed and the steps required.
— *Establish a collection system.* How will the contributor be approached, by wham and how will they be held accountable?
— *Conduct the collection drive.* Put strategies and plans into action.
— *Allocate the resources.* Use the funds raised as promised.
— *Monitor utilisation.* Collect information on what is being done and how it is achieved.
— *Communicate back to contributors.* Build towards a longer-term relationship by informing contributors how their help has made a difference.

Fund-raising is a profession distinct from writing project proposals. Because they have evolved within the framework of aid, Southern or Eastern NGDOs seldom have this type of competence. In the North, some NGDOs have built up significant expertise in mobilising funds from the public and the market: It is time this capacity was prioritised and experiences shared, which is now beginning to happen. The odd case needs to become a standard component in NGDO relationships between North, South and East. Moreover, given the difference in environments, South-South exchanges would be particularly useful.

Barring the fund-raising strategies or methods employed outside of investments, any contributor naturally wants as much of their support as possible to go towards the goal they have been 'sold'. Making this (appear to be) the case—the art of minimising overheads—is both a skill and a trap for NGDOs. This, then, is the final element in resource mobilisation.

NGO Finance and the Dangerous Myth

NGDOs want and need their supporters to believe that they are effective at minimum cost. To this end, the ratio of administrative costs to total income is used as a proxy for efficiency, irrespective of the product. NGDOs have been so successful that, irrespective of the type of development work they do, low overheads are apparently always possible. The American financial magazine *Money* produces a yearly value-for-money ranking of US charitable organisations using one criteria only -administrative costs. 1994 saw the International Rescue Committee at 7.7 per cent, followed by the Mennonites and Save the Children Fund at 11.8 and 17.9 per cent respectively. The magazine has no idea what they actually achieve, which is a vital criteria. Similarly, *Henderson Top 2000 Charities*, a UK publication, 'guarantees you the answer!' about non-profits, again apart from what they achieve.

NGDOs, especially in the North, are in a bind when it comes to the false image they have created—that development itself is easy and can be done on the cheap. So how do they square the circle? The answer is that they fudge by using creative public financial reporting. There are no standardised or legally binding formats or ratios, such as the generally accepted accounting principles (GAAP) used by businesses and their auditors. Only when media disaster strikes is the curtain lifted, shedding light on the way NGDOs allocate expenditures to show themselves in the best possible way.

Whichever techniques are adopted, they are all counterproductive in one way or another. First, they leave the NGDO vulnerable to detailed enquiry and negative publicity. Second, by obscuring the real costs of doing development work, management is rendered less effective because an important foundation for informed decision-making is missing. Third, by ignoring the fact that different types of activity carry different cost structures, donors can get away with misusing their position. Some donors, such as USAID, do establish realistic overheads through a Negotiated Indirect Cost Rate Agreement for an agreed programme. This is an exception, with UN agencies, such as UNHCR, being apparently the worst at accepting the full costs of the work they fund NGDOs to do.

None of these tricks solve the essential problem which is the calculation and allocation of true costs associated with different types of development work, combined with public honesty. The most critical cause of today's difficulties is that the process costs of development are denied, ignored or just not considered 'real' development. And sadly, this perspective can still be found in professional donors who should know better. Ignorance is no longer an excuse for understanding what sustainable development means in all its dimensions and costs. It really is incumbent on NGDOs, say through their co-ordinating bodies, to confront this issue collectively.

With respect to Northern NGDOs, adherence to the myth indicates that leaders/ managers make an internal calculation that the risks of discovery and negative publicity do not outweigh the benefit of keeping things as they are. This calculation may be faulty; the few NGDOs who are transparent about their costs do not necessarily suffer from it. For example. World Vision Australia has published overheads of 33.7 per cent and has still managed to be the largest public fund-raiser in the country.

In Europe, no individual NGDO or grouping is taking the lead in developing standards for overhead calculations which others could adopt on a voluntary basis. The probable reason is fear of being undercut promotionally by those who keep to their old 'untransparent' practices. Change, if it comes, is more likely to result from external rather than internal pressures. The UK has a Charity Commission which is drafting proposals for accounting standards which it can enforce. Other countries do not have such a body. Another type of initiative is to establish a *Guide to Good Giving*- a sort of consumer's guide to NGDO effectiveness and costs. This move is likely to be actively contested ami declared technically impossible by insecure NGDOs who have the most to hide.

Are there basic principles which could justify categories of expenditure which NGDOs could agree to apply, allowing the public to make a fair comparison of overheads and enabling managers to do their jobs more effectively? At the risk of gross oversimplification in a very complicated area, the following principles are suggested. They flow from the understanding that NGDO work in sustainable development contains the micro-macro, North-South, product-process dimensions explained in previous chapters.

— NGDO expenditures should be categorised according to their interaction with the primary stakeholder.

- Because of their intermediary position between giver and beneficiary, NGDO fund-raising should be treated as a direct cost. Without the poor, NGDOs cannot exist; without donors they cannot serve the poor. The costs involved at both extremes mirror each other in terms of primary interaction, but not in terms of their proportions, which should be low at the income and high at the expenditure end.

It may be unrealistic to expect Northern (and in the future Southern and Eastern) NGDOs to struggle with the re-education needed for the general public to understand why professional development work is not simply a case of shipping money overseas. Altering the public's perception of what development is about—from quick, cheap and easy to slow, costly and complex—has to happen sooner or later. The trouble is, who will take the lead at the risk of losing market share?

But, let's be optimistic and say that reeducation does occur and NGDOs provide fair, comparable accounts of their expenditure. Even with new understanding and better figures, the public, and NGDOs themselves, still lack a vital piece of information—what has actually been achieved? Without this measure, high or low overhead percentages are meaningless.

CHAPTER 10

Rural Development Through NGOs

The voluntary sector is an important source of developmental initiatives; in particular, the non-governmental organizations (NGOs) articulate more at the local level than at that of the state or regional level. Hence, the local administration bears a special responsibility as a listening post for incorporating people's views that are made available via NGOs.

People's participation is not a new concept in the Indian setting. Of course, scope and content of it, have been different at different times of history or in different regions or communities. For traditional communities, it was the management of communal properties and resources which extended to forestland, village land, water harvesting systems and village common cattle, grazing pastures, etc. For religious groups or communities it is a matter of providing and pooling labour and wealth for religious or even social functions. For patriotic groups, it is pooling people in movements such as Dandi March or, Quit India or electoral participation. In the context of rural development, however, the term participation has a specific meaning. Participation is the introduction of a new set of people into the decision-making process with regard to resource allocation or distribution. By people we mean here those who have been victims of their exclusion from the development process and those who are likely to emerge as the beneficiaries of participation. In view of the complementary relationship between development and preservation of natural resources people's participation should involve the management of natural resources as well. The community organizations should be able to reinforce the existing structures of authority as long as tradition and authority are upheld. The community should feel empowered, and be independent of outsider's (including government) intervention. The set of rules and norms of cooperation should be such as to meet the felt-needs of the people. The above concept and definition of participation in management of natural resources in a way, covers the entire gamut of development activities at the rural/village level. It may, however, operate at different levels of intensity, measured by the kind of activities in which the beneficiaries participate.

There are reported to be somewhere one million development oriented NGOs in Asia. They are highly heterogeneous in character, varying considerably in character, geographic scope and sectoral interests. The overwhelming majority of the Asian NGOs are very small, employing generally only one or two staff, rarely more than ten. Frequently, they are the results of the efforts one—often charismatic-individual who draws together others for the purpose of ameliorating some social or economic need. The motivation is commonly charitable and the technical resources available are of a low order. The hope that such groups may make a contribution to development rests on the belief that it may be possible to reinforce them with insight, appropriate intervention techniques and adoption.

Non-governmental development organizations (NGDOs, or NGOs) constitute a potentially important vehicle by which social and economic development can be promoted in developing countries, especially at the micro level. At the same time it is recognized that NGOs too depend largely on people's participation in accomplishing their objectives. Mid-1970s witnessed a revival of voluntary activity, largely attributable to:

(a) The sense of mission which imbued social workers for the betterment of the underprivileged and deprived sections of society;

(b) The need for intervention in areas of public life which were suffering from the effects of official apathy and evils associated with the misuse of power.

(c) The elective local democracy's failure to satisfy the aspirations of the people;

Since then we observe the birth of a number of commendable voluntary ventures engaged in a variety of activities. A brief analysis of some of them will help in understanding the stimulant forces which gave them birth and the purposes for which they exist. To a casual observer, the strength of the NGOs lie in their ability to effectively motivate people to undertake some development initiatives at the village level, and serve as a intermediary for the government to understand people's needs and priorities. Generally, the voluntary agencies fulfil several tasks apart from the usual service provision for the needy; these main tasks could be classified into two categories: animation and facilitation. In reality, one cannot clearly be distinguished from each other. Animation means, first of all, conscientisation of the poor. Animators help the poor to regain their self-confidence and self-assertiveness. Only when the poor regard themselves as equal human beings and citizens do they question the reasons behind their poverty, realize their rights, request changes, discover the abilities and capacities at their disposal, have the confidence to change established patterns of behaviour.

If the poor have been motivated and activated through a process of conscientisation, the animator changes into the role of the facilitator. One assists the poor in forming groups, in decision which measures should be taken and in executing the same. He/she acts as an intermediary to get access to governmental or commercial services. One, for example, manages to establish first contacts between the poor and the officials by facilitating to provide the securities banks require (i.e., seed money, incentive deposits or group guarantees), and by helping the banks to change their procedures in such a way that they meet the requirements and abilities of the poor. NGOs also provide legal aid to the poor and their groups in their disputes with the rich and the government authorities, they encourage them to unite in federations or to take part in support networks in order to promote common interests collectively, and establish themselves as institutions at the service of those of the poor who have no access whatsoever to any services.

NGOs, serious about grassroots development are aware that they themselves could not specifically predict the direction in which the poor will move. They present themselves, therefore, not as teachers and know-alls, but as equal partners and, by skilful questioning, make them conscious of their problems, prompt them to identify the causes and to propose solutions. Such a process provides a code of conduct for the organization rather than hierarchy that is conducive to participation. We can understand this by scrutinizing some movements in Asia.

Conclusion

We observe that the voluntarism in Asia has passed through a number of stages. The Gandhian (peace loving, silent strugglers) and other types of voluntary agencies that existed prior to the phasing out of Colonialism in the region, on receiving government grants started working closely with and under the broad guidance of the government. They had lost the pioneering independent spirit that they had come to symbolize during the freedom struggle. In the second stage, there came a shift back to constructive work from "progress" or development work, as conceived by the government. The next phase saw a new genre of activist groups came up, ready to struggle on behalf of the poor, landless, *dalits* and other minority groups, against the State and dominant interests. There is a wide variety of such groups working in as different sectors as forestry, migrant labour, women, child labour and so on.

Thus a people-centred approach is not a utopia; it is the way out of poverty and underdevelopment. Already links appear with larger national struggles. One example is that of anti-nuclear popular actions in Asia. Local experiments with soft energies are also linked with a wider social movement which, in the final analysis, is challenging the whole system of values of the consumer society.

CHAPTER 11

Challenges to NGOs

Of late, hot discussion has been made about the Voluntary Council of India and the Code of Conduct proposed to be imposed on the voluntary sector through a law of the Parliament. While some have viewed this attempt only as an intrusion into the voluntary (viewed as private) sector, others have thought of it as one more way of controlling the activists who have been struggling with the marginalised groups and, as such, posing a threat to the vested interests whose economic and political power depend on the poverty and exploitation of the poor. In other words, it is important not to see these attempts in isolation but to view them within the historical process both as a part of the changes that have been taking place in the voluntary sector.

One can mention in particular two viz. the interest shown by international organisations in involving the voluntary sector in the implementation of projects and the threat many vested interests feel in the involvement of activists in rural development.

For the first, the involvement of the voluntary sector has become a part of many contracts signed by international aid-giving agencies with the Government of India and various State Governments. Among these one can mention social forestry sponsored or funded by agencies such as the World Bank, US Aid, SIDA and others. In some of these contracts, there is a clause stipulating that voluntary organisations be involved in the implementation of these projects. Similarly, the international agencies want to ensure people's participation in the implementation of projects. Thus, according to the agreement on the SIDA-funded social forestry project in Orissa, most decisions have to be taken by village committees.

The implementation by governmental agencies is unsatisfactory. The funding agencies assume that the voluntary sector can implement the programmes more effectively. An underlying assumption is that the voluntary sector can implement the projects without questioning the thinking behind them.

The voluntary sector is not homogeneous but has many tendencies. As Rajni Kothari mentions in his paper published in this Monograph, there are major differences between the voluntary organisations that work closely with the Government, those that are involved in relief and economic projects and the activists who struggle with the poor. In other words, over the last 15 years or so, there has been a major change in the type of voluntary organisations. The evolution of many of them poses a threat to the vested interests.

Voluntary Sector under Change

According to one estimate till the 1960s over 80% of the voluntary organisations were either Gandhian or Church-related (Fernandes 1983). In the 1950s most of them were either in relief (satisfying the immediate needs of the people) or in institutionalised programmes such as schools and hospitals. Most Gandhian organisations were those that responded to the call of Mahatma Gandhi that the Congress Party dissolve itself and that its workers go to the rural areas and work for the economic improvement of the poor. Many of them got involved in these programmes and in the implementation of projects initiated by the five year plans. Their focus was mainly on productivity-oriented technology and on functional literacy-oriented extension work.

By the 1970s many young persons who experienced the ill effects (such as unemployment) of a GNP-based growth model began to question the very system and the pattern of development and began to ask whether economic inputs alone could overcome poverty. They felt that poverty itself was the result of the oppressive social structures that marginalised the weaker sections. The dominant sections tended to get most benefits of the economic growth-oriented technical and other organisational inputs (Arora 1979: 27-35). They felt that they needed to support a new type of education geared to making the weakest sections aware of their situation in order to help them become active agents of their own development and change in their society. They viewed this type of education as an essential element in the process of enabling them to acquire their rights.

Another set of professionals began to emerge in the field of development. Convinced that the present systems such as medicine, architecture, education, etc. benefit only the rich, they began to search for low-priced technical alternatives that would be accessible to the poor. Hence, several medical professionals initiated community health programmes, and many of them got into associations such as Medico Friends Circle, and encouraged the people to find their own solutions to their health problems. Others like the architects in the Ahmedabad Study Action Group, searched for low-priced housing solutions. Some of these groups of professionals, particularly those in the medical and legal fields, have gone beyond the technical inputs and have begun to view the health, legal and other problems (to which till then technical solutions were sought) as structural. As such, they view these aspects as political and access to them as a right which the poor are deprived of, by the few who get the benefits of the present pattern of development.

In recent years there have been many other attempts at finding alternatives. Some of them are an offshoot of the "Total Revolution" launched by Jayaprakash Narayan and the disillusionment that followed. Some others emerged from the Naxalite groups that moved away from the strategy and the type of violence practised by them. Many others have been able to politicise issues that were so far considered non-political and have used them as rallying points. Among these we can mention groups that have rallied the people around issues such as the environment, women's rights, health, etc. (Fernandes and Lobo 1986: 318).

A result of such an approach has been several struggles of the weaker sections against the vested interests. There have been struggles against land alienation, against deforestation, for minimum wages, against caste discrimination, etc. This analysis and struggles have also affected many traditional organisations, most of them Gandhian or Church-related. A large number of them have got involved in these struggles and they extend support to the weaker sections.

Briefly, though one often speaks of the voluntary sector as a homogeneous unit, the reality is considerably different. On one side are the traditional organisations that have been implementing economic programmes. On the other side are the activist groups. Even these are not homogeneous. Though most of them are called "action groups" and may take a radical approach, they may be revolving around one or two highly motivated individuals and may not be having the historical perspective needed for radical social change. Others begin with economic or welfare programmes and the growing contradictions of such an approach raises many questions in their mind. Thus they develop their own critique and launch into the activity of organising the people. Others may originate in the context of a political debate and slowly enter areas where the parties do not go and eventually link the grassroots with the main political streams (Nayak 1985: 318).

Together with the proliferation of actions groups, one can also see the somewhat easy availability of money, particularly in the form of foreign funds. Among these changes, one cannot but expect abuses and the proliferation of those who view development only as a job or power. To those who want to control the genuine activists, the organisations that abuse the easy availability of money provide a good pretext to control the activists who threaten the vested interests. In other words, it is the *bona fide* organisations that are sought to be controlled.

Mechanisms of Control

The reaction of the Government and of the vested interests has been repression against those who have been threatening their domination. The activists are often called Naxalites and pseudo-encounters in which they are killed are not uncommon. Besides, the people are often the victims. The recent Arwal massacre in Bihar (Mathew 1936: 334-338), the killing of the Santal tribals in April 1985 (Kavalackatt 1985: 278-283), the Gua firing, the Pipra and Belchi massacres (Das 1979) are among other examples of extreme repression taking the form of the physical elimination of those who pose the threat.

However, physical elimination of the enemy cannot be the everyday remedy. Other methods have to be found to divide and slowly weaken the sector. These have been found in the form of the control of funds, allegations and commissions and finally the efforts to bring them under a centrally controlled organisation. The first efforts were made during the Emergency in 1976 when the Foreign Contributions Regulation Act (FCRA) was enacted. Thus, an effort was made to keep track of those who received foreign funds for fear that they may be misusing them for anti-national activities. On the pretext of national security, at a moment when few dared contest the claim following upon Operation Blue Star and the assassination of Mrs Indira Gandhi, the same law was amended to make its provisions stricter and to ensure better control. All foreign money had to got through only one account and a report had to be presented to the Home Ministry every six months. Moreover, the Government could name organisations which it considered political and ban all foreign funds to them. 142 organisations were thus named and others have been added recently, including civil liberties organisations such as PUCL and PUDR who have never received foreign funds and do not even have a registration number for this purpose.

Others could be forced to restrict the inflow of funds and accept conditions from the Government, by forcing them to ask for official permission for each project. This would ensure that the project in no way went against the dominant interests. Twenty-seven organisations have been brought under the purview of this clause in 1986, as many as 23 of them Christian.

Together with that, efforts have been made to control the flow of Indian funds. The 1983 Financial Act removed income tax exemption given to industries that made donations for rural development. However, the same law made such exemption available to them if they made contributions to a rural development fund to be set up by the Prime Minister. It has not been set up even 3 years later. Similarly, tax exemption was removed from all income generating activities of Charitable Trusts. Many of them had tried to be self-sufficient by setting up income generating activities. These were to be treated as commercial propositions and taxed accordingly. Thus, if they wanted Indian funds, they had to receive them from the Government on terms to be determined by it.

Together with this one has to see the setting up of the Kudal Commission to inquire into the working of the Gandhi Peace Foundation. Its terms of reference are extremely vague and its life has been extended continuously over the last five years. Thus, it has been able to make many allegations against as many as 945 organisations of Gandhian inspiration. The exact amounts involved in the allegations or the expenses of the Commission are not known. But one estimate puts the expenses at between 1.5 and 2.5 crores and the funds supposed to have been misused by these organisations over a 30 year period at two or three lakhs. Whether this calculation is exact or not is irrelevant. The fact is that the commission has kept many Gandhian organisations busy defending themselves against these allegations and bas affected their work considerably.

Introduction of communalism is not uncommon in order to discredit the activists. The vested interests that cannot defend their exploitation, often divert attention from this injustice by accusing the activists of being missionaries attempting to convert the poor (Fernandes and Lobo 1986): 314-315. At least three states viz. Arunachal Pradesh, Madhya Pradesh and Orissa have "Freedom of Religion" Acts that deprive the people of the possibilities of education and other benefits by alleging that these are inducements for conversion. When the tribals demand their right to be human, efforts are made to divert attention from these struggles by pressurising them by introducing other religious issues at it has happened recently in Chotanagpur in Bihar and Chattisgarh in Madhya Pradesh (Anon 1986).

Briefly, the small activist groups that could have been effective are forced to spend much of their time in administration to send regular reports to the Government. Since Indian funds are not easily available, red tapism forces them to go in search of foreign funds. Much of their activity is affected by the administrative work involved. Thus, their effectiveness in supporting the struggles of the oppressed is reduced. These are mostly the recent organisations that can be called activist. The financial controls, the Kudal Commission and similar enquiries have attempted to control the organisations of Christian and Gandhian inspiration. Thus a "divide and rule" policy is introduced.

Briefly, one notices that the effort has been to control the organisations rather than to support them. It is in this context that other moves such as the Voluntary Council of India need to be situated. All these measures have a common factor viz. influence and control and attempts at cooptation.

Rajni Kothari situates the voluntary sector within the context of the international economy and studies the factors that motivate the funding agencies to stipulate that they be the implementing agencies. He makes a distinction between the voluntary and the activist sectors and also analyses the growth of what he calls Government Organised Non-Governmental Organisations (CONGO). It is the CONGO and voluntary NGOs that the funding agencies would like to coopt, but not the activists. The Government in its turn tries to control the activist groups to stop any threat to the vested interests. Hence, he suggests that a distinction be made between the voluntary and activist groups and that the latter stop calling themselves voluntary. Upendra Baxi continues in the same strain and situates the recent moves within the context of the efforts to control the struggles for social change. L.C. Jain has a similar analysis while Rama Reddy shows how a vibrant cooperative sector was brought under the control of the administrator and the politician through legislation. This should be a lesson for those in the voluntary sector who think that the abuses among social workers can be corrected through a law of the Parliament.

Summing Up

In nutshell, the opposition of the activists is not to the Voluntary Council of India (VCI) but to the efforts at controlling them. They themselves would like to come together and they hope that the discussion on the VCI will provide them with an opportunity to begin a reflection on their own shortcomings. It is possible that they will, over a period of time, evolve a code of conduct suited to their needs. But they fear that any code of conduct imposed from above will, in practice, mean their depotiticisation when in fact the struggles they are involved in are political though not necessarily linked to parties.

Their opposition is not a struggle for their own survival but an attempt to keep the efforts at social change going. Thus, they do not pay much attention today to the moves to form such a council but look deeper at all the combined efforts at controlling them. They hope that this discussion will provide them with an opportunity to look at abuses in their own sector and correct them.

NGOs are also aware that through their inaction they have allowed themselves to be controlled. Little attention was paid to the Kudal Commission and nearly 1000 organisations were allowed to be blackmailed for what appear to be political purposes. Within the national security atmosphere prevailing at the end of 1984, very few of them dared to analyse the effects of the amendments to FCRA and other laws that tried to control their funds. Very few of them protested when activists were arrested under the anti-terrorist acts and were killed as Naxalites. The religious element introduced in their reaction and the efforts to treat the Gandhian, Christian and other groups separately were successful to a great extent. By and large, activist groups did not know how to respond to these moves. They were thus exploited through this "divide and rule" policy. But they are also aware that every move has its right time and space. Many of them think that such a time has come for them to sit together, reflect on their own situation and on the threats coming from within and without and act in unison. Whether this will bring them together into a federation or not is a minor question.

REFERENCES

Arora, L.S., *Rural Development in India.* (New Delhi: S. Chand & Co, 1979).

Fernadnes, Walter, Geeta Menon and Philip Viegas, *Forests, Environment and Forest Dweller Economy in Orissa* (New Delhi: Indian Social Institute, 1984), mimeo.

Fernandes, Walter and R.G. Lobo, "Social Action Groups and the Search for Alternatives," in Walter Fernandes (ed) *Inequality,*

Its Bases and Search for Solutions: Dr Alfred de Souza Memorial Essays (New Delhi: Indian Social Institute, 1986).

Kavalackatt, Thomas, "The Killing of Santal Tribals," *Social Action,* 35 (n.3, July-Sept. 1985), pp. 278-282.

Mathew, Mammen, "Roots of Rural Violence in Bihar: A Case Study of Arwal," *Social Action,* 36 (n.3, July-Sept. 1986), pp. 333-342.

Nayak, Nalini, "Where are the Action Groups Today?" in Walter Fernandes (ed). *Social Activists and People's Movements: Search for Political and Economic Alternatives.* (New Delhi: Indian Social Institute 1985).

Sen, Jai, "On Anti-Voluntarism: The PADI Committee Proposals for the Protection and Regulation of Voluntary Organisations" in Harsh Sethi and Smita Kothari (eds) *On Anti-Voluntarism* (Delhi: Lokayan, 1986), pp. 8-36.

CHAPTER 12

NGOs: Performance Appraisal

The experience of voluntary organisations and other non-governmental organisations in India has become so diverse and multi-faceted that there is a need to systematise and classify this vast range. In some ways the label "non-governmental organisation" is a negative, non-explanatory label. Under this label, private sector institutions and a host of other formations are being included. There is considerable debate about the meaning of the word "voluntary" or "voluntarism" in the contemporary context. It has nothing to do with being honorary, which may have been its historical roots; it has more to do with a combination of self-initiative and social commitment.

The purpose of evolving typology is to attempt differentiation between one type of voluntary organisation from another and to understand implications of these differences. Why is a voluntary initiative needed? It is almost like a statement of belief from the "founder's)" about what needs to be done in society for an appropriate change to occur. If we examine the range of voluntary organisations, three types emerge under this:

(a) The first type is based on the rationale that people need help, that the poor, downtrodden and weak need assistance and help. They need material assistance and resources, they need assistance of knowledge and ideas and skill. But the fact remains that they are poor because they have not had the "help". This help or assistance could also be temporary, during times of extreme crises or hardship. This phase was from 1840 to 1950.

(b) The third type is based on the theme of empowerment. It assumes that the poor need to get organised and struggle in order to bring about an appropriate change. The focus of intervention, therefore, becomes the conscientisation and organisation of certain sections, viz., tribals, scheduled castes, landless, women, etc. The ultimate purpose of the strategy is empowerment. The struggle of the target population may be catalyzed through a variety of activities which may focus on acquisition of assets, wages, implementation of certain progressive legislations, education, etc.

(c) The second type comprises a worldview which could be called developmentalist. Here the focus is on the people who could do it on their own but with "our" support, particularly support in the form of programmes, resources, ideas and skills. It is under this category that we may place programmes of health, education, agriculture, forestry, economic activities, appropriate technology, etc.

These three types described a wide variety of programmes and activities that voluntary organisations undertake. We find that a health programme carried out with first rationale of "help" tends to provide medicines and treatment, while another one carried out with the rationale of "development" tends to educate people and solve other non-health related problems in an integrated manner. Therefore, these distinctions are important not merely in their underlying belief but in the outcome as reflected in the manner in which programmes and activities are carried out by such voluntary organisations.

Some organisations focus on one constituency—let us say tribals or landless in a given geographic area. Some organisations focus on multiple consitituencies.Thus, it is possible to find different types of voluntary organisations carrying out the same sectoral work with similar constituencies but having totally different orientation, approach and activities.

The oldest batch of agencies to come up in the 1950s and 1960s were usually the products of post-independence revolutions in new free India. The veteran freedom fighters who had put all their energy and enthusiasm into the independence struggle now channelised their energy towards rural development and in upliftment of the poor. Mentionable were especially those who were followers of Vinobha Bhave and were active participants of the Bhoodan Movement.

Origin and Development

The spirit of freedom behind the concept of development in Himachal Pradesh can be traced back to the very first organisation, the SWARAJ which was established in the year 1868 in district Chamba since the formation of the Societies Registration Act of I860. Not much is known about this organisation which to the best of is it our knowledge and belief is redundant now.

An institute was established in 1952 in Kalsi, district Dehra Dun (UP) by the name of "Ashok Ashram". Some of the workers of this institute started coming to Himachal Pradesh and helped the inhabitants in solving their problems like water scarcity, getting loans, etc. The same institute was offered a house at Salogra, district Solan (Himachal Pradesh) by the local people for development work. On coming here, it was found that the people were leading a nomadic life (including Gujjars, Pangwals, Sarperas, etc.). Thereafter, an organisation was established by the name of Parvatiya Adam Jati Sewa Sangh (PAJSS) to cater to the needs of the backward communities leading a miserable life. The workers of PAJSS started doing different types of development work besides their projects. Any minor problem encountered by a local family was a problem for the PAJSS workers, from writing letters and application for loans, to getting treatment for an unwell child; just about anything and everything.

In the district of Kinnaur, there existed a practice of maintaining *jomas*, a tradition very similar to that of *devadasis* of South India. These young girls were given to the temple deity at a very early age, and naturally, educating them was unheard of. In fact, it was thought of as a crime. The PAJSS revolutionised this practice by opening schools exclusively for them in Kinnaur. Till date a few Jomas's can be found in some remote areas. This organisation was registered on November 14th, 1956 in Rampur Bushair (Himachal Pradesh). Another organisation named Harijan Sevak Sangh started the developmental work in Himachal Pradesh in 1954. This organisation started work on the line of Gandhiji's work on Harijans.

Now, the PAJSS has merged into the Bhartiya Adim Jati Sevak Sangh, New Delhi and is working as a branch of BAJSS in Himachal Pradesh.

After SWARAJ there is a large gap of about 84 years for which there is no authentic record or mention of the formulation or functioning of any welfare society till the establishment of the PAJSS or HSS.

Seven of the oldest organisations have been established between 1956 and 1966 and are still continuing with their work giving them a functional age of 36 to 26 years. Ten of these organisations are about 18-12 years old having started between the years, 1974 to 1985. Fourteen organisations are 10-7 years old (1982-1985). Fifteen agencies are younger at with 6-2 years of work experience and with the neo-group, which is hardly one year old, there are only four such organisations. There are more than ten organisations which are under the process of registration in Himachal Pradesh.

Nine organisations were first established in Himachal Pradesh. These were registered with the Societies Act of 1860 working in the area for 1-6 years. The rest of the organisations were registered first and then started their development work.

Even among these organisations there exists a wide variation with reference to their sizes, aims, functions and spheres of activities as well as their success in it.

Financial Classification

Using the financial criteria, seven out of 50 voluntary organisations have an annual budget of more than Rs. 6 lakhs and can be classified as large voluntary organisations. Twenty-two voluntary organisations, having an annual budget ranging from fifty thousand rupees to six lakhs, can be classified as medium-sized voluntary organisations. Thirteen voluntary organisations, having a smaller annual budget of fifty thousand rupees or less, can be given the status of smaller NGOs. The level of activities are limited to blocks/villages, in the case of smaller NGOs and the activities of larger NGOs are expanding to other districts and also to other north Indian states.

Funding Agencies

The major sources of funds for the NGOs seem to be the central government. Thirty-three NGOs are getting grants from the central government (15% to 100% grant for projects). The state government is funding only 22 NGOs, from 25 per cent to 100 per cent. Only 10 NGOs are getting foreign grants (10% to 100%). Ten NGOs are getting grants from national level NGOs (10-99%). Fifteen NGOs are running their limited programmes on the basis of donation from people, *panchayats*, villages; two NGOs, from sale of their products, etc.

Some of the central and state level departments who are funding different organisation are: CAPART; State Social Welfare Board, Central Social Welfare Board, Ministry of Health and Family Welfare, New Delhi; Ministry of Human Resources Development; Ministry of Environment and Forestry, New Delhi; Department of Education and Himachal Pradesh. Also important are private sources like charitable trust; welfare organisations; Indian Environmental Society,

Delhi; IGSSS, Delhi; APPRO; big companies and bureaucrats interested in a cause and even personal donations which could be in the form of cash, property, equipment or in kind.

Foreign agencies like CHF (Canada); NORAD; SIDA; FPP International; LWR, West Germany; CASA; Netherland Embassy; SAP; UNICEF (Canada); Action Aid (UK); Community Aid Abroad (Australia), WHO; Ford Foundation, Terre-des-Homes and OXFAM are funding these organisations in Himachal Pradesh for various rural developmental programmes. One major problem faced by the organisations with smaller budget to receive foreign funds is the need for legal formalities under the Foreign Contribution Act of the Government of India.

Aims and Objectives

The objectives of the organisations are generally to promote all aspects of social work/development, in accordance with the national policy. They adopt an integrated approach to solve the problems of rural communities and provide facilities for community development of backward areas. They also provide adequate incentives to attract educated and dedicated youths to rural development services and to undertake research work related to the function and work of the organisations. They work to raise consciousness among the underprivileged to promote self-reliance and to organise them against exploitation and social evils and in furtherance of above objectives:

1. to establish multipurpose training for grassroot workers in the areas of cottage or small industries, social welfare, education, health, nutrition, childcare, etc.;
2. to promote and provide increasing awareness of ecological balance;
3. to set up day care centres including creches, *balwadis*, nurseries, ashram, school or hostel for handicapped, etc.; and

4. to organise *mahila mandals* for all-round development of women.

In addition to the above objectives the following objectives are included while implementing various programmes and self-evaluation at the grassroots level:

1. to organise people, especially the weaker sections, at the grassroots level against the socio-economic inequalities and injustice and to make people aware of these things;
2. to work for all round human development at village level; and
3. to seek effective involvement and participation of target groups in planning, implementation and evaluation of all activities and programmes.

Though the area of operation of organisation is whole of Himachal Pradesh, a few of them are carrying out their activities in Uttar Pradesh and other states of North India whose border area adjoins Himachal Pradesh.

At the beginning a block/village was adopted by different organisations in their respective districts initiating their activities. The block/village was adopted because:

1. it is one of the most backward and interior areas,
2. its unique socio-economic cultural problems,
3. it is entirely a rural block/village having large scheduled caste or tribe population, and
4. there is no other voluntary agency working in the area.

The activities of these organisations spread out to adjoining blocks of the district as well as in other districts.

Operational Sectors

Over the wide and varied areas of operation of the gamut of organisations, the following major sectors can be identified:

1. social awareness,
2. economic development,
3. legal aid,
4. environmental issues,
5. providing economic and social self-sufficiency,
6. health care services,
7. social forestry,
8. animal husbandry,
9. non-formal education,
10. non-conventional energy sources,
11. water management for local consumption and irrigation,
12. vocational training,
13. networking including dissemination of technology/information,
14. income generating activities (sericulture, breeding rabbits, goat, cow, etc.),
15. children holiday camps, and
16. marketing of handicrafts.

While some of the organisations try various permutations and combinations from the above mentioned set of functions, there are others, especially the large organisations, which have the capacity and specialise in highly specific fields requiring sophisticated technical knowledge, skilled workers, expensive equipment, etc. Some of these fields are:

1. research in science and technology,
2. fellowships in journalism and publication,
3. dissemination of information,
4. catalysing rural change,
5. land water management,
6. rain water harvesting,
7. watershed management,

8. improved mud solar cooker,
9. horticulture (for marketing),
10. ferro-cement technology,
11. research in ayurvedic medicine, and
12. computer training

It has been observed that most of the organisations started their programmes firstly with creches and *balwadis*, nutrition-programmes, organising mahila mandals, awareness campaigns, etc., and now they are also focusing on vocational training, environmental issues, watershed management, income generation, appropriate technology, legal advice, health care services and computer training for, the development of rural poor. It could be due to the enhanced educational standard and broader world view of the executive heads of the various organisations.

Those voluntary organisations which specialise in certain working spheres need not necessarily absolve their responsibility of all other sectors. They do involve themselves but this can also be in the form of collaborations or helping other fledglings to do the same. After the depth of similar activities being conducted by different organisations also differs in accordance with their methodology, made of action and expertise available.

Also just because an organisation has been functioning for years and has a massive infrastructure with an equally magnanimous budget to, match, it does not mean that all its programmes would be effective, good and fault-free. Suffice it to say that the size and budget of the organisation does not necessarily reflect the efficacy of its programmes. Also this factor of reviewing the effectiveness of the agencies is outside the purview of this study.

Although a large area of action has been mentioned, almost all the organisations work towards the betterment of mankind by creating awareness and self sufficiency. These two results are obtained primarily through socio-cultural activities and economic development activities.

The former consisting of awareness camps, literacy campaigns, adult education centres, non-formal education classes, practical demonstrations of problems etc., have their impact on the people, if slowly, then surely, and at its best. It stays with the people and shape the personality of the future generation.

The latter, on the other hand, can include anything from among giving information, generating task forces, creating programmes, designing and implementing, production units, giving interest free loans, providing funds, training and imparting skill.

These facilities, however, are not so lucrative unless they have some back-up system for support and multiple avenues ahead of them for marketing, further investment, growth and development. It is quite easy to understand that without these facilities prefixing and suffixing these economic developmental activities they are going to be absolutely redundant and a complete wastage of the invested precious resources and manpower.

Programmes/Activities and Achievements

A brief summary of programmes and activities which are going on in each district by various organisations are given below:

District	Programmes/Activities
1. Chamba	— Creche and Balwadis — Training to Young People on Tibetan Tradition Trades — Production of Carpets, Painting and Dresses, etc. — Nutrition Programmes — Family Welfare — Adult Education — Sanitation and Health — Appropriate Technology

2.	Kangra	— Multipurpose Workers female): Health Guides and Traditional Birth Attendants — Environment — Health and Sanitation — Wasteland Development — Women Awareness Camps — Organisation of Mahila Mandals — Vocational Training — Social Animators Training Camp — Running Balwadis etc. — Drinking Water Awareness Camps — Adolescent Programmes for Girls — Alcoholism Anonymous Programme — Rehabilitation of Displaced Refugees (Tibetans only)
3.	Solan	— Environment Issues — Appropriate Technology — Sanitation — Adult Education — Children's Home — Income Generating Units — Community Health and Mother and Child Care — Drinking Water — National Unity Camp — To Generate Self Sufficiency and to Remove Exploitation — Environment Protection — Awareness Generation for Rural and Poor Women — Education (running Balwadis, Creche, etc.) — Day Care Centre for Old People — Vocational Training to Women — Children Holiday Camp, Ashram School — Welfare of Scheduled Caste and Socio-economically Backward People. — Mahila Mandal, Youth Club.
4.	Kullu	— Restoring Ecological Balance and Environment Issues — Plant and Saving Trees

		— Holiday Camps
		— Assess and Monitor Environment
		— Vocational Training
		— Promote Horticultural Produce
		— Creches and Balwadis
		— Health and Family Planning
		— Marketing of Agricultural Produce Women Awareness Camps
5.	Sirmaur	— Organisation of Economic Development Camps
		— Adult Education Centres
		— Children Holiday Camps
		— National Environmental Awareness Campaign
		— Community Health and Mother and Child Care
		— Developing Local Skills for Propagation of Rural Technologies to Reduce the Drudgery of Rural Women
		— Awareness Camps
		— Rabbit Rearing Unit
		— Income Generating Units
		— Education (Creches, Balwadis, etc.)
		— Drinking Water Awareness Camps
		— Mahila Mandal, Horticulture, Forestry and Plantation
		— Small Savings
		— Small Scale Industry
		— Vocational Training and Master Masons Training
		— Bio-gas Technology Extension
		— Rural Sanitation Programmes
		— Youth Leadership Training
		— Communication
		— Watershed Development
		— Networking of NGOs
		— Rain Water Harvesting
		— Ferrocement Technology
6.	Una	— Education and Awareness Programme
		— Holiday Camp
		— Computer Training
		— Vocational Training Programme

		— Income-Generating Programme
		— Health, Eye Camp, Family Planning
		— Ayurvedic and Herbal Medicines
		— Drinking Water Awareness
		— Energy Saving
		— National Environment Awareness Campaign and Environmental Programme
		— Dissemination of Information
		— Research in Science and Technology
		— Income Generation Activities
		— Land Water Management
		— Animal Husbandry
		— Horticulture, Tree Plantation
		— Fellowships in Journalism, Publication, etc.
		— Imparting and Raising Skills
7.	Mandi	— Educational (Balwadis, Balashram, etc.)
		— Short Stay Home for Poor Girls/Women
		— Holiday Camps
		— Awareness Generation for Rural Poor Women
		— Promoting Rural Industry
		— Low Cost Cold Storage
		— Fruit Cost Cold Storage
		— Fruit Processing
		— Literacy Campaign and Adult Education
		— Sericulture
		— Environment Issues
		— Help Age Project
		— Goat Rearing and Dairy Unit
		— Nutrition Programmes
		— Income Generating Units
		— Social Awareness Camps
8.	Bilaspur	— Organisation of Eco Development Camps
		— Environment
		— Awareness Camps
		— Education
		— Family Planning and Health
		— Eradication of Social Evils
		— Child and Women Development
		— Small Savings Campaign

9.	Hamirpur	— Rehabilitation of Destitute Women
		— Training Camps
		— Free Eye Camps and Nutrition
		— Legal Advice
		— Sanitation
		— National Awareness Camp
		— Rural Houses for Houseless
		— Social Awareness
		— Balwadis and Creches
		— Vocational Training
		— Education
		— Drinking Water Camps
10.	Shimla	— Legal Advice to Women
		— Income Generating Activities
		— Agriculture and Horticulture
		— Education and Literacy Drive
		— Handicrafts
		— Eye Camps, Health and Child Care programmes
		— Sanitation
		— Ecology
		— Mahila Mandals and Youth Cubs
		— Social Awareness and Social Evils (e.g. Child Marriage, Drug Abuse)
		— Social Forestry
		— Holiday Camps
		— Sports and Cultural Programme
		— Environment Promotion
		Child Development Programme
		— Vocational Training

The problems are multidimensional in the sense that they range from socio-economic, medical and health, nutritional, agricultural, employment and educational to ecological problems in all the districts of Himachal Pradesh. However, all the problems are interrelated and are the products, directly or indirectly of economic and social backwardness.

From the commonness of some of the programmes as

indicated from districtwise programme classification it seems that few organisations have finally identified independently the crucial issues which are most important for the development of a population. These issues are: (i) bringing in awareness among masses without which no development work is possible; (ii) health and family planning because, as for a sound mind a healthy body is required, and for a better distribution of limited resources the family size is of utmost importance; (iii) education, women and training of almost each organisation is busy in organising one or the other vocational training programme to educate the women to be independent economically; and lastly, (iv) the importance of environment in one's life.

The scattered and scantily populated villages in Himachal Pradesh have considerable implications for service delivery as well as they emphasise the need to strengthen local groups and workers. In Himachal Pradesh, 63 per cent of the villages have a total population of less than 2,000, another 23 per cent have a population between 200 and 250 and only .9 per cent of its villages have a population over 500. Ninety-five per cent of Himachal Pradesh's total population lives in the villages as compared to 77 per cent in the rest of the country. This pattern of population distribution in the villages associated with inaccessibility, difficult communication, difficult transport, unpredictable weather condition, with heavy rainfall (second highest in the world) makes delivery of services a task to be reckoned with and these facts need to be given due consideration in our plans of outreach services by involving the local people more and more.

The innovation scheme is one of such programme, this scheme includes alcoholic anonymous programmes, adolescent programme, networking of intersector and intrasectoral departments and social animators scheme and is being implemented by Chinmaya Rural Primary Health Care and Training Centre, Kangra.

For the first time in the state of Himachal Pradesh, RUCHI has introduced rain water harvesting technique to collect roof water for drinking purposes into ferrocement tank. This has also been successfully demonstrated at its own complex. About 70,000 litres of water is stored here making reliant on this front and is being propagated in the field also. Some of the non-conventional programmes started by RUCHI in the state includes rearing of angora rabbits and spinning and weaving. A research project to convert biomass into biogas is also under way.

Every man fears the unknown, so is the case with the rural folk. The Awareness Generation Programme (Samaj Kalyan Sabha, Shimla) provides information on varied topics from legal aspects and environmental issues to knowledge on governmental offices and procedures. The information gained during these programmes will shield the innocent villagers from exploitation by corrupt officials and other vested interests, by making him/her aware of his/her rights and duties as a citizen of India.

It has been found that Himalayan environment is being degrading due to massive developmental works engineered by man to loot its wealth unceremoniously. The development which is ushered is lop-sided. Environmentalists and social workers have for the last several years been criticising the development of the Himalayas through roads strategy. The people of the region have seen with their own eyes the tragedies wrought by the roads. There has been no check as well as conscientious efforts to educate people linked with this degradation. The Society of Reassemblement of Western Himalayan Ecology, Mandi, under their programme 'Ecology' is trying to overcome it through setting up information centres and involving agricultural universities, research institutes and government departments. Their aim is to provide better understanding of man-environment relationship and to assess likely impact of human activities on environment of the western the Himalayan region and suggest ways for bringing about ecological balance in the region.

Children's home was set up for the orphan, semi-orphan and deserted children by *Deenbandhu Sewa Mandal,* Mandi, with the financial assistance of 45 per cent from Ministry of Human Resource Development, Department of Women and Child Development, Government of India, Shastri Bhavan, New Delhi, and 45 per cent from the State Government, Department of Welfare, Himachal Pradesh. They are also making 'short-stay home for women/girls' of poor families.

Free eye camps, functional literacy centres, many sports, cultural and national integration programmes, work camps to build bamboo bridge over the Nangal river. *Sahayata cell* to help the rural people in various programmes run by different government departments were organised by the Society for Environmental and Rural Awakening, Kangra. ERA has started preparing ayurvedic medicine also.

Under the "Energy Saving Programme", the Energy Environment Group, Una, is making mud solar cookers and low cost pour-flush toilet for the people.

The above few important programmes which have been started recently by the organisations in their respective areas show that these organisations are using latest techniques and concepts for the development of rural people along with the old concept of development. It has been observed that few organisations are still sticking to stereotyped programmes because of certain limitations.

Attitude of the People Towards Organisational Operations

To know about the status of any development programme or organisation it is imperative to know about the attitude of people effected as well as not affected (directly) by it. A favourable public opinion on a developmental programme or on the operation of a voluntary agency would itself be considered an achievement. The public opinion indicates the level of acceptability of the agency's function to the beneficiary groups and also the potential success of the future programmers. Apart from interviewing the beneficiaries, some of those people were also interviewed in each district, who were not getting any benefit or they were living in non-project areas. These people were interviewed mostly in groups.

CHAPTER 13

NGO and Rashtriya Mahila Kosh (RMK)

Introduction

1.1 It has been felt for some time that the credit needs of poor women, particularly those in the unorganised sector, have not been addressed adequately by the formal financial institutions in the country. Varied experiences in this sector have established a need for a quasi-informal credit delivery mechanism, which should be client friendly, has simple and minimal procedures, disburses quickly and repeatedly, has flexible repayment schedules, links thrift and savings with credit and has low transaction costs for both the borrower and the lender. With this in mind, the Govt. of India has established a Rashtriya Mahila Kosh with the main objective of women empowerment. The other details of objectives are given in the Operational Guidelines of Rashtriya Mahila Kosh.

1.2 *Rashtriya* Mahila Kosh (RMK) for the furtherance of its objectives provides financial assistance mainly through NGOs/SHGs to poor women both in rural and urban areas. The Kosh also strives to go beyond credit delivery and provide services for integrated development centered around the needs of poor women. Credit will be linked mainly to production and economic activitiy.

2. Self-Help Groups (SHGs) Definition of SHG

2.1 It is a homogenous group of 10 to 20 women having clear understanding about the main objectives of SHG, including thrift and credit. These women select their own leader and also frame other rules/terms and tenure of leadership, etc.

2.2 Self Help Groups are extremely helpful in allowing the NGOs to know a large number of individuals intimately and to relate to them in a variety of ways including facilitating credit availability. Through peer pressures exercised by the members, each member can be made to feel keenly, individually and severally responsible for using and returning credit made available to them through a financial institution. They (SHGs) also serve as decentralised centres of administration for NGOs who take responsibility for forming these SHGs.

2.3 After formation and stabilisation, these SHGs become significant agents for bringing about changes in the lives of the members. They may also make a difference to the lives of others around them.

3. Important steps for formation of SHGs:-

(a) The most important step for formation of SHGs is to conduct a socio-economic survey of the village. The survey report would enable the NGO to identify the needy economic groups in the village and the crafts/business they want to follow.

(b) Conducting of the first meeting in the village.

(c) Dissemination of information about principal purposes and the procedures of setting up a SHG for saving and credit through group leaders in the villages.

(d) Opinion leaders should spread the concept of group savings and credit to their friends, relatives and other people.

(e) Identification of other problems of the women, including social and medical problems, if any.

(f) Building a consensus for working together, defining group dynamics and rules which will develop the group on a sound basis.

(g) Discussions and determination of the programmes that will be undertaken by the members of the group.

(h) Identification of an effective and appropriate group leader for conducting group activities.

(i) Steps for ensuring effective working of group by participation in open, friendly and congenial atmosphere, giving respect to the views of all members and to ensure that the group stands by itself.

An explanatory note on formation of SHGs is given at Annexure 'A'.

4. Specific Functions to be Performed by SHGs

4.1 The groups are supposed to perform the following important functions:-

i) Emphasising that there is a great strength in getting united;

ii) Effecting regular savings and credit activity within the group, which would follow explanatory sessions on the difference between consumer credit, production credit and the use of credit for socio-economic transformation in the lives of the members of the SHG;

iii) Analysis of the existing formal and non-formal credit systems;

iv) Articulation of the group's requirements in terms of credit and enhancement of skills required for income generation activity;

v) Facilitating easy access to credit and instituting the mechanism for its effective channelisation;

vi) Teaching importance of regular repayment and using group dynamics for the same;

vii) Applying viable norms for interest rates, repayment schedules, gestation period, extension, writing off bad debts and the requirements for communication with the financial institution;

viii) Serving as a platform for review of the cost benefit of the income generation activities being undertaken;

ix) Undertaking identification of needs for upgradation of technical skills in the Income Generation activity undertaken;

x) Any other activity including review of social issues impinging on the lives of women.

5. Stabilisation of SHGs

5.1 The following important checks should be applied to test the stabilisation of a group:

a) constant membership of not less than 5;

b) depiction of common understanding about who are the members;

c) clear understanding among the members about the main objectives of the group;

d) initiative in regularly attending meetings;

e) high and shared participation in the meetings;

f) free and open communication and feedback among members;

g) consensus in decision making;

h) realisation for a structure of the group and action on group decisions;

i) reasonable level of on-going activity in the group;

j) shared leadership in the group, will to improve and develop;

k) conflict resolving by discussions/mutual appreciation of ideas.

7. Accounting procedure of SHGs/NGOs

Notes are enclosed—Annexures B and C.

8. Principles of Saving

8.1 In any credit programme, savings are the mainstay

as these constitute its life blood. This is equally true for NGO run savings and credit programmes (SCP). Savings are either received by NGOs as part of internal resources mobilisation for funding their credit programmes directly or through the self-help credit groups which keep their funds with the NGO banks. The unique feature of SCP is that the saver and borrower being the same, there is a direct relationship between them. The savings serve a wide range of purposes other than the immediate investments as indicated below:

i) Savings impose a discipline on the group members in developing a savings habit;

ii) Savings enhance self-confidence. An individual who is not used to saving, finds it a great source of encouragement to become a habitual saver;

iii) Savings cover normal business risks, seasonal variations in income, natural calamities like flood, famine, cyclone, draught, disease and political disturbances. Members of the group can undertake risk decisions because they find some cushion in the savings;

iv) Group savings of the poor could demonstrate that their number is a great source of strength to themselves and also to the Nation. Small amounts saved each week regularly add up to a large amount;

v) Savings eliminate dependence on money lenders and contribute to the formation of a new team perspective.

Ground Rules for Deposits

a) Features of an efficient deposit management

i) The deposits should be on a regular basis and be accepted even for small amounts;

ii) Terms and conditions should be clearly spelt out and pass books showing details of deposits received and withdrawn, interest credited etc., should be given to each depositor;

iii) Depositors should have easy access to deposits and should be made to feel assured that their deposits are safe and will be repaid to them even earlier, if so required;

iv) Interest rates should be market rates to compare favourably with the rates given by banks.

b) Compulsory Deposits/Thrift

i) The deposits could be even for the smallest amount in the beginning but in due course it should be related with the amount of loan at a suitable rate, say 1 per cent of the loan per year.

ii) The deposits should be collected along with the monthly instalment for repayment of principal and interest. Arrears in this regard should not generally be allowed and amount should be collected at a later date with penal interest.

iii) Interest could be allowed on such deposits at rates which should normally be less by 6 to 8% over the lending rate adopted by NGO/Group.

iv) Where no interest is allowed, (which is not very desirable) the net surplus of the interest earned on funds could be either proportionately credited to the deposit account of each member or to a common fund. Accretion of surplus may not be allowed to be withdrawn. It will be better if it is used for increasing the common fund.

v) Withdrawals say 50% of the amount may be allowed out of deposits only after the beneficiary has repaid the principal and the interest under loan.

vi) Emergency loans could be given out of compulsory deposits at 50% of the deposit at rate of interest applicable to consumption loans.

vii) Refund of deposits and interest could be allowed when the member ceases his membership or asks to leave the Group/NGO for any reason. Such member, if allowed to rejoin the group, should bring back the total amount of deposit refunded to him. The practice followed by depositor needs to be re-examined.

viii) One time deposit say Rs. 10 or Rs. 20 per member could be collected for crediting the amount to the account of Cluster Committee or Federation, if these exist.

c) Optional Deposits

i) Such deposits could be either in the type of savings bank deposit or term for 1-3 years, depending on the fund requirements of NGOs for term loans. If the NGOs are not issuing loans for more than 2 years, deposit should not be accepted for a term exceeding 3 years. There should be co-relation between the collection of term deposit and loans portfolio of the NGO for term loans.

ii) Rates of interest on such deposits should normally be equal to about market rates. These could even be ½% to 1% per cent more than the rate allowed by the banks in the area.

iii) Withdrawal of the optional deposit could be allowed in the case of saving deposit say once in a week as per requirement of the local area and in the case of term deposit, the deposit should be repaid as per tenure of the deposit even if depositor ceases to be a member of NGO.

iv) Premature withdrawals of the term deposit could be allowed in very special circumstances but in such cases the interest paid should be 2% less than the rate applicable to the deposit.

v) Loans against term deposit could be allowed at the rate of 75 per cent of the deposit amount and rate of interest could be 2 per cent higher than the rate applicable to the relative deposit. The interest accrued on deposit should be credited to the loans account in such cases.

vi) Interest on savings bank deposit should be paid on the minimum balance held in the account in the month. Interest may not be allowed if the balance is Rs. 50 or less.

The above are only important broad principles but these could be modified as per the felt needs of the area.

d) Important points to be noted

i) It is to be noted that the deposits should be accepted by the NGOs or groups only from members (regular, associate, nominal as per provisions of bye-laws) and not from public since the latter proposition would require the approval of RBI. Similarly, withdrawal slips only have to be used for getting payment of the deposits and not cheque, as defined in the Negotiable Instruments Act.

ii) Although there is no requirement to maintain liquid assets to meet the claims of the depositors (under withdrawal deposits) as and when these accrue or earlier on demand, it is always advisable to keep some 25 per cent to 30 per cent of the total amount of deposits in liquid form, i.e., cash, or bank balance in fixed or savings deposit account so that these would be available for meeting the demand of depositors.

e) Utilisation of deposits

i) Compulsory deposits normally form part of the lendable fund and, hence, could be used for lending purposes. But the deposit collected on optional basis, cannot be so liberallly used by NGOs for lending purposes. NGOs should study the position and decide the extent of optional deposit which could be used for lending. Normally 60% to 70% of such deposits could be used for lending purposes.

ii) When a group has surplus resources these could be kept as fixed deposit with banks or if considered proper by all the members of the Group, the amount could be lent to other Groups at a suitable rate or interest provided the creditability of the borrowing groups is beyond doubt.

9. Principles of sound lending

a) *The established principles of sound lending are*

i) the lending must conform to the requirements of the accepted policy of an organisation;

ii) there should not be any diversion of finance for anti-social, less productive or unapproved purposes;

iii) the borrowings must be right for the borrower and be of real help in his financial problem. It must not assist him on courses which will lead to further financial embarrassment;

iv) to the extent possible, advances should be production oriented (barring a few loans for consumption purposes); and

v) every loan should be for a clearly disclosed and approved purpose to an approved borrower whose character holds out an assurance that arrangement made will be faithfully and successfully adhered to.

These are some of the sound principles to be acted upon while making loans. A lender cannot always be a genius but he should use his common sense to reconcile personalities and propositions with principles.

b) *Features of credit delivery for poor*

A successful micro lending credit system particularly for the poor run by a NGO should be run on a quasi-informal pattern. It should have the following characteristics:

i) organisation delivering credit and its staff should be involved actively in community outreach through local organisation in fora, where the staff works in the village and meets borrowers almost daily explaining their requirements, assisting them, etc.

ii) the application form should be simple and procedures should have minimum paper work;

iii) loans should be disbursed quickly even for the smallest activities and also for start up business. Initially, loans should be for working capital, which will help testing the borrowers conduct and seeing whether the loan will help the growth of business or not;

iv) loans should not generally require collaterals and guarantees. Emphasis should be on individual's own reputation and preference should be given to groups or borrowers to have the benefit of joint liability and peer pressure;

v) savings should be compulsory for all as this will help building up local commitment of the programme whether they ask for a loan or not;

vi) transaction costs, i.e., cost of administering the credit programme should be minimum both to the borrowers and lenders. To the borrowers in the form of no delay in sanction, simple procedures and flexibility and to the lender, less paper work and hence low cost of operations;

vii) interest should be charged at market rates with no subsidies and or subventions, overt or covert;

viii) there should be mutual interaction between borrowers for better use of funds, problem solving, periodical counselling, etc.; and

ix) links should be developed with the normal sector on selective basis particularly for bigger and profitable projects.

c) Need for a policy

A proper policy of loans criteria and portfolio parameters should be laid down at the beginning of every year by the NGO for itself as also for its affiliated groups taking into account the local factors, needs of the area, human and financial resources available, etc. The policy should lay down the following:

i) total lending to be done under short term, medium term loans, etc., depending on the resources, both existing and expected. The total lending to be done in each month of the year should be estimated; and

ii) sector-wise allotment of funds to avoid concentration in certain sectors like trade and small business. Sector-wise allotment should be made as per the priorities of the area and experience of previous year and linkages available-both backward and forward-and existence of other government, semi-government programmes. Thus, if a dairy development programme is run by the government in an area where the NGO is working, a lower sectoral allotment for this should be made. The backward linkage in this case means availability of animals, fodder, medicines, etc. While forward linkage will mean arrangements for roads, milk collection, marketing etc., for their successful operation.

d) Eligibility criteria

This is an important area where the following should be seen:-

i) Prospective borrowers are to be judged very discreetly for their character, capital, capacity, financial position, size of the family, willingness to work with honesty and frankness, health, temperament, life style, relationship in society, etc. These aspects should be looked into by having some sort of informal survey. The preference of the client for the economic activity should be carefully assessed since this will have effect on the utilisation and recovery of loans. The above criteria should apply to individuals whether they are financed directly by the NGOs or through the SHGs.

ii) While selecting the SHGs as clients for lending, their quality of group activity, image, size and working should be looked into. Only well established, homogenous and socially viable groups should be made eligible for lending.

iii) SHGs to be selected for lending should have done savings programmes at least for six to twelve months or even more, if considered necessary.

iv) It will be better if some broad ceiling is prescribed in terms of the annual income of a family to be supported by credit by the NGOs.

v) Cases of defaulters of loans taken from banks under various Government programmes should be carefully examined and decided on merit. Default of the husband and or other family members should not come in the way of advancing fresh loans to member women beneficiary of the SHG.

A Note on Cash Flow

i) Cash flow means a detailed break-up of all cash inflows and cash outflows. This facilitates planning for all income and the expenses, loans and recoveries. It also helps to plan for investments of surplus funds, and to keep a check on expenses.

ii) The cash flow statements should be prepared at the beginning of the financial year atleast for one year. We have to project the possible income and recoveries of loans and issue of loans and expenses for the whole year on a monthly basis. Once it is prepared, it could be used as a budget. If the expenses/outgo for a given item increases over the amount allotted for a particular month, one should try to find out the reasons for that and take appropriate action as soon as possible.

Similarly, if receipts/income is more than what was planned, then one must find out the best way to utilise it or invest it in ways permissible for voluntary organisations. A specimen of cash flow is given at Appendix I.

Points to remember

a) It is necessary to prepare a budget of expected lendings/recoveries and deposits savings under each type of loans and deposits. The extent of net surplus available for lending (after meeting the expenses and making the provision) should also be taken into account. The overall aim is to ensure optimum utilisation of funds and to increase the yield an funds consistent with sufficient liquidity for meeting the claims of depositors and others. The progress achieved in the last year should be critically examined and projection for the ensuring year should be based on, realistic estimate of demand for loans and the expected deposits keeping in view the improvement in the economic condition of the beneficiaries in the area.

b) Due notice should also be taken of uncertainties and the time gap involved in getting grants and donations from the Government and other agencies so that availability of cash could be timed accordingly.

c) Extent of funds available for lending out of recoveries of old and current loans should also be taken into account. Very often, it happens that small loans are issued to beneficiaries for 3 to 6 months and these are recovered within the year and as such these are available for lending. On an average, 30% of the ST loans issued in a year could be taken as recoverable within the year while out of the loans outstanding at the beginning of the year and falling due during the current year, some 60-70% could be taken for purpose of estimating recovery. The estimate of recovery percentage should be reviewed year after year and suitable changes made in working future projections in this regard.

d) Defaults in recoveries of loans should be critically examined to find out reasons for taking corrective steps. Similarly, deficits in getting targetted amount of deposits should be looked into to see if the deposit scheme needs to be made more attractive.

Clarifications and explanations on various matters relating to Application Form and other formats prescribed by RMK and Its loaning procedures.

A. Application Form for Credit Limit

1. *Lending done in the last 3 years:* This represents the loans issued either by the NGO directly or through the Self-Help Groups. In the case of loans issued directly, the loans outstanding at the end of the year should tally with the figures given in the balance-sheet for such loans. In the case of lendings done through SHGs, there need not be any mention in the balance-sheet. NGO should have reliable data about the working of the SHGs to indicate the total lendings done, recoveries made during each of the last 3 years for our general scheme and at least for one year for loan promotion scheme.

2. *(a) Demand for recovery:* It indicates the actual amount which has fallen due for recovery during a particular year and not the total loans issued. Similarly, the recoveries to be shown in the application form are the recoveries actually effected, including advance recoveries, if any. The percentage of recoveries has to be calculated with reference to the demand and not with reference to outstandings of loans or to loans issued.

   (b) Wherever, the NGO has given extensions in the due dates of recovery of loans because of failure of crops, the amount of loans so extended or rescheduled will be deemed to have been recovered for the purpose of calculation of demand and recoveries.

3. *Audit Report:*
   (a) What is required is Audit certificate given by Auditors for Income-tax purposes as also the Audit Report containing the important observations of the Auditors on the audit of the annual accounts of the NGO and his certificate in the prescribed form prescribed by the Income Tax department, but in actual practice such reports have not been sent to the RMK. Only the balance-sheet is certified which does not serve the purpose.
   (b) Auditor's certificate should also indicate the Registration No. of the Auditor.

4. *Surplus of expenditure over income:*
   (i) Wherever such situations are shown in the balance-sheet, the NGO should give proper explanation as to how it proposes to meet the excess expenditure incurred during a particular year either from out of grants which it hopes to receive during the next year or from some other funds.
   (ii) Details of borrowings from members/other institutions should be indicated in the loan application. Defaults, if any, should also be shown indicating the reasons for defaults and the time-frame to clear it.

5. *Testimonials about the working of the NGO:*
   (a) Many NGOs receive certificates about their performance from donors as also from the Government departments. It will be worthwhile to send copies of such certificates along with the credit limit application.

(b) Copies of important sanctions received by NGO recently from CAPART/Govt. of India/State Govt/ District Admn. etc., may also be enclosed.

6. *Eligibility of women borrowers for loan under RMK:*

   It should be ensured that the identified borrowers for RMK loan are not covered by any scheme of the banks for extending the credit to the poor and that the proposed women borrowers were not defaulters to Banks.

7. *Purpose of loans:*

   NGOs or the SHGs are giving loans for various purposes. It will be worthwhile to calculate the cost and benefit of each such activity so as to ensure that the activity proposed to be undertaken is financially viable. A few such calculations made for the most usual types of activities undertaken by women borrowers should be enclosed with the loan application. Further, the economic activity should be supported by proper backward and forward linkage for ensuring supply of raw-material, marketing etc.

8. *Lending Programme:*

   (a) While calculating lending programme for next year, what is required to be given is the additional lending programme which the NGO proposes to undertake out of RMK funds for which it will have to keep separate accounts. Similarly, the amount of savings and thrift to be used while making advances out of RMK funds will have to be separately computed while indicating the availability of funds with the NGO for making lending under the RMK scheme.

   (b) The NGO should always make a realistic estimate of the number of borrowers and specific purposes for which loan will be given during the year. This should be done area/village-wise. The lending programme posed for RMK support should be realistic and within the managerial capacity of the NGO keeping in view the performance in the last year.

(c) The unit cost of each purpose should also be specifically determined as per local conditions. If necessary, a reference could be made in this regard to the unit cost norms prescribed under IRDP, etc. programmes in the District. The total lending programme will be the number of borrowers multiplied by the unit cost for each of the purposes for which loans will be given.

(d) In the beginning, the lending programme should be drawn mostly for the short-term loans so as to test the borrowers before giving them medium-term loan. However, a limited medium-term loan programme could be accepted even in the initial stages.

(e) Specific purposes of loan should be mentioned under agriculture and non-agriculture sections Mentioning the broad categories as 'agriculture' and 'non-agriculture' does not serve the purpose.

(f) Loans, e.g. crop loans which require longer gestation period, i.e. more than three months under short-term loan and six months under medium-term loan should be indicated in the application, so that these could be taken into account while issuing sanction.

9. *Bye-laws*—It has to be ensured that there is a specific provision for borrowing from institutions. Indirect or general provision saying that the NGO could do all activities leading to achievement of its objectives will not do.

10. *System of Thrift and Savings:* It will be better if NGO furnishes details of the system of thrift collection of savings obtaining with it and the SHGs. The system

should clearly spell out the norms for savings, periodicity, rate of interest allowed on savings, system of withdrawal and the present position of total amount of thrift collected by the NGO/ SHGs.

11. *Consumption loans:* Normally consumption loans including loans for house repairs are supposed to be met by the SHGs from out of their own resources and, as such, the funds from RMK are not to be utilised for these purposes, except when these are so specifically sanctioned by the RMK based on the non-availability of resources with the organisation for which suitable explanation will have to be, given.

B. Documentation

(i) The guarantee deed prescribed by RMK is an organisation guarantee i.e. on behalf of NGO as such. It is not a personal guarantee of Secretary, Managing Director or the President of the NGO.

(ii) The loan agreement and the guarantee deed have to be typed fully on stamp paper and under no circumstances, photostat copies of pages should be attached to the application.

(iii) Loan agreement to be taken by NGO from SHG/ borrower should provide for proper ghypothecation of the assets to NGO till such time loans are repaid with a provision to reassign the charge in favour of RMK in case of need.

C. Drawals and Disbursements

(i) Drawals should be made only after the NGO/SHGs have completely identified and firmed up the list of borrowers indicating the amount required by each and purpose thereof. NGO should also see that the formalities of calling the meetings for sanction of loans etc. are completed and a probable date of disbursement is fixed for each of the areas. The date of disbursement could be indicated in the drawal application so that the proceeds of the drawals are sent to reach the NGO well on time. This process will, to a great extent, avoid delays which are presently occuring in disbursement of funds to the borrowers. In certain cases, delays have also occured in reaching the funds to the borrowers because of the time taken by the bankers in collecting the drafts from the local branches of the State Bank of India Normally, local collection of drafts should not take more than a day. It will, however, be better if the NGOs could indicate to RMK the nearest branch of the SBI located in their area so that draft could be sent on that branch to avoid the time taken in collection. NGO may also consider opening a separate RMK loan account with SBI to avoid the formalities of sending the drafts for collection.

(ii) It should be ensured that SHGs disburse the loans to their members without delay preferably on the same day they get funds from NGO. All disbursements should be made in open meeting of SHGs, preferably in the presence of a representative of NGO/office bearers of SHGs.

(iii) Utilisation of all loans S.T./M.T. must be verified though field staff within a reasonable time after disbursement.

(iv) The disbursement of loans to members should be as per drawal application submitted to RMK. However, if for certain unavoidable reasons, deviations become absolutely necessary in terms of the names of the borrowers or amounts or purpose, these could be done by the NGOs within a reasonable limit of, say 5% of the total drawal made, while MT loans sanctioned by RMK could be converted into ST loans, ST loans should not be converted into MT loans without the prior approval of RMK.

D. Remittance of recoveries to RMK

a) Loans could be recovered from members/SHGs daily, weekly, monthly or quarterly depending on the practices followed in the area and also the purpose for which the loans were advanced. The main point is that recoveries of the loan should come out of the income-generated by the activities undertaken through credit. It should not happen that a borrower has to borrow again from outside to repay her loan.

b) Repayments to RMK should be made on the due dates indicated in the sanction letter. These are quarterly, for short-term loans and at half-yearly intervals for medium term loan. There is, however, no objection to NGOs remitting the funds representing recoveries of loans to RMK, even earlier which will go to save interest charges for them.

c) Any recoveries received by the NGO but not remitted to RMK because of the due dates falling later in the month/quarter should be used judiciously by the NGO for making short loans for a month or two to the eligible women borrowers for justifiable purposes. But it should be ensured that on the due date of the payment to RMK, the NGO is having funds to meet its applications. In no circumstances, the recoveries of loan received by NGOs should be used for any other purpose/activity of the NGOs which may jeopardise the repayment programme.

E. Charging of interest by NGOs

(a) Whatever system is followed by NGOs in disbursing loans either directly or through SHGs, it has to be ensured that the ultimate rate of interest to the borrower does not exceed 12% per annum. The interest spread available presently at 4% could be shared between SHGs and NGOs by mutual agreement depending on the items of work/services to be rendered by the NGOs and SHGs.

(b) The system followed by some of the NGOs in levying interest on the original amount of the loan and recovering it in monthly instalment was not proper. As per RMK policy, interest has to be charged only on the reduced balances after adjusting the recoveries every week, month or quarter as the case may be. There is also no system of compounding interest under the RMK scheme at any level.

(c) Penal interest for delayed payments could be charged by the NGO from SHGs/borrowers at the rate to be decided between the NGO/SHG.

F. Charging of Interest by RMK

(i) Interest is applied to the loan accounts of NGOs on the basis of number of days a loan amount has remained outstanding taking into account repayments received in the account. Interest is required to be paid every quarter independently of the repayments under principal. The due dates for payment for interest are first week of July, October, January and last week of March of the year.

(ii) RMK will not charge interest on loans advanced to the NGOs for the stipulated period for disbursements provided the amount of loans are disbursed by the NGO to the SHGs/Member of the SHGs within the time stipulated in the sanction letter. The time given for disbursement is usually 30 days from the date of sending in demand draft by the RMK. In case disbursement is delayed beyond the stipulated date referred to above, no concession of interest is given to the NGO and RMK may charge penal interest.

(iii) RMK also provides relief on account of interest on repayments if the bank draft for the repayment of principal amount due on a particular date is purchased on the above date and sent to RMK immediately thereafter so as to reach RMK office say within 6 days. If there are delays in receiving the draft, interest concession will not be available to the NGO.

G. Maintenance of 10% margin

10% margin stipulated by RMK, the minimum thrift required to be mobilised before a borrower is advanced a loan. The amount of thrift collected from the members could be used by the SHG or NGO for providing loans for consumption purposes and other purposes also on which the interest ceiling of 12% is not applicable. In due course, with the increase of credit-flow and consequent better income, savings are expected to grow and proportion of loans to savings presently 10 times would diminish to reach a ratio of 50 : 50 to be achieved in the course of next 3-4 years.

H. Periodical Returns

(a) The NGOs should ensure that the disbursement certificate and utilisation certificate are submitted on time.

(b) Monthly progress report. RMK has prescribed a monthly/quarterly progress report (overview report) to be submitted to it on the working of SHGs to indicate the total disbursement of loans, repayments, defaults, etc. The purpose is to keep the NGO informed of the operations of SHGs and hence this report is considered necessary.

RASHTRIYA MAHILA KOSH

RMK Scheme—A Scheme to ensure direct involvement of women in income generation activities

The Department of Women and Child Development of the Government of India has constituted the Rashtriya Mahila Kosh (RMK)—which is a scheme to ensure full participation of women below poverty line in income generation activities. The removal of red-tapism and the direct availability of funds to the needy women are receiving overwhelmingly high appreciation from all quarters. In fact, the World Bank has also recently appreciated the constitution of RMK for channelising credit to poor women on a more participatory basis.

Under the scheme, any voluntary organisation, which has some experience of formation of Self-Help Group (SHG) of poor women in its area and of mobilising a saving and credit programme with these funds or with funds made available elsewhere, can apply to RMK for loan at 8% interest for further on-lending to poor women at a rate not exceeding 12%. NOGs with 3 years experience of these activities would be very welcome to participate in this field. The amount of maximum loan for short-term (S.T.) is Rs. 2500/- and for medium-term (M.T.) loan is Rs. 5000/- per borrower.

These amounts are given to women for carrying on their day-to-day income generation activities or for creation of assets which can lead to income generation. The advantage of the scheme has so far been allowed to be taken by 97 NGOs belonging to 14 States in the country to benefit 98,000 women. However, the number of applications being received from Himachal Pradesh, Punjab, Rajasthan, Haryana, Gujarat is very small. RMK is making efforts to get the elements of the scheme widely known so that NGOs which are not eligible for loans today may become eligible tomorrow.

The total loans sanctioned so far are about 19 crores. About 70% of this amount has also been disbursed. In other words, more than 62,000 women have already taken advantage of this scheme.

Experience has shown that depending on the local requirements, raw material availability and marketing opportunities, women are using this money for generation of income in diverse ways ranging from catering for mill workers (Annapurna Mahila Mandal, Bombay), support to footpath dwellers for petty vending (SPARC, Bombay) preparation of beautiful Sujni items (ADITHI, Patna), dairying

(SEWA, Bhopal), improvement of agricultural yield (ASSEFA, Madurai), garment preparation (SEWA, Lucknow). As a matter of fact, this list is only illustrative and not exhaustive.

The amounts of credit have deliberately not been kept high. The reason is that the number of women in need of small amounts for occupations, such as vegetable, fruits and fish vending, petty shop, embroidery work, preparation of handicraft items, agricultural inputs required for small land holdings etc., is very large. If large amounts are concentrated in a fewer hands, the creative energies of a vast number of women in the country will remain untapped.

RMK does not charge any collateral from the NGOs or members. It simply makes sure that the NGO is sincere and knows its job and has roots close to the people.

The concept of Self-Help Group for operations under the scheme is also a very interesting example of decentralisation of administration of the scheme. It is much easier for voluntary organisation to deal with Self-Help Group leaders of every group of about 10 women rather than to deal with every individual member for the purposes of frequent guidance, disbursal of loan money and for recovery. Besides, since every group member is individually and severally responsible for returning the instalments, peer pressure of the members is also very helpful in appropriate use of money. RMK is very particular about the recoveries as it intends to re-cycle the amount of Rs. 31 crores given to it, in the course of next 5 years to the extent of 100 to 150 crores.

People are beginning to find quite a lot of sense and significance in this new scheme which teaches women to receive credit and not grant and, in turn, to live with dignity and not with compassion shown by others. Besides, women who by nature exhibit sufficient alertness in returning the RMK money in time, are eligible to have repeat sanctions. Repeated sanctions may also one day lead them to come above the poverty line.

The office of the Rashtriya Mahila Kosh is situated at 4, Deen Dayal Upadhyaya Marg (ICCW Building), New Delhi -110002.

(by Smt. Indira Misra C-11/18,
Bapa Nagar, New Delhi)
(The Author is the Executive Director of RMK)

ANNEXURE 'A'

EXPLANATORY NOTE ON FORMATION OF SHGS

1. *Village survey:* A quick participatory survey could be made to find out the nature of environments and resources in the village, particularly the number of families, their economic status, land holdings, type of land, annual income, expenditure etc. This apart, the survey should also find out potential for goods which could be produced by the women borrowers, availability of markets, social structure of the society, the present system of money lender's debt etc. What is important is to ascertain how the community members participate in socio-economic development programmes and who are the known opinion makers in the area.
2. *Training of Leaders:* The leaders of the groups should be properly trained in group dynamics, conduct of meetings with discipline, proper conduct of savings and credit business, i.e. sanctions, disbursements, utilisation, recovery, resource mobilistion as also keeping of proper records. The leaders should be specifically trained in methods of developing linkages and liaison with the local Govt. department and building up of capacity of leadership in other members of the group.

   The extension workers should also be properly trained in the above aspects so as to guide and advise the group leaders. The extension workers training should include knowledge about such aspects as process of decision making, rotation of common fund, basic rules of savings and credit, various aspects of women development inside home and outside home, conflict resolution and basics of the type of income generation activities being run in the group.

3. *Group Meetings:* The monthly or fortnightly meetings of the group should be facilitated by the extension workers by ensuring that the group discusses the problem by itself and finds solution. The facilitator needs to give only advice on certain issues where the group is struck up. Under no circumstances, the facilitator or coordinator should dominate the group meetings. The extension workers should also keep close contact with beneficiaries and others so as to get information directly or indirectly about the working of the groups, the income generation activity undertaken by the members, their difficulties and financial position. In case of difficulties, contact could be made with local authorities and other available experts.
4. *Exposure visits:* Exposure visits of the leaders and members should be conducted to really good working NGOs and Self Help Groups which are stabilised in their operations and the facilitator/coordinator should properly explain the system and procedures of the group, the type of account being maintained and also how difficulties and problems faced in group formation were sorted out by the leaders of the group visited by the new members.
5. *Annual Meeting:* The annual meetings of all members of the group should be held invariably where the yearly performance should be critically examined to learn lessons for the future and take such corrective steps as are considered necessary.
6. *Cluster Approach and Cluster Committee:* NGO should,

find it easier to form new group in areas/villages which can form clusters making it easier for the extension staff to supervise the groups. At appropriate time in due course, the groups should consider to have a block level cluster committee for 10 to 15 groups. This cluster committee may undertake common functions like surveys, audit, training etc. and also act as an institutional mechanism to gradually take over on the functions presently performed by the NGOs.

ANNEXURE 'B'

SUGGESTED GUIDELINES FOR AN ACCOUNTING SYSTEM FOR SELF-HELP GROUPS (SHGS)

1. The common transactions which normally take place in a group has an independent identity by itself keeping record of all its transactions are normally the following:-

1. Deposits, receipts and payments;
2. Borrowing from NGOs/Others;
3. Loans, disbursements and repayments;
4. Interest received on loans and interest paid on deposits;
5. Interest earned on investments;
6. Expenses on stationery, TA/DA, salary, education and others;
7. Transfer of funds from one group to another group if that takes place;
8. Amount deposited and kept in the bank;
9. Amount payable, i.e. where money is due but has not been paid;
10. Amount receivable, i.e. amount due but not received.

2. The following books of accounts may have to be maintained by the Self-Help Group:-

(i) Cash Book/Day Book

(a) This is a book of records, receipts and payments of all moneys under various Heads as and when these happen. A broad proforma of the column cash book is given in Appendix II. These accounts are maintained on a system called single entry system of book keeping. While cash transactions will be recorded under the cash column, transactions with the bank will be recorded in the bank column. Whenever cash is deposited in the bank, it will be shown in two columns i.e. cash payments will be shown in the cash column of payment side and deposit in bank will be shown in the bank column on receipt side.

(b) All the columns of cash book should be totalled every month and progressive total of each month added up at the end of the year which will indicate the total receipts and payments under each of the important heads.

(ii) Ledger

(a) From various entries made in the Cash Book regarding the borrowing from the NGO under the RMK scheme/loans issued, saving etc. of the member, a separate ledger account will be opened for RMK loan, as also for each of the borrowing member in respect of his savings and loans. Entries from the cash book will be transferred to the specific ledger account and no entry will be made direct in the ledger.

(b) Interest on loans and deposits will be suitably incorporated in the relative columns in the cash book as indicated in the proforma.

(c) There is, perhaps, no need for an SHG to have separate ledger account for furniture, expenses, interest, income etc. These can be separately recorded in a passbook and yearly position calculated by placing the opening balance as per last balance-sheet and adding to it total receipts deducting all payments which will then depict the balance at the end of the year.

3. All accounts in the cash book relating to income and expenditure will go to income and expenditure account, while the accounts relating to assets and liabilities i.e. furniture, fixtures, cash balance, bank deposits, and loan accounts, RMK loans outstanding etc. will go to the balance-sheet.

4. *Income and Expenditure Account & Balance-Sheet:* This is prepared at the end of the year to show the total receipt of income/interest on the credit side and all expenses incurred and interest paid on debit side. SHG should make an assessment of all its expenses/interest payable on deposits borrowings at the end of the year as also its income/ interest etc. receivable on loans which should also be shown in the Income and Expenditure account and also in the balance-sheet. Surplus of total income over expenditure will show the surplus of the year while the excess of expenses over income will show the loss.

CHAPTER 14

Toward Future

Indian society for centuries survived the vicissitudes of history without a centralized political system. Except for short periods, it lacked a clear centre. Even those short periods had a rather limited reach and proved to be transitions in the long march of Indian civilization. The core of the civilization was cultural rather than political. Its 'State' was intermittent, scattered and multipolar, an arena of conflicting claims of a large number of clans and regimes. The real 'action' was by voluntary entities representing trade and commerce and the 'mahajans' governing them, and cultural, religious and caste and caste-like organizations. The view often held by Westerners, that India consisted of a series of republics, represents a misreading of this voluntary, non-political, non-State cultural terrain.

In its core manifestations, voluntary effort is initiated by diverse individuals and groups; its distinctive features lie in its being autonomous, relatively independent and self-propelled. Indeed, as one surveys the Indian reality, one finds that a large part of innovative and creative endeavour in many fields is voluntary in nature, not a result of external incentives. Thus, if one says that voluntarism has been an enduring feature of India, it only means that many people at many places are engaged in multifarious action without being asked to do so by an external agent—political, bureaucratic or market-propelled.

The perception of a dichotomy between State-directed and voluntary initiatives has arisen only in recent decades *after* the modern State and its institutions either began to impede the voluntary ethos of Indian society or forced themselves on what people did on their own. The contemporary interest, both scholarly and political/bureaucratic, in voluntary action has arisen because of this imposition, for long accepted as beneficial but which in the long run has proved to be largely (though not wholly) inimical to people's interests with the result that large sections of people are once again forced to rely on their own methods of resolving their problems. Not that this is always to their liking. Often they are compelled to fend for themselves, whereas they would have liked to participate in the formal structures of the modern State, to benefit from the opportunities it promises to offer. Hence the recurring image of voluntary action as a response and reaction to the failure of the State and its policies and programmes. However, even while returning to the voluntary terrain in ways that may appear reactive, we are soon likely to discover a more positive and liberated sense of what voluntarism involves. The model of development which we adopted on achieving Independence—and for which we 'fought' during the freedom struggle —was one in which the government was seen as the key to social change and to improving the life chances of the mass of the people. Unfortunately, the focus of the movement became merely 'capture of power' from the British. This largely meant capture of governmental power, not *swaraj* in its full-blown sense as was conceived by Gandhi and other leaders of the movement.

There was, however, a school of thought which gave priority to social reform, viz., the early liberals as well as the later radical thinkers engaged in social emancipation of the oppressed classes, who considered it to be more important that any premature rush for political independence.

Ambedkar was foremost among such leaders, as were Phule and other predecessors of his. There were others too, such as M.N. Roy, for whom waging a war against fascist tendencies at both global and national levels assumed greater importance than any formal transfer of power from the British to the Indians. In the model adopted, not only was the government central to bringing about social change; so too was a conception of 'democracy' in which political parties were to be the basic units for choosing those who were to be in power and who were to be in opposition. In structuring the relationship between the institutions of governance and the people, this model relied essentially on parties and the party system in which elections were to play the main role. Similarly, a new set of political parties were seen to provide alternatives to the prevailing order fashioned by the 'ruling' party.

Thus, both for creating a consensus on critical issues and for challenging current policies and ideological positions, parties were meant to be the key actors. The people were left to exercise choices between given sets of parties and their candidates. There was no provision for them to initiate the process themselves or even to participate in the selection of candidates. They were expected merely to put their mark on the ballot paper consisting of names of candidates selected by political parties. They were not even given the choice of rejecting all the candidates proposed.

In fact, the only decisive role that the voters have is to reject a government in power. They have little say in what the incoming government or party (or coalition of parties) is to do. They have in effect little say in the governance of the country in any positive manner. The only rights that they enjoy are of a negative kind. This is what the model of governance and dissent that we gave to ourselves upon becoming independent has brought us to. This model has increasingly led to discontent and disillusionment with the operating system over the last quarter of a century.

Not all the micro efforts at voluntary action are, however, political. Some of the macro efforts too are of a non-political nature. Indeed, some of them deliberately keep away from the political process, particularly the voluntary organizations with a Gandhian origin or those of the liberal vintage, which chose instead to focus on certain ethical norms or the defence of civil rights. At the other end of the spectrum are groups that take a more radical and often 'revolutionary' stance—from the Naxalites to the regionally-based militant formations found in Punjab, Kashmir and the North-East and in a different way, those offering sustained resistance to State repression and armed assaults of the upper classes in Andhra Pradesh, Bihar and parts of Maharashtra. Together, the 'voluntary sector' consists of diverse groups engaged in a variety of activities and forums of assertion and espousing varied causes, and yet somehow together presenting a challenge to the political and economic model that continues to inform the Indian State and its key institutions.

Simultaneously the growth of non-party and non-governmental action was a highlighting of a series of issues not confined to a mere expression of dissent and protest. Examples of these various issues include: the state of the environment, the condition of women, preservation of tribal and other ethnic identities and resistance to their displacement and eviction as a result of the building of large dams and thermal plants, the arena of dalit politics following growing atrocities and violence against them, struggles against different forms of social exploitation such as bonded labour, position of migrant labour and the horrendous condition in which children and especially the girls are placed.

NGOs and Popular Movements

As struggles on these issues gained strength, voluntarism emerged in a new form of 'movements'. It took two shapes—specific movements such as the environment movement, the women's movement, the dalit movement, and the movements of the tribals, and, a broader networking of issues through macro formations such as the Jan Vikas Andolan, the Bharat Jan Andolan, the Azadi Bachao Andolan, and the most recent and comprehensive of them all, the National Alliance of People's Movements.

Simultaneously, the non-party and non-governmental organizations have also been metamorphosing into what are called the NGOs, currently the most widespread form of voluntary action. This is partly because several developments at the international level have given rise to the emergence of a new corporatist model of capitalism. Institutions like the World Bank, IMF and WTO; major UN bodies such as UNDP, UNICEF and FAO; and donor agencies are showing a preference for the transfer of technology, development funds and in some instances even finance capital to NGOs at the national and local levels alongside governments. Similarly, a series of international 'summit' conferences on environment, human rights, population, social dimensions of development (known as the social summit) and women have all been followed up by massive transfer of funds to NGOs, either directly or through ministries in national governments. This new constellation of 'voluntary' effort, encompassing funding agencies and international NGOs, units within government bureaucracies and the Planning Commission meant to assist national and local NGOs provides a completely new model of both joining in and containing, co-opting and corrupting the large mass of genuine, grassroots based, activist efforts. Whether this NGO model of voluntarism will further accentuate the great divides between the haves and the have-nots, or ameliorate the condition of the latter, is still an open question. It will depend on how the people respond to them, just as the fate of the dominant model of governance will depend upon how the people, increasingly getting disenchanted and alienated with it, will respond to it over time. On this depends the future of voluntary action in India. Many of the voluntary, non-governmental and non-party responses to the established order, led by activists and in some cases backed by radical intellectuals, have also been sought to be incorporated in the NGO framework, gradually losing their militant and dissenting stance as well as their pursuit of an alternative political process. However, some of them still continue, despite difficulties, to launch struggles on behalf of the poor and marginalized social strata.

While the activist arena is entering this ambivalent phase, a new upsurge of both consciousness and action from the grassroots has been under way, which, if successful, may lead to highly innovative strides towards genuine voluntarism. It consists of the rise of the poor and the oppressed themselves (not just on behalf of them as is the case with the activists), who are tired of waiting for the system to deliver the goods. They are already showing their disdain for parties and governing elites, who prefer to take advantage of the increasingly regionalized and decentralized structure of the Indian polity and who, far more than the urban middle class, have found a stake in the democratic political process and are participating in large numbers in it. As this process gains ground, they would be willing to challenge the established institutions and replace them with not only a new system of governance and representation but also a new model of organizing civic affairs. For this they will need to draw increasingly upon their own innate confidence, their ecological resource base, their ethnic, caste-like, tribal and other indigenous identities, all this as part of engaging in the transformation of the system. This is both in terms of moving away from the Western-inspired models of governance and competition and in terms of giving greater salience to the institutions, systems of knowledge and technical know-how which had evolved over the centuries but had been allowed to wither under the impact of imported and alien ideas of organizing society, economy, polity administration and law.

Emergence of New Voluntarism

Voluntarism has, over the centuries, been the hallmark of Indian society. The new upsurge holds the promise of returning our country and our culture to its basic genius.

But we live in an uncertain world and therefore face an uncertain future. Much will depend on how we respond to not only the political crisis that we face but, even more importantly, the intellectual crisis generated by the collapse of all ideologies and the all-round erosion of self-confidence. Fortunately, there are still a number of conscientious men and women who can take up the challenge, along with literally thousands of others—women and youth in particular— who would be willing to join them in creating a social order.

Many forces are at work with which the prevailing system has not been able to cope. This period of erosion of parliamentary institutions, parlies and the authority of the State and of the national political leadership has also seen the rise of new actors on the scene, a new style in the conduct of public affairs, and new definitions of the content of politics.

The essence of such a transition has to be a new order based on a new consensus. The political system and its socio-economic counterparts that were put in place by the Congress after Independence, though based on a consensus, were soon overtaken by the Western-inspired (Fabian) model of development and the attempt to centralize power and homogenize the diversity of cultures. Fortunately, the scope for dissent and expectations for change built into the Congress system and the democratic process in course of time called for the need to restructure the consensus. Political consensus is an on-going process; it has to be revived constantly and provided with new meaning.

Democracy poses both an opportunity for creating and recreating consensus and a challenge to its mechanical continuation based on what is called the 'demand explosion' of our times. The new turmoil among the Indian masses, like the new forms of expressing demands through engaging in protest and struggle, is part of the continuing commitment to democracy— indeed a further deepening and broadening of its base. It needs to be located in the larger context of a world in transformation, to be seen as an expression of new stirrings of consciousness engulfing large sections of society, a new conception of rights and responsibilities. It also signifies a new understanding of the democratic process, moving from an almost exclusive preoccupation with parries and elections to deeper currents of change involving millions of people. Only thus can the new voluntarism become a catalyst of human liberation and genuine freedom. In its absence, mere voluntary action arising from the erosion of the modern State and its institutions can easily degenerate into uncontained violence or other forms of anarchy and decay and disintegration which may once again pave the way for an authoritarian or fascist intervention.

Select Bibliography

Arora, L.S., *Rural Development in India.* (New Delhi: S. Chand & Co, 1979).

Bhatt, Anil (1995). 'Voluntary action in India', *Economic and Political Weekly,* Vol. 30, No. 16, pp 870-76.

Bonner, Arthur (1990). *Averting the Apocalypse: Social Movement in India Today.* Durham: Duke University Press.

Chambers, Robert (1995). *Poverty and livelihood: Whose reality counts,* IDS discussion paper, Sussex, December.

Clark, Peter B. and James Q. Wilson (1961). 'Incentive systems: A theory of organisations', *Administrative Science Quarterly* 6, pp. 129-66.

Dreze, Jean and Amartya Sen ,(1995). *India: Economic Development and Social Opportunity,* Delhi: Oxford University Press.

Dua, M. R. and Gupta V. S. (Ed.) *Media and Development: Theories in Communication and Extension.* New Delhi, Har-Anand Publication, 1994.

Eldridge, Philip (1984/5). 'The political role of community action groups in India and Indonesia: In search of a general *theory'. Alternatives* 10, pp. 401-34.

Fernadnes, Walter, Geeta Menon and Philip Viegas, *Forests, Environment and Forest Dweller Economy in Orissa* (New Delhi: Indian Social Institute, 1984), mimeo.

Fernandes, Walter and R.G. Lobo, "Social Action Groups and the Search for Alternatives," in Walter Fernandes (ed) *Inequality, Its Bases and Search for Solutions: Dr Alfred de Souza Memorial Essays* (New Delhi: Indian Social Institute, 1986).

Fernandez, Aloysius P. (1996). *Working with Government.* Bangalore: MYRADA (Mysore Resettlement and Development Agency).

Ferrington, John and Anthony Babington (1993). *Reluctant Partners.* New York: Routledge.

Gulati, Ravi and Kaval Gulati (1996). *Strengthening Voluntary Action in India.* Delhi: Konark.

Hansman, H. (1979/80). 'The role of non-profit enterprise', *Yale Law Journal* 89, pp. 835-901.

Hardgrave, Robert L., Jr and Stanley A. Kochanek (1986). *India: Government and Politics in a Developing Nation.* San Diego: Harcourt Brace.

India, Ministry of Human Resource Development, Department of Women and Child Development. Universal Children's Day 14 Nov. 1994, Rights of the Child: A Commitment. New Delhi, the author, 1994.

India, Ministry of Information and Broadcasting. *India 1993: A Reference Manual.* New Delhi, Ministry of Information and Broadcasting, Publication Division, 1994.

Indian Journal of Public Administration (1987). Special number on 'Voluntary organisations and development: Their role', July-September.

Jain, Devaki (1956).'Struggle against power: Notes on Indian political behavior', *World Politics* 7, pp. 393-96.

Jhunjhunwala, Bharat (1986). 'Voluntary work as countervailing power,' *Economic and Political Weekly* 21.

Karat, Prakash (1984). 'Action groups/voluntary organisations: A factor in imperialist strategy', *The Marxist*, April-June, pp. 19-54.

Kavalackatt, Thomas, "The Killing of Santal Tribals," *Social Action*, 35 (n.3, July-Sept. 1985), pp. 278-282.

Kochanek, Stanley A. (1974). *Business and Politics in India.* Berkeley: University of California Press.

Korten, David C. (1986). 'Micro-policy reforms: The role of private voluntary agencies', working paper no. 12, The

National Association of Schools of Public Administration, Washington, D.C.

Maheshwar, Madan Lal. Role of Media in Creating Awareness for Children Rights in *A Report of the Workshop on the Rights of the Child,* 1994 August 30-31, Jabalpur, M.P.

Mahila Dakshata Samithi. *State Level Workshop on Rights of the Child: A Report.* 1994, Sep. 27-28, Hyderabad. Hyderabad, the author, 1994.

Marx, Karl (1983). "Theses on Feuerbach' in Eugene Kamenka (ed.), *The Portable Karl Marx.* New York: Viking.

Mathew, Mammen, "Roots of Rural Violence in Bihar: A Case Study of Arwal," *Social Action,* 36 (n.3, July-Sept. 1986), pp. 333-342.

Mathur, Kanwar B. *Communication for Development and Social Change.* New Delhi, Allied Publishers, 1994.

Mitra, Subrata Kumar (1991). 'Crisis and resilience in Indian democracy', *International Social Science Journal* 43, p. 565.

Nayak, Nalini, "Where are the Action Groups Today?" in Walter Fernandes (ed). *Social Activists and People's Movements: Search for Political and Economic Alternatives.* (New Delhi: Indian Social Institute 1985).

Pandey, Shashi Ranjan (1991). *Community Action far Social Justice: Grassroots Organisution in India.* New Delhi: Sage Publications.

Patel, Rohini (1995). 'The pressure group role of voluntary associations: A case study of the Ahmedabad's Women's Action Group and the Self Employed Women's Association' unpublished Ph.D. dissertation, Pennsylvania State University.

Ramachandran, Vimala (1996). 'NGOs in the time of globalisation', *Seminar,* November.

Saint, Kishore (1974).'The role of the catalyst institution' in John Sommer, Pratima Kale and Ranjit Gupta (eds), *Rural Development at the Grassroots: The Catalyst Role.* New Delhi: Ford Foundation.

Salisburg, Robert (1969). 'An exchange theory of interest groups', *Midwest Journal* of Political Science 13, no. 1, pp. 1-32.

Sen, Jai, "On Anti-Voluntarism: The PADI Committee Proposals for the Protection and Regulation of Voluntary Organisations" in Harsh Sethi and Smita Kothari (eds) *On Anti-Voluntarism* (Delhi: Lokayan, 1986), pp. 8-36.

Sen, K.M. (1961). *Hinduism.* Baltimore: Penguin Books.

Sethi, Harsh (1935). 'Whither voluntary action?', *Seminar,* May, pp. 18-23.

Sethi, Harsh (1987). *Refocussing Praxis.* New Delhi: SETU-Lokayan.

Shah, Dinesh (1985). 'Voluntary agencies in the seventh plan', *Voluntary Action* 27, nos. 9-10, p. 259.

Shah, Ghanshyam and H.R. Chaturvedi (1983). *Gandhian Approach to Rural Development: The Valod Experiment.* New Delhi: Ajanta.

Sharma, S.L. (1992). 'Social action groups as harbingers of silent revolution', *Economic and* Political *Weekly* pp. 2557-61.

Viswanath, Vanita (1991) *Non-governmental Organisations and imen's Development in South Asia: A Comparative Analysis.* Boulder, CO: Westview Press.

Index